BLENDED

edited by samantha waltz

BLENDED

writers on the
stepfamily experience

SEAL

Seal Press

Blended
Writers on the Stepfamily Experience

Copyright © 2015 by Samantha Waltz

Published by
SEAL PRESS
A Member of the Perseus Books Group
1700 Fourth Street
Berkeley, California

Library of Congress Cataloging-in-Publication Data

Blended : writers on the stepfamily experience / edited by Samantha Waltz.
      pages cm

 ISBN 978-1-58005-557-4 (paperback)
 1. Stepfamilies. I. Waltz, Samantha, 1945-
 HQ759.92.B547 2015
 306.874'7--dc23

                                        2014038097

Cover design by Faceout Studios, Kara Davison
Interior design by Kate Basart/Union Pageworks
Printed in the United States of America
Distributed by Publishers Group West

To those whose love brings families together

ooooo

contents

Part 5 | *Reflections*

note from the editor

samantha waltz

More than a decade ago, when I was working as a family therapist, I hadn't yet become part of a blended family. I looked into the faces of thirty stepparents gathered for my workshop on step-parenting, all of them leaning forward on folding chairs, eager for the new insights that I would surely offer to help them in their family relationships.

At the time, my book on parenting styles had recently been released. I was confident my information on setting appropriate expectations, improving communication skills, and utilizing effective problem-solving tools would help them. After all, I'd keynoted a regional early childhood conference a few weeks earlier, and I'd previously presented numerous workshops on parenting topics. True, this was the first workshop targeted to stepparents, but I wasn't expecting it to be that different from the others.

I was so wrong.

As I taped large sheets of butcher paper to the walls, I asked the participants to call out the issues they most wanted to discuss. The words flew at me from every part of the room: loyalty, jealousy, displacement, grief, guilt. How to deal with biological parents, visitation schedules, multiple parents at holidays, different surnames? What to do about expectations from a spouse, the kids, society, and oneself? How to set boundaries with children one wants desperately to win over?

When I listened to the fears and heartache of these parents, I began to understand the unique difficulties they faced. Part of every stepfamily member's memories and even his or her heart is often in another home. The words *stepfather*, *stepmother*, and *stepchild* exist in Old English forms related to the word *ástieped*, meaning "bereaved." Visitation is not the same as having the mother or father a child bonded with in infancy living with him or her on a daily basis, tucking them in at night, and sharing a story or secret. When a parent passes away, all possibility of playing ball or making Christmas cookies together is gone. So despite a tremendous desire to please, a stepparent can come off as a poor second to a beloved birth parent.

A stepparent can also become the target of a stepchild's displaced anger with a mother or father. Unfair? Of course. A difficulty that can be overcome? Sometimes, but not always. The stepparent has usually done nothing except stand in the line of fire.

And then there is the power of the mythology about evil stepmothers and wicked stepfathers that has existed since before the Brothers Grimm. Family problems feel clammy on stepparents' skin and they aren't sure what they've done wrong or how to proceed, but they must somehow prove themselves the good guy over and over.

Every step situation is different. The family may have a traditional or nontraditional configuration. A child's age and experience with a biological parent will bring a unique perspective of the stepparent. Irrational as it seems, a child may choose to like or dislike a stepparent before ever meeting him or her.

Until I taught that workshop for stepparents, I envisioned stepfamilies as bigger and better. Complicated, sure, but worth it. I had wanted to be part of a large family since the spring break of fifth grade when I stayed on my cousins' farm. I could still picture those mornings when I joined my ten cousins, ages three to twenty-two, forming a line down the hall outside the farmhouse's single bathroom, toothbrushes in hand, everyone cracking jokes as we waited. My stomach had ached from laughing so much.

Years later, when I became a stepmom, I learned that *more* is not always *merrier*. A patchwork family needs extra effort and care, and even then there is no guarantee of *happily ever after*. Today I have more wisdom and less advice.

As a stepmother to six adult children, I care passionately about the challenges and successes of stepfamilies. More than half the families in America are living in step. Some work beautifully, but more than 60 percent are torn with conflict and will end in dissolution. Parents and children currently living in stepfamilies, or coming from them and making their way in their own families, have stories that will entertain, inform, perhaps trouble, but ultimately inspire us.

When I met and fell in love with my husband Ray, I asked the officiate for our wedding if I could plan a ceremony that united not only Ray and me, but also my three grown children and his six, three each from his two former marriages. I assumed that although we wouldn't all live under the same roof, our new family would be a big, bustling, jovial brood like my cousins. I arranged for all our children to precede me down the aisle, except his oldest son who couldn't be with us because of health issues. Each of my children was on the arm of one of Ray's, with a daughter from his first family on the arm of the son from his second. Tears of happiness washed down my face at the celebration of our marriage and blending of our families. I hadn't a clue what challenges we would face.

My first hint came when Ray and I bought a house together and showed his youngest daughter and my youngest son, home from college for the summer, the two bedrooms they could use. One bedroom had a double closet and both our kids wanted it.

"Let's flip for it," my son suggested, taking a quarter from his pocket.

"I'm sorry, but I want it." My stepdaughter flashed a smile of self-reproach, but her tone of voice was firm.

"I'll pay extra on the mortgage," Ray offered.

My breath caught in my chest. Would this stepdaughter always insist on her way, and would her father always jump to her defense, ignoring what my children and I might want?

Ray's oldest son Mark moved into the large bonus room in our daylight basement. Having used drugs from the age of twelve, he was now clean and waiting for a kidney transplant. I enjoyed his quick humor and his eagerness to help as we set up the house. He filled us all with his optimism, assuring us that he would enroll in college after his transplant and pursue a career. I was with him when he got the call that there was a kidney available, and I rushed him to the hospital.

I hadn't counted on the power of addiction.

A few months after his successful transplant, Mark began using again. His personality changed dramatically. Grunts or hostile silence met my efforts to talk with him. Ray couldn't express his anger toward his son, so he buffeted me with it. When the tension in the house grew unbearable, I saw that I had two choices: I could leave or I could ask Mark to leave. I was afraid if I asked Mark to leave, my stepfamily, reluctant to acknowledge his using again, would be furious with me. And indeed, when I did have him leave, some of them hardly spoke to me for months, even though Mark moved in with an uncle around the corner from us.

And then there were the step-grandchildren. I'd never been any kind of grandma, and the name hung on me like a garment that doesn't quite fit. Did these five children, ages three to nine, want another grandmother? Did the young ones want to sit in my lap and read books, or whisper what happened during their day? Did the older ones' parents push them to wrap their arms around my waist in quick hugs? How important was it to them that I attend their soccer and baseball games and their birthday parties? Could I sometimes go on a bike ride with friends or work on a writing project instead and still be loved?

I struggled to feel part of a large family with a common history, but more often felt excluded. I was the new kid on the team and the rest had been holding practice for decades. At every family gathering I smiled bravely through story after story from the life they shared before I arrived on the scene. Frequent talk of exes especially hurt. Sometimes I tried to join in the conversation. Other times I slipped out of the room, blinking back tears. No one seemed to notice.

Gradually I built a relationship with each member of our combined family. Ray's four daughters consistently touched my heart with warm hugs, thank-you notes for family gatherings, and gifts on my birthday. One became a virtual daughter when she moved to another city and we kept in touch through a flurry of emails. The stepdaughter who had demanded the bedroom with double closets became a true daughter to me, sharing confidences and dreams. I spent her wedding day by her side, her own mother distracted with personal concerns, and smoothed her dark hair from her damp face when she was in labor with her son, and again with her daughter. Ray's youngest son offered assistance with anything we needed, from planning family reunions to brokering the sale of our car. He was the first one we called when Mark's kidney failure and heart problems threatened his life. He called Ray's other children who immediately joined us to mourn Mark's passing.

I am fortunate. Everyone in our family works hard to keep lines of communication open—even when feelings run high and hot—to make time for each other, to treat each other with respect, to grieve each other's disappointments, and to celebrate each other's successes.

Ray and I had imagined our children becoming best friends. That hasn't happened. They simply don't have much in common. But they like each other and some of them keep in touch on Facebook or through email. The stepdaughters in town attend my daughter-in-law's fashion shows. Everyone makes a determined effort to attend family events.

We are one of thousands of stepfamilies facing enormous challenges. In the following pages, thirty stepparents and stepchildren, some prominent writers, some new, share their experiences.

Blended takes readers from the first blush of a new relationship, through the often intense experiences that buffet family members as they struggle to meet the challenges unique to stepfamilies, to a place where stepparents and stepchildren can look back and celebrate or grieve their stepfamily journeys.

When organizing these poignant stories, it became clear that there are natural progressions members of blended families go through. The stories seem to organize themselves around the part of the journey that the story's writer is sharing.

In "Coming Together" the authors take us from first meetings through a stepfamily marriage and honeymoon. In "Self-Discovery" they share their honest insights as they relinquish myths of what families should be and embrace their new realities. In "Evolution" writers reveal the difficult process of building step-relationships. In "Acceptance" they rise above what could be crushing circumstances to find resolution. In "Reflections" they look back at their experiences and celebrate or mourn the influence of stepfamilies on their lives.

From these writers who have given us their deeply personal stories with honesty, candor, and even humor, we can gather insights and inspiration, and know we are not alone on our own stepfamily journeys.

Some stories in this book offer a model for creating order and peace out of a tangle of step-relationships, and others let us know it isn't always possible. Some warm your heart and make you smile. Others spark tears of empathy. All of them will broaden your understanding of stepfamilies and offer guidance, compassion, and hope.

foreword

ariel gore

In my family, we don't have children who are reared in one household by their two biological parents. It's just not the way we do things. We stay single or we marry, have kids when we choose. We have affairs, adopt, give birth out of wedlock. Grandmothers aren't required to have been mothers first. We divorce. We get knocked up by donors. Custody arrangements are made in courthouses or at picnic tables. Sometimes biological parents wander away, or get deported. Sometimes they die. Our families flow on, expanding and contracting like rivers on a changing earth.

I wish I could say that every blending follows the same basic trajectory—that if you do a, b, and c you're guaranteed success—but, alas, when it comes to family, there never seem to be any universal answers. Lucky for us, however, there are the wise and honest voices of parents and kids who've done it before. And sometimes that's what we really need.

Like the authors in this vibrant collection, what I know about blended families doesn't come from studies or "expert" advice. It comes from the real and lived.

My first stepdad eased himself into my life with a warm smile and few expectations. He'd been a college-campus Catholic priest before he was excommunicated for marrying my mom, so I guess he'd had a lot of practice serving as a father figure to people who didn't necessarily serve as son and daughter figures.

My stepdad brought structure to our family in the form of reliability rather than sudden rules. I called him John. He treated me like a short adult. I was five years old. And I loved him immediately, like apple pie.

He and my mom stayed married for more than thirty years—until his death—but I suspect that even if they'd divorced, he would have stayed my dad forever. He made this fluid family thing look so easy.

But not all of us can be priests.

The first time I had a partner move in, I'd lived alone with my daughter for almost twelve years. I was a good mother by most people's standards, but sometimes the two of us ate dinner in front of the television. Bedtime was when we got tired. Some nights we let the dishes sit in the sink until morning.

My new partner decided that she'd make herself useful: she'd impose some much-needed order on our chaotic single-parent household. Yes, she'd make some rules. She'd show my daughter some structure. Maybe she'd even save us from ourselves.

Predictably, my preteen daughter snarled and called this new adult a bitch.

My partner stomped her foot and called my daughter homophobic. I poured myself a glass of wine and drank it too fast.

We were not off to a good start.

Over those first months and years, my heart went out to my partner as she tried to make a place for herself in our little family, but I wondered, too, if she held some basic belief that every family needed a firm dad figure. I wondered if her anxiety and jealousy about my close bond with my daughter were, in fact, running the show.

The truth is that single-parent families don't necessarily "need" anything they don't already have. And a truth for me is that I would throw myself in front of a train for either of my children, but can't say the same thing about any partner I've ever lived with.

I fall in love, I want to cohabit, but I don't ever want my kids to suffer for that.

My sister's the same way. When explaining to me why she'd kicked a new boyfriend out, she said: "I guess he thought it was a good idea to get between a mammal and her offspring."

"Harsh," I said. But I understood.

If you ask a parent to choose between you and the children, you have to be prepared for the answer to be "the children." Sometimes this is as it should be. Sometimes it's unfair.

As a mother, it's always been hard for me to see the difference between putting my kids first and irrationally siding with them. It may be a very bad idea to get between a mammal and her offspring, but that's true, in part, because mammals have a hard time backing off and letting other mammals have their own relationships.

That partner who moved in with me when my daughter was almost twelve lasted a decade with me. Things between her and my daughter were always tense. My guilt about the ways it hadn't worked kept me up nights, my heart contracting in my chest. So it was bittersweet the first Thanksgiving after we'd broken up that my ex and my daughter decided to get together without me for an afternoon.

"Wow," my daughter said when she got home. "The two of us just had our first chill conversation ever. She actually treated me like a normal human being. She's kind of . . . cool."

I shook my head. I mean, seriously? They could have just gotten along?

I couldn't help but wonder at how things might have gone differently. What if we'd treated each other more like normal human beings from the start instead of as generic players in our own preconceived notions of what "family" ought to look like, of how children ought to act, of where a new partner has a right to tread?

Rivers and priests make it all look so easy, but for most of us this flowing on involves a lot of guesswork and panic. When it works, I think it involves a lot of faith and letting go.

In my family, we don't have children who are reared in one household by their two biological parents. It's just not the way we do things. So we learn as we go. We make mistakes, and try to imagine what it's like to stand in each other's shoes. New commitments are fragile, exciting, terrifying. Old bonds are complicated. And as our love for each other flows on in all its changing forms—easy and tense—we grow up. And that's the goal with all of this, isn't it? Growing up and learning to see and accept our families for what they are rather than getting stuck in our individual and preconceived ideas about what "family" should be like. Your family "should" be just as it is—ever changing and delicious.

Part 1 | *Coming Together*

TWO DOGS, THREE CATS, TWO GIRLS

• • •

ellen sussman

What I brought to the new relationship:

Two daughters, ages nine and eleven, both angry about the end
of my marriage.

One badly trained but sweet Golden Retriever.

A 500-square-foot cottage that was already stuffed full of daughters, a dog, and me.

What he brought to the relationship:

A dog, three cats, and two horses.

A gorgeous ranch in Washington that we couldn't move to
because of the joint custody agreement with my ex.

What happened when we bought a new house together and brought my daughters, my dog, his dog, his cats, and the two of us into a new blended family:

My older daughter emailed Neal right before he moved down and said: Don't come. My mother is a witch and you won't want to live with her. He wrote back: My family comes from Transylvania (true) and as a vampire I have no problem living with a witch.

I hate cats. They walked all over me while we slept. They peed on the new rug. They preened in the middle of the dining room table, fur flying into our food.

My younger daughter, who adores cats, didn't know that chasing them isn't the way to get them to love you. And since she wasn't going to listen to Neal about anything at all, she kept chasing them.

He didn't like my dog very much. Neal's a guy who lived on a ranch. Madison, the Golden, was pathetically suburban, spoiled and lazy. She spent most of her day with her head on someone's knee, waiting for a treat.

I loved his dog, a big mixed-breed ranch dog with brindle-colored fur and soulful eyes. She immediately became my dog, following me everywhere, ignoring him in the same way my daughters did.

He missed his horses. Or so I imagined as I watched him ferry the girls to school and ballet and basketball; as he cooked pasta every night since it was the only thing everyone would eat; as he worked in his shop, building furniture for the girls and bookshelves for us. I tried to rent a horse for him one Christmas, but he watched it wistfully for a while as it trotted around the ring and then told me that horses were a part of his old life, not his new one.

How things changed:

Our house is still filled with animals, fifteen years later. We've chosen them together. My youngest daughter has stopped chasing the cats.

The girls and I bought Neal a Christmas kitten after the last of his ranch cats died, and now even I have fallen in love with Emma.

When we first moved our families in together—my girl family and his animal family—I knew it wouldn't be easy. He hadn't raised kids. They didn't want some new guy telling them what to do. The first time he disciplined one of the girls—telling her not to talk to me in such a nasty way (Yes! Why hadn't I thought of that?)—I was more surprised than my daughter. "I'm a part of this family," he told me. "I have a say in how the girls behave." And so he did.

Over the years, the girls have fallen in love with Neal and he with them. He's a true dad with them, a dad who puts them at the center of his life. He's flown cross-country to bail one daughter out of a bad situation. He was the road trip companion for the other daughter's college drives from San Francisco to Tacoma. He tells them how to deal with cranky computers, tough bosses, and silly boys. He teaches them to cook fish now that we've moved beyond pasta.

Our girls have moved into apartments of their own, both within an hour of our house. When one of them is upset over a fight with a boyfriend or bad day at work, she'll come over to visit the animals. Or so she says. We'll all gather in the living room, dogs at our feet, cat on a lucky lap. It's the animals that draw them home, the love they get from sprawling on the floor with the very big dog or tumbling into bed with the pound puppy. Emma can cure all ills with a cuddle.

Maybe, in the end, the vampire and the witch have cast their spells and created a home.

WHO WILL THIS BE TO ME

• • •

betsy graziani fasbinder

One afternoon a few months before Tom and I were to be married, Max wandered into the dining room of the house we all shared. I was sorting through a box of old photographs and, when he entered the room, I turned to him. He tossed a bright orange Nerf ball over and over, said nothing, didn't look at me, just focused completely on the ball. Though he was barely seven, I could already recognize in the way he threw the ball straight up and caught it the quick reflexes and fast hands of the athlete he would become. Soon he began to twirl around after each toss, catching the spongy ball behind his back. Then he bounced the ball off the wall over the table, then off the ceiling.

"Hi, Bud," I said. "Nice moves."

No reply. Wall. Ceiling. Twirl. Wall.

"Whatcha doin'?" he finally asked.

"Just trying to organize some of my pictures."

In my months of living with Tom and Max, I'd learned to let the boy come close on his own. If I crowded him or moved too quickly, he skittered away, his tolerance for closeness dissipating like so much water vapor. If I was patient, though, we often ended up playing, laughing, and, recently, even snuggling on the couch with a book or a TV show.

"Who's that?" he asked, peeking around my shoulder.

"My mom when she was young."

"What's she sitting on?"

"A paper moon. They used to have them at fairs and carnivals. People liked to pose for pictures on them."

"That's dumb. It doesn't even look like a real moon."

"After the wedding, I suppose she'll be your grandma Sylvia."

"Cool." Wall. Ceiling. Wall. Wall. Twirl.

He caught the ball and then sidled up beside me, leaning his warm body against my arm and pressing a dirt-smudged finger on another photo. "Who will that be to me?" he asked.

"That was my grandfather, the one who died a few months ago."

Max shrugged and resumed his tossing, this time switching hands. Right. Left. Right. "I already got a grandfather," he said, not unkindly.

"Lots of kids have two grandpas. I guess my grandfather would have been your great-grandfather."

"Hmm. Too bad he had to die. I coulda used one of those."

As I continued my sorting and stacking, I felt a pinch in my chest. Death is always a barbed topic, but is particularly so for a child who lost his mother only two years before. I shuffled quickly past the pictures of dead relatives.

The Nerf ball stilled again and Max propped his elbows on the table, resting his chin on his upturned palms. "What about them?" he asked, pointing to a picture of my sister and her family. He'd known them his whole life, just as he had known me, played with my niece and nephew regularly, attended birthday parties and family dinners. But I could see that he was beginning to grasp the change that was coming. The difference in how he knew me before and how he would know me in the future.

"Di and Jim will be your aunt and uncle. Megan and Matt will be your cousins."

"Sweet," he said, looking into my face for the first time since he'd entered the room. His eyes were chocolate pools, his thick dark hair a sleek, shiny coat that made me want to run my fingers over it. "I don't have any boy cousins. And how about him?"

"That's my brother John. He'll be another uncle."

We sorted stacks of aunts and uncles, cousins and friends.

"Wow, you have a lot of people," Max sighed.

"I suppose I do."

He began to finger through the stacks, messing up what I'd already sorted, but that was all right. My original task no longer mattered. As we neared the bottom of the stack, a honey-thick warmth began to fill me. Perhaps my family was to be the dowry I'd bring to this little boy who had lost so much.

"Whoa," he exclaimed, laughing at my third-grade photo, the one where my hair had been expanded to new dimensions by an especially humid Indiana day.

At moments like those, Max was just a little boy, buoyant with energy, easy with a laugh. He played Legos and watched *Teenage Mutant Ninja Turtles*. And he tossed balls. At other times, when he was still or thought no one was looking, it seemed that the earth's pull was just a little stronger where he stood, tugging the corners of his mouth downward, making his eyes years older than seven birthdays would imply.

Just as I was about to put the last of the pictures in the box, Max pressed his finger once more to a face. "And who will this be to me?"

Beneath his finger I could see the edges of my own face. I was suddenly flooded with a heart-swell for which I had no name. This son of the man I loved was becoming my son. We'd have family Christmas cards and school art stuck with magnets to the fridge. I'd make goodie bags at birthday parties, snap pictures at graduations. All these things I'd never allowed myself to want, thinking that perhaps my own parents had left me so wounded that I could not allow myself children of my own. Now I was becoming a mother, but without the benefit of a growing belly or a baby shower to prepare me.

I should have known the answer to his simple question. I should have known how to say just the right, wise, magical thing. But I didn't. So I offered the therapist's cop-out question.

"Well, what do you think?"

Max shrugged. Then he looked away and I knew it was my job to field this one. Jumbled words bobbed to the surface of my mind, like those triangled answers floating in the blue waters in a Magic 8 Ball.

Finally the image rose to the surface. "I'll be your second mom," I said.

"Oh."

"I'm sorry that your first mom died. I liked her."

"What should I call you?" he asked.

My heart pounded against the cage of my ribs, and my stomach turned over. *Mama,* I wanted to cry. *I'll be your mama and you'll be my son.* I resisted. "You can call me Mom, or Mama. You can also call me Betsy, if you'd rather. Whatever feels okay for you."

He stood there a minute, and I waited, expecting a pronouncement of my new title.

"What's for dinner?" he asked picking up his ball.

"Burgers."

"Sweet," he said, tossing the ball as he walked out of the room.

At our wedding a few months later, Tom and I said our vows to one another. Then Max was invited to stand beside us and I made vows to him. I promised to step into the shoes his mother had been forced to leave behind, to help him remember her, and to be the best mother I could be.

After the wedding, for the next few days, Max tried out a new title for me. "Can we go bowling?" he'd ask, and then follow the question by mouthing the word *mom*. Or, "Can we go to the store?" And the mouthed word, *mom*. *Mom* was always silent. It seemed he was trying it on, seeing how it felt in his mouth. "Whatcha doin', *Mom*?" "Can I watch TV now, *Mom*?"

My hopes floated like a pink helium balloon. Then, like a thousand hornets, guilt attacked the balloon, piercing it until it lost its air and sank. It felt wrong to take such pleasure in seeing his little plum lips form that singular syllable. After all, this new son of mine was an inheritance I would not have if he and Tom hadn't sustained such an enormous loss. I felt small . . . and smaller still when old habits resumed and Betsy was once again my only title. I tucked this shameful disappointment away, telling no one.

Weeks later as I drove him home from school, Max pulled a baggie full of Cheez-Its from his *Teenage Mutant Ninja Turtles* lunch box. He munched away, licking the orange dust off each finger. With his focus deep inside the near-empty snack bag, he suddenly said, "I notice I don't call you Mom."

Oof. Who threw that rock at my chest? Dead hit. I breathed to calm my voice. "I noticed that."

One last cracker, then four fingers to lick. "When I say Betsy, I mean Mom."

I swallowed past the dry dirt clod that formed in my throat. "Thanks," I said. "That's nice to know."

He looked out the window. "Moms die, you know. I think it's maybe safer if you're just Betsy."

We could have a long talk about magical thinking and death and how nothing he could say, or not say, could cause me to die, or could have caused his mother to die. But this just didn't seem like the time for all of that.

I willed tears away, not wanting to overwhelm him. He had enough to carry. "Thanks, Bud. I appreciate you telling me."

Those big chocolate eyes found mine. I waited.

"Hey, Betsy?"

"Yeah," I said, delighted with the new sound of my old name.

"What's for dinner?" he asked.

BLENDED

• • •

marcelle soviero

The bus carrying our children, who made up most of the wedding party, and a number of guests, was more than an hour late getting to our house, the spot we'd chosen for the ceremony and reception. Eric and I waited. Today, after three years of dating, we were getting married, joining our hearts, homes, and five children: Johnny, Jamie, Olivia, Sophia, and Luke—ages four to nine.

The children had been excited since our engagement five months before, wondering where we'd go on our honeymoon. After the announcement, we all moved into the historic Henry Finch House, circa 1842, Eric and I having passed on purchasing one of the cookie-cutter colonials that had closets and updated plumbing. The Finch House had character: thick moldings, a *Harry Potter* closet under the stairs, and four chimneys to give Santa options. All this and our own slice of the Saugatuck River, which cut through our backyard, where there was now an arbor, rows of wooden white chairs, and a piano set up for the ceremony, which was supposed to start an hour ago.

With the children at the hotel the previous night, I'd imagined a leisurely morning, a long hot shower, a chance to comb my hair. Instead, I was a sack of mud until noon. Eric and I moved the trampoline, in the drizzle, to the neighbor's yard. While Eric fixed the party tent that had blown down in a storm during the night, I drove Lemon, our oversized Brittany Spaniel, to Dog Gone Smart, the pet hotel, since he gets hyper around a host of people. Lemon was short a shot required for admission, so I'd raced him to the vet and waited an hour for Dr. Noonan to immunize him.

Eventually I did get dressed. I wore a fitted ivory gown, nipped at the waist. The gown held in every inch of me except for my calves, where the dress flared, producing what I felt was the look of a mermaid, not the look of an hourglass, as my mother had insisted in the bridal shop. I'd curled my long blonde hair, normally straight as uncooked spaghetti. I put on pink lipstick. Then, feeling I had to jazz it up somehow, I tried the false eyelashes, ultimately flushing them down the toilet in frustration. Other than those lashes, I did not fuss much. I had no time until I suddenly had hours as I waited for the bus.

I stood at the kitchen window in the mermaid gown. The servers flew in and out the screen door, keeping the salmon crepes warm, moving everything into a second kitchen they'd set up in the garage. I took a small sip of Scotch, straight from the bottle.

Clearly, at some point in the wee hours I'd fallen through the rabbit hole and, like Alice, woke in a nonsensical place with strange characters surrounding me. The justice of the peace, a top-heavy middle-aged woman whom I had a bad feeling about from the start, but who was available on this date, paced in the living room, tapping her silver wristwatch. The DJ, a substitute for the man I hired, blew by me. "Everything's cool!" he said, positioning his ponytail.

I was a spectator in my own home and I did not fight it. My sister-in-law, a woman who can manage twelve tasks at once, breezed by holding organza bows and a hammer. "You look beautiful, Marcelle," she said.

Antonio, the cook, passed by. "*Bellissimo, Marcelle!*" he said, blowing me a kiss and waving the carving knife he'd finally found. I laughed out loud, feeling sillier by the minute in the gown. I took another small swig and considered changing into my jeans.

Out back, the river swelled with rain and the September air swooned with the smell of butterfly bushes, penne pasta sauce, and a hint of hornet spray. Dozens of our local guests sipped blue martinis in the backyard under the fixed white tent whose tiered tips poked into the late afternoon sky.

At last, brakes wheezing, the bus pulled up along the fence, taking up half the street, stopping cars in both directions. The people in paused cars watched my beautiful children, wrinkled but finely dressed, race in the front door.

"Mommy! Your hair is excited!" Johnny, just four, stuck his hand in the pocket of his pinstripe seersucker jacket, his light blue tie touching his belt buckle. He was referring, I think, to the curls in my hair. "I ate twelve Twizzlers and two Gobstoppers on the bus," he said, passing me a purple jawbreaker he'd held the entire ride, which had made a lavender stain on his palm. I popped it into my mouth.

The girls swooned around me like bees to a petal. "Mommy, you're a fairy queen," Olivia said, touching a thin line of beads at the waist of my dress.

My eyes dropped to Sophia and Olivia, ages nine and eight, and my stepdaughter Jamie, just seven, in mismatched white dresses they'd chosen from the sale rack at the Lollipop Guild. Just last night, they'd tried the dresses on again, dancing like debutantes spinning in front of the full-length mirror in my bedroom, skirts blooming.

"It's hard to believe I'll love you even more tomorrow than I do right this minute," I said to them.

The guests filed into the folding chairs and Leonard Bernstein's "Make Our Garden Grow" played through the speakers, the notes gently pulling Eric and his little best man, Luke, beside him toward the arbor under which we would be married.

They walked down the makeshift grassy isle in matching blue blazers, a slice of sun catching the silver in Eric's hair. I remembered our first date at the SoHo Grande, two hearts winking tears, lips in a kiss under a plaid umbrella. He was the good guy in every movie I'd ever seen, the one the Hollywood starlets wished they'd chosen once the bad boys broke their heart. He was mine now. Always would be.

Jamie entered stage left, her click-clack shoes tinkling on the slate pathway, tiara tucked into a blonde bun. Awestruck by the crowd that filled the chairs, she forgot to drop even one of the silk flower petals from the white woven basket, though for weeks she'd practiced throwing big bunches at a time. Johnny, the tiny ring bearer, followed close behind steadying the ring on the small pillow I'd stitched from the plaid flannel robe my father wore for at least thirty of his short fifty-six years.

My maids of honor, Sophia and Olivia, came next, holding hands. Their long dark hair, secured with faux diamond clips, scrolled down their backs. The children surrounded Eric at the arbor. I took them all in, considered my life in that instant, not precisely what I had planned, but perfectly imperfect.

STEPFAMILY HONEYMOON

• • •

rebecca payne

The first test of our newly blended life came with the chewing gum. Tomás thumped a pack down on the dash of the rented minivan as we pulled out of the driveway on our family vacation/honeymoon.

"Better hide that," I said, sticking with the promise I had made to myself.

That promise was one I'd made on our wedding day, that from here on out my kids and I would be on our best behavior. Jack, Katie, and I would be neat, polite, and quiet(er).

Tomás had advantages on me in the parenting department. At twelve, Jessica was slightly the oldest. Being female made her more socially adept to start with, and she was an only child, who had been raised in the quieter adult world of her parents.

At ages nine and eleven, my children, Katie and Jack, were nothing if not rambunctious and loud. Chewing gum was definitely not going to help with the neatness.

"Jessica likes chewing gum." Tomás didn't even cast a glance in my direction.

"Well, let's put it away for this trip," I countered. "If my kids see that, they'll want some too, and they're pretty messy."

"Then don't give them any." My dearly betrothed shrugged.

I should have pursued the divorce right then—if I were not hypnotized by that magic state of blissful love.

So now, my promise met its first test. I was madly in love, but I was not about to let my children be treated like second-class citizens.

Pretty soon Jessica spied the gum and asked for a piece. Then Jack and Katie asked too. I handed a piece to each of them without glancing at my husband. *Hmm*, I thought, *I guess we have a thing or two to learn about co-parenting.*

Half an hour later, Jessica neatly rolled her gum up in its original paper and deposited it in the cup holder. Jack rolled down the window and spat.

"Don't!" I cried too late, looking to see if his gum had landed on a car behind us. Tomás raised an eyebrow nervously.

Before I could stop her, Katie stuck her head out the window, hair blowing wildly into her eyes, and spat too, but her gum stuck to the window ledge. She picked it up and tossed it, leaving little streamers behind. The bits left on her fingers she wiped on the outside of the van.

I looked at Tomás and smiled. He was staring in the rearview mirror in panic.

At the next stop, Tomás took me aside to show me the damage.

"Look, it's here . . . and here . . . and here. I've tried to wipe it and it just smears." He frowned.

"I can get it off," I said calmly. I'd had plenty of practice removing stains. "In the meantime, maybe you'd better put that away." I felt a surge of triumph as he slipped the gum into his pocket.

Our destination was a cabin by the ocean in North Carolina. The owners, friends of my mother, had offered it to us for free. A great deal—except it was a two-day drive from our Michigan home. The ocean seemed a perfect place to take a pack of energetic kids. I had visions of them rolling in the surf, and Tomás and I taking moonlit walks as the tides washed in.

After two days of driving in summer's ferocious heat, we were cranky and exhausted, but that changed when we approached the little town. I rolled down the window. "Wow, smell that sea air! You kids are gonna love swimming in the ocean!

"Here's what we're going to do," I continued, as we turned onto the street. "When we get to the house, we'll jump into our swimsuits and then drive to the ocean as fast as we can, okay? We'll unpack later."

We were five limp and soggy beings when we finally stopped in front of the cabin. As soon as we opened the doors, the oppressive heat hit us in the face.

"Ouch! It's hot!" Katie cried, curling her toes as her bare feet hit the sand.

I carried her to the porch, then noticed Tomás looking over the rickety shelter with shock on his face.

It was more dilapidated than I'd remembered. Fifty years earlier, Mary and Earl had bought this small lot in the middle of a grove of pines. They parked an Airstream trailer in the middle of a cement pad, and built crude walls around it—that was our cabin.

The backyard sported a hammock and an open-air shower, complete with tree frogs that hopped across the rough board walls. As a child, I had thought this place was perfect. Now, it looked like a good wind would blow the whole thing over.

"Hey, Tomás, it's beautiful, isn't it?" I joked. "Fine-quality construction, huh?"

He shook his head. "Guess it won't fall on us. It's been here a long time, anyway."

His confidence was one reason I loved him. I gave him a peck on the cheek, then turned to the kids.

"Okay, grab your suitcases and let's get out those swimsuits." I felt like a camp counselor. "I'll get some water in the thermos. Just a suit and a towel and off we go!"

The kids and I walked inside with our bags.

"You girls, go there in the bedroom and change." I pointed to the shiny metal Airstream sitting like a blimp in the middle of the shelter.

I took Katie and her pink suitcase and climbed the three stairs into the camper with Jessica following.

"Isn't this fun?" I ducked my head to get inside. "I haven't been here in years."

The inside of the camper was one big knotty pine bedroom.

At one end was Mary and Earl's large bed, with a green chenille bedspread. At the other end was a lumpy twin-sized mattress on a frame.

"Which bed is mine?" Jessica asked.

"Um," I looked at the two beds, "I guess you girls will sleep in the big bed and Jack will have the little one."

"Daaad!" Jessica looked imploringly at her dad, who was peeking inside.

She took him by the hand and ran outside, where there was some whispered conversation while I helped Katie and Jack into their swimsuits.

Pretty soon, Tomás came back inside. "Jessica isn't used to sleeping with anyone. She needs a bed alone." He was looking at a spot over my head, avoiding my eyes.

"She can't sleep with anyone? We're on vacation! She'll sleep like a log!"

Remembering that until this week Jessica had been an only child, I whispered, "Has she ever *tried*?"

Tomás looked pained. "She needs her own bed."

"Okay," I said, "then she can have the little bed and my two will sleep together in the big one."

The big bed had heaps of lacy ruffled pillows. The smaller one was stained and lumpy. Jessica came in and sat on the big bed looking imploringly at her dad.

"Jessica can't sleep in that little bed," Tomás said. "She has a big bed at home and she needs a big bed. Maybe you can put one of your kids in the little one and one on that roll-out cot." He pointed toward a cot in the corner.

I raised an eyebrow. "That's crazy, Tomás. There are three kids here. They need to share."

"Well, they can share on some other things, but Jessica needs this bed. I'm sorry, honey, but she'll just have to have this one."

"Okay . . ." I said very slowly. "She can have it the first night, but then they can switch. That's just not fair." I looked at Jessica, "Is it?"

Kids understand fair—they challenge adults on fairness all the time. Surely she would understand. She rushed out of the room and Tomás followed with her swimsuit. I shrugged.

We'd deal with beds later. I was certain that a few hours at the beach would tire them to the point they didn't care where they slept.

I slid into my own swimsuit. When I returned to the front of the cabin, Jessica was in her swimsuit looking out the front door.

"Oh, wow, that was fast!" I said. "Let's get in the van!"

"We can't go until Dad gets my other stuff out," she said.

"What stuff? Let's go jump in the water. It's too hot here!"

Jack, Katie, and I walked out while Jessica waited inside by the door. Tomás had opened the car top carrier and was tossing down bags and boxes. He had loaded Jessica's bags at her mom's house, so I had not seen what she'd brought.

"What are you looking for?" I asked him as I corralled my kids before they headed into the street.

"Jessica's beach stuff."

"Oh, she can use mine," I said. "I have some drinking water and sunscreen. See? We have towels. We can get all the other stuff out later. Let's just go!"

"No," he said with a calm, steady voice.

Jessica started grabbing bags and taking them into the house. When everything was out of the carrier, I walked back inside and looked around in awe. Spread out in the entrance was an inflatable raft, flippers, masks, water wings, a giant inner tube, folding chairs, a Frisbee, a beach ball, a water cannon. There was also a radio and a beach umbrella.

I hadn't brought a thing, not even a blow-up ducky for my kids. When I was a kid, I'd contented myself with collecting shells on the corner of a beach towel and playing in the water. I made sand castles with pieces of shell. And that was fine. It doesn't take much to entertain kids at the beach. It hadn't even occurred to me to buy stuff.

Jessica started pulling more things out of a small bag, sunglasses and sun hat, bottles of sunscreen, suntan lotion, and bug spray.

Now, before we go on, I need to insert a public service announcement in support of my new stepdaughter. There are millions of families who go to the beach with lots of gear. There are a lot of folks who wouldn't dream of stepping in the water without a chair, umbrella, and cooler waiting for them a few steps away. Jessica's supply of consumer goods put her more squarely in the middle of mainstream America than my barebones plan. But for me, barefoot with only a towel and a thermos of water, seeing all this gear plopped in the living room of our tumble-down beach house was about as shocking as watching a helicopter arrive to transport us to the beach.

"Can we go?" Jack tugged at my swimsuit.

"Sure, honey." I couldn't stop staring.

"We're almost ready," Tomás said, smiling.

We waited long minutes while Tomás helped Jessica apply sunscreen and braid her hair. Jack and Katie were nearing tantrum stage. We walked around the yard, looking at the unfamiliar plants and lizards, and feeling the sandy soil under our feet. We could hear the surf, but couldn't quite see the ocean. The childish side of me wanted to just take off on foot, but the grown-up side of me knew I needed to stay and guide Tomás and Jessica.

Finally they emerged, Jessica in swimsuit, cover-up, sunglasses, hat, and water shoes. She carried a big tote bag and a camera. Tomás carried towels, goggles, fins, masks, and the blow-up raft with a pump all balanced on top of a cooler.

We drove silently the few blocks down the public access road to the waterfront. I felt a sense of betrayal that Tomás had not warned me of all the stuff Jessica was bringing. We could have coordinated better. My half of the family looked a little shabby.

Neither Tomás nor I had much money. Our whole wedding had probably cost as much as this newly purchased beach gear.

When we parked, I ran into the surf with Jack and Katie and quickly forgot the two coming slowly down the sand behind us, their arms loaded down. The crashing waves knocked us down. We stood up, laughing and splashing. Ah, paradise! Two days cooped up in a smelly minivan, all the stress, all the fuss and muss—this was worth it!

Tomás and Jessica joined us. Leaving all the stuff behind, soon Jessica was squealing and jumping with Jack and Katie.

Tomás and I held hands in the water and smiled. Our relationship had a few bugs to work out, but all in all, this was going to be a great trip!

When we were tired out, we returned to the cabin to change for dinner. This time it was Jessica who was nearing a tantrum. While we washed off under the outdoor shower, Tomás turned to me.

"Jessica's homesick. We're going to drive downtown to find a phone and call her mom."

"Um, well, why don't we all go together on our way out to eat? We're starving!"

"This won't take long. I need to do it with Jessica. Just let us do this alone, and then we'll get something to eat."

"Okay," I sighed, not knowing what else to say. "But hurry."

Marriage is about compromise, right?

Tomás was a great dad. He truly was. And Jessica was a great kid. A bit sheltered from being an only child, I thought, but if she stuck around this family, that wouldn't last long.

After they left, Jack, Katie, and I played a few hands of cards. After we tired of Rummy, we turned on the tiny television. The children settled onto the musty sofa, curled around each other. I wandered around putting away gear.

"Can I have a hot dog?" Katie asked.

"Honey, we haven't been to the store yet. Tomás and Jessica will be back soon and we'll go out for dinner."

I looked down the road in the lengthening shadows for the van.

"Can I have a cookie?" Jack asked.

"No. We're going out to supper, so no more snacks."

"But I'm hungry," he whined, and I knew his little stomach was empty. Denying him food made me anxious.

"No," I said angrily. "Stop asking!"

They grew silent, and as the minutes rolled by I felt guilty for yelling.

After the TV show ended I noticed Katie's eyes drooping. These kids weren't going to make it through dinner in a restaurant. I had to feed them or deal with a meltdown if we tried to go out.

I made sandwiches from the doughy bread and limp cheese slices that had survived two days in the cooler. *Some supper*, I thought, still looking out at every passing car for the one that would turn into our driveway. *Where could they be?*

After eating, I pulled out the small cot in the Airstream and grumbled as I prepped it for sleeping. As the time lengthened, I became more distracted.

I alternated between worry—*Are they lost? Did Tomás wreck the van?*—and anger—*Did they eat without us? How dare they leave us here without food!*

Anger won out over worry. They couldn't be hurt. We were on a small island where there was almost zero crime. The speed limit on the main road was 25 mph.

I cleaned up the kitchen, put away the snacks, and surveyed the contents of the cupboards.

No van.

I helped the kids brush their teeth and put on pajamas.

Still no van.

I went to the back bedroom and put on my nightgown, the new nightgown I had bought for my honeymoon. *Ha! Some honeymoon!* I got angrier as I put clothes away, remembering the chewing gum incident and compounding it with the massive amount of stuff Tomás had brought for Jessica. *He's not going to treat me this way! My kids deserve everything he can buy for his daughter.* I loudly snapped sheets onto the bed.

Buddyrow, if you think this is the way our marriage is going to go, I have another think for you. I found myself using the same vocabulary my mother used to use against my father.

Furious, I kept glancing around the corner looking for headlights turning into the driveway. *How dare he leave me here with two hungry kids! It's pitch dark!*

My mind reeled. *I left my kids hungry so I could wait for HIM! I snapped at them!*

Still there was the nagging question, *Are they okay?*

Finally, I saw lights turn into the drive. The last nibble of worry dissolved and left in its place a pure white anger. I walked around the corner and stood facing the front door with my hands on my hips. My face was flushed and my eyes were blazing. *Whatever excuse he has, it is not going to be enough!*

Sweet little Katie looked up, her eyes heavy with sleep. "Mom," she said. "I've never noticed before, but you are really beautiful!"

I won't bore you with the details of what happened next other than to report we had the first fight of our marriage. Or at least I had a fight. After we'd put the kids to bed, Tomás sat with me on the outdoor swing and listened calmly while I spouted all the words my mother used and more. He weakly defended himself, saying only that Jessica had never been so far away from her mother. He had tried to distract her by walking on the beach and looking around the town.

After a while, I ran out of steam. Tomás apologized, and we let the sound of the surf calm us again.

"We have a lot to learn about each other, huh?" Tomás stroked my hair.

"Yeah. Next time, let's talk this out a little better, okay?"

"Till death do us part, right?" he asked.

"If it kills us," I answered smiling.

The next day, limited budget be damned, I bought beach gear for my kids, grumbling as I paid for plastic toys and cheap sunglasses. Why crowd the beach with so much junk? There were so many other exciting things to do. We could walk on the piers and look in the fishermen's baskets. We could put coins in the pinball machines in the arcade, make sand castles, or look for the crabs burrowing in the sand.

Luckily, my children weren't the type to feel slighted. They were content with what they had, even though Jessica had more and better stuff. She ended up keeping the big bed all to herself for the whole week—and they didn't complain. But just as with the chewing gum incident, I didn't want my kids to feel lesser because they didn't have the same as their stepsister—and I didn't want them to resent Jessica. We five were in this life together now, so we'd all have to be on the same page. I could embrace a little of this materialistic side of Tomás and Jessica. I had loved my simple life, but I could splurge sometimes, too.

I felt like an entertainer, tap dancing across the stage of our family, trying to put happiness in the place of insults or hurts. I had thought that this marriage would bring some calm to the chaotic lives that my kids and I'd been leading. Raising kids as a single person was exhausting.

Tomás was so protective and caring to Jessica—I'd dreamed of how nice it would be for all of us to share that feeling. I would never have guessed that the chaos would get worse. Now suddenly it seemed as if, far from being able to relax, I needed to stay more alert to keep his wall of protection for Jessica from harming my kids.

At least I didn't need to add Jessica to my mothering duties. Tomás made sure that he was always available for her. She was afraid of the frogs in the outdoor shower, so Tomás stood by the door while she showered. She didn't like the meals I prepared, so he fixed food especially for her. She needed longer to dress, to eat, to do everything, and she needed her dad at her side to do it.

By the end of the week, we were all ready to go home. We'd visited museums and learned about the ecosystem of the shoreline. We'd seen sand sharks and pelicans diving for fish and had watched the little plovers running up and down in the surf. We'd built sand castles and jumped in the waves—with and without the balls and rafts and other plastic gizmos.

On our last afternoon, we sat quietly in the shallow surf watching the sun go down, until an especially large wave sent us tumbling. When Tomás got his balance, he stood up and looked at me quizzically.

"Did I just have my glasses on?"

"Ummm, did you?" I asked.

"Ahhh! Dad lost his glasses!" Jessica shrieked.

"Maybe I left them by the blankets. Let's go see if they're there."
He and all three kids took off up the beach.

My heart sank. Tomás couldn't function without glasses. The next
day we faced a fifteen-hour drive home. If his glasses were gone, I'd
have to do all the driving and also tend to the maps, the radio, anything that took vision.

We have to find those glasses, I told myself. *Think, think.*

I was still in the water where we had been when the wave struck.
The glasses would probably have sunk straight to the bottom. If I
could feel around on the ocean floor, maybe I could find them.

I got down on all fours in the tumbling surf and started crawling
back and forth, fingering each of the rocks and broken shells for
something that felt like eyeglasses. A wave rolled me over, but I clambered back to where I had been, trying not to miss any spots.

"Mom, what are you doing?" Jack called.

"I'm trying to find the glasses," I said between mouthfuls of foam.
"Come help me."

"I don't think they're here," Tomás said. "I'm going to look in
the van."

"Tomás, come help me look. They have to be here!" I shouted.

"It's no use." He looked out at the vast expanse of ocean. "I'm
going to the van."

I thought of the next day's drive home and doubled my concen-
tration.

Tomás was halfway to the van when my fingers touched them.
Relief surged through me. I whooped and held the glasses over my
head.

"Dad!" Jessica cried, pointing at me. "Look. There they are!"

Tomás walked back toward me, beaming. "You found them! How
did you know . . . how did you do . . . what made you think . . ." He
looked at me admiringly.

I walked out of the water toward him, grinning. "Well, mister, you didn't think you were going to get out of driving that easily, now did you?"

The children jumped with glee. As the sun sank toward the horizon, we began gathering our gear for the last time.

Honeymoon—that blissful "honeyed moon" when a newly-wed couple gets to know each other more intimately. Well, I couldn't speak to the "honeyed" part, but this getting-to-know-you period had certainly opened our eyes to the challenges we faced. How funny that a mere week ago I'd believed we were going to live out a fairy-tale life! Blending these two families and maintaining our love and respect for each other, I now realized, were going to take hard work, fast reflexes, and tough skins.

But we weren't going to crack at the first bump in the road. We were both too stubborn to quit.

For better or worse? I looked around at these four happy, sunburnt faces and smiled. You bet.

NATURE'S PERFECT BLEND:
A WORK IN PROGRESS

• • •

lizabeth p. kingsley

In the summer of 2008, I fell in love. Sounds simple, right? Not so much. I was thirty-nine, married to a man I'd known since eighth grade, and raising two young sons (seven and nine). I was busily going on about my life, patching together part-time jobs to feel productive in the present, pursuing a teaching degree to become productive in the future, driving children to practices and parties in my suburban New Jersey town, trying to cultivate the writing career about which I'd dreamed since I was a little girl, and being a dutiful you-name-it: wife, mother, daughter, sister, daughter-in-law, sister-in-law, aunt, friend, and neighbor.

It started on the last day of school. My older son had finished second grade. A friend with a son the same age invited my kids and me to the zoo the following day. On the drive home from the monkeys and the snakes, she invited me to her patio for drinks with some women I'd met once or twice, most with sons in second grade. I felt at ease with these women and had visions of frequent get-togethers and lasting friendships in the making. The next week, several of us got an email from one of the women, G, asking us to write letters of support for our boys' teacher. That was our beginning.

G and I have a mutual love of writing—everything from comprehensive, persuasive letters to clever, amusing emails—and that love changed our lives. She and I spent the next month exchanging emails throughout the days and nights. My boys were in camp and we both worked from home, so we gave many, many hours to the keyboard. Something about the initial vibe between us on the patio, and the sharing of those teacher recommendation letters, had me hooked, but in a way I hadn't quite defined. All I knew was that I wanted to know everything about her and I wanted to entertain, impress, and entice her with every detail about me.

After hundreds of what I later realized were shamelessly flirty emails, we decided to take our friendship live and meet for dinner. Would our connection translate face-to-face or was it just a writing thing? We ate, drank, talked, and closed the restaurant down. We started playing tennis. Singles led to intimate discussions and painful good-byes in the doorway of her minivan. Toward the end of summer, G was going to Cape May for a week with her husband and three children. The morning they were leaving, we met for a quick tennis game. Then I crashed her quiet pre-departure work time at Starbucks because I just had to see her. I told her, with my heart pounding, my skin salty and rank, my hair slapped back in a sloppy ponytail, and no idea of what was to come, that I had feelings for her. I had a hunch it might be mutual, but I figured that even if it wasn't, it would be okay to put myself out there. She told me she felt the same way and asked if I was scared. Scared? I felt everything but scared . . . excited, bold, flattered, overcome. In that moment, fear was the farthest thing from my mind.

That wouldn't last long.

That fall, G and I spent every spare second together. I was student teaching, G was writing articles in her home office, and we were caring for our children and our husbands. Mostly, though, we were caring for the overwhelming, empowering, and overpowering love we felt for each other. We revealed our relationship to our husbands in November, and we were faced with their devastation and what to do with our lives.

G was unflinching in her certainty that she and I could build a life together, blend ourselves and our five kids into a family of our own, and usher all nine of us through this huge change so that we'd remain intact. To put it lightly, I was apprehensive. I knew I wanted to be with her, but I had tremendous difficulty believing we could make it work. Before long, I'd made a three-page list of the hurdles we might encounter and the challenges we'd undoubtedly face . . . everything from religious differences to financial struggles to creating something approaching a harmonious household with our five very different children and our two very (how very) different ways of dealing with them. Then, there were our husbands.

In the fall of 2009, just over a year after we'd first met and after months of crying, sleeping way too much, barely eating, and growing sick of being so afraid, I took a leap—a leap of faith, a leap into her strong, confident, determined, and loving arms. We could figure this out. We were creative, bright, educated, and passionate, and we wanted this so very badly. In June 2010, we moved into a house together. My two boys shared a room, G's two boys shared a room, and G's daughter, the oldest of the five, had a room to herself.

It took a very short time to realize just how hard this blending would be. I know nothing's perfect and things aren't always (ever?) what they seem. Particularly stepfamilies, which, according to the several therapists helping me navigate my life, are the hardest family incarnations going. We have wonderful moments, but much of the time, life in our house is hard. We have a few major issues that pop up again and again. We make headway with them and then regress.

First, the good news: There were issues that we thought would be huge stumbling blocks but that have turned out fine. We are two stepmothers; we're women in a gay relationship raising five children (with their fathers' substantial involvement) from the ages of nine to fourteen, ages during which there are all kinds of awareness and maturing and coming into one's sexual own. We worried that our kids might be ridiculed in school for having two moms or gay moms or whatever spin mean kids would put on that. We worried that people who'd been our friends when we were heterosexually married would turn their backs. None of that has happened.

Another example: In our household, three of us are Jewish and four are Episcopalian. I imagined these religious and cultural differences could cause rifts between us. My older son was a bit troubled by the sight of our first Christmas tree, and G's kids felt a little odd lighting Chanukah candles, but now, my stepdaughter, who lights altar candles as an acolyte at Sunday church services, wants to be lifted into the air on a chair during my son's upcoming bar mitzvah.

Finances are an area that can tear stepfamilies (and all families) apart. In books about the issues that plague stepfamilies, finances are always right at the top. Fortunately, even this isn't one of our big struggles. G is the primary earner in our house and she can earn from home, so she's around for school drop-off and pickup and anyone who develops a sore throat during school hours. I work as well, partly at home and partly away from home. We manage to pay the bills, live in a comfortable house, and eat out now and then without feeling strapped. We worry about money like most people do, but no more as a function of our step-ness.

And now, the not-so-good news. Part of the reason this relative comfort level is possible is that G and her ex-husband, who earns more than both of us combined, continue to operate from joint bank accounts. Everything financial between them is as it was before, only now there are three extra people and one extra house on the scene. The way G and her ex-husband support and care for each other and collaboratively raise their children in a state of divorce brought about by G leaving the marriage for another woman is astonishing. My cadre of therapists regularly acknowledge the unique and extraordinary quality of their relationship. What they've been able to achieve, the trails they blaze as they define what it looks like to be amicably, even lovingly divorced, work fabulously for almost everyone involved. I am the exception. While their closeness is admirable and I want that for G and her kids, it can be hard for me, sometimes wrenching. Certain interactions between them roll right off me while others knot my intestines. They have a history with which I can't compete. G and I have been living together for over two years now and still this issue pops up. I'm working on it; we both are.

The thing is, I like her ex-husband and I'm grateful for him. He's a salt-of-the-earth person with a big, forgiving heart and great comic timing who's important to G and their children. She wouldn't be happy if he weren't around. He's also generous with my children; a lifelong Mets fan, he bought my sons giant Yankee Fatheads for their bedroom walls. He's generous with me; I doubt he envisioned commuting to and from New York City every day to help support a woman and her sons who, despite his great resistance, became part of the fabric of his family and helped undo his marriage. He's even said that he and I are now family. I want to be über-tolerant, über-understanding, über-appreciative, über-secure, but if my new life has taught me anything, I have über-limitations.

A parallel issue is that my relationship with my ex-husband has drastically deteriorated. He and I have known each other most of our lives, and while he wanted very much to save our marriage, once he realized that wasn't going to happen, he decided we were finished . . . finished as friends, finished as individuals who greet each other at baseball games, finished as humans who exchange small courtesies. Our mode of communication is restricted to email and the content of our communication is restricted to our boys. He and I spent thousands of dollars and about as many hours constructing a precise divorce agreement that we refer to often, as compared with G and her ex-husband who spent negligible money on legal fees and came up with a written document only because the court system requires it. My loss isn't easy, not easy for me to sustain and not easy for G to watch. Most of all, it's not easy for my boys. One only knows his parents as virtual strangers, and the other may (or may not) remember a time when his father and I made eye contact and conversation.

Another relentlessly recurring issue is our kids, who are as different as any five kids could be. I can come up with varied adjectives to describe them, but more than just their individual differences, it's probably the cultures in their early households that have shaped them and how we relate to them. G wields a swift decision-making ability to fantastic effect when our kids do something that warrants it. I like to talk things through and give warnings about the next time. The culture she's used to has clearly drawn lines between adults and children, both of whom know their place. I don't know that I recognized this before, but our many hard talks about the mothers we are have shown me that the lines between parent and child have been much more blurred in my houses, both as a child and as a mom. G's kids sing along with Disney movies. Mine vie to watch *Contagion* and *The Terminator*. Hers drink milk with dinner. Mine offer to "make our drinks," which may include wine or vodka. My kids negotiate and deal-make. They want explanations. They hear "no" as "let's figure out a compromise."

Did I create this? I'm sure I played a role, along with the rest of the village it's taken to get them where they are. G and I have talked a great deal about imposing appropriate consequences only to have one of my therapists advise us that consequences don't necessarily get us the end result we want: happy children. It's about getting to the root of bad behavior rather than sticking a soapy Band-Aid over a fresh mouth. Among us, we have moodiness, even tempers, sensitivity, arrogance, reluctance to take responsibility, self-punishers, inclusiveness, frustration, video games, adolescence, goofiness, and five kids who would probably jump at the chance to have things go back to the way they were, when, as the youngest among them says, "there's a house with a mom and a dad."

G tends to treat all those at the kid table equally, whether she pushed them out after fifteen laboring hours or met them, potty trained, a few years ago. I love egalitarianism. I think I'd be a good Communist. But I watch myself in action (and so do G and the kids), and I have a hard time treating everyone the same. I'm instinctively tougher on my kids and more lenient with G's (let's ignore for the moment the reality that my kids more often warrant toughness). I mean no manipulation or subliminal favoritism. I just have a particular knack for quickly reaching orange-alert levels of annoyance with my own kids. I think it's a logical extension of our tendency to be self-critical. They are me. If they've screwed up, I have too.

It also complicates things, as strange as that may sound, that G's kids and I get along very well. We don't butt heads, we don't lock horns, we don't have tension. G has told me many times how warmly they feel toward me and I consider it the highest compliment. You can't force that. If I've behaved in a way that's endeared them to me, it's a great source of pride. Maybe if I raised my voice more, that would change. Someone, likely a therapist, told me that the job of a stepparent is to be liked by her stepchildren. I'm sure it helps that my steps have a father who treats me with acceptance (as hard as that may be for him), so they have both of their parents to look to as models if they're not sure what to make of me. My kids get no such positive reinforcement from their dad.

Here's the thing. These challenges are stubborn, but as I said, along with them come incredibly rewarding moments when we palpably feel that we're building something. This is what I do—turn to the bright side when things get heavy, and we really do have one. We've taken many a deafening minivan ride with five children singing a song parody in unison, waving their arms and giggling. We've (well, they've) ridden death-defying roller coasters together in amusement parks from Dorney Park to Disney World (can you say "Expedition Everest" thirteen times?). The kids speak about each other as steps and describe each other that way in writing assignments for school. When my younger son turned ten last year, his stepsister drew a card and covered every inch of white space on the envelope with inside jokes and song lyrics and *Harry Potter* references. As he turned it around and around to read every inch of writing, he smiled wider and wider.

People in town tell me what a talented singer and actress my step-daughter is or what nice people or gifted athletes my stepsons are, because they know how important they are to me. G's mother changed her car's license plate to reflect her current number of grandchildren. G buys my kids fizzy drinks or large boxer briefs when they need them or just because, and I leave chocolate surprises on her kids' beds when the mood strikes. G had ankle surgery this summer and when my son called from a vacation in Israel, he asked how she was feeling. When I come home exhausted after a writing class, G's youngest asks me how it went. All three of G's kids have sought me out to share good news: a pitching victory, a nailed audition, a great weather forecast for a day at Six Flags. These are small moments, unplanned and fleeting. I know they don't obliterate the big stuff, unplanned and much less fleeting, but I am proud of every single one.

I've read a lot of literature about blending families, hundreds of success stories and some of failure, where the parties gave up and went their separate ways. One statistic that sticks to my ribs is that the average blended family takes between four and seven years to find its groove (the scientific term). I think that's good news and bad news. On the one hand, our plodding pace to harmony is par for the course (we've logged about two years so far), but on the other, there's no shortcut, as with anything worth having.

Not that I'm an expert on anything, really, but blending has brought out in me new and deeper levels of humility (aka cluelessness). I make much of this up as I go: how to be supportive and stern with my kids while they're adjusting to something they didn't ask for and while only living with them half the week; how to meld my styles of thinking and living and mothering with another thinker and liver and mother, who's got her own way of doing things; how to maintain trust among stepchildren who may still be figuring me out; how to strengthen my rubber exterior so the disrespect lobbed at me by my ex-husband, or occasionally my kids, bounces off; how to know when to advocate for us as a family and when to back off if one of us doesn't feel quite on board with that designation; and how to get out of my head and put my relationship first, which is something that is vitally important and incredibly satisfying.

G and I argue. We unintentionally hurt each other. We spend days merely coexisting while working through angry, guilty, or confused feelings. We marvel at how hard our lives can be. We watch our kids, our ex-husbands, and ourselves struggle, but without fail we come back to each other and remember why we're here.

FAMILY ROLE PLAY

• • •

c. s. o'cinneide

What can I say? I brought home an Irishman.

I hadn't meant to do it. I was traveling to Europe on behalf of a software company I was working for at the time, with a programmer in tow and a client on the warpath. Romance was the last thing on my mind. I'd been divorced for close to nine years, with two children almost out of elementary school. I was secure in my new job, with a financial freedom previously unheard of in our modest little gable-roofed home, where my kids Alex, eleven, and Laura, ten, had been known to busk on the front stoop for spare change with a guitar and an upturned hat.

The fact is: I wasn't on the lookout for a permanent relationship. When I made that fateful business trip to Europe, I was both emotionally and financially secure, and let's be frank, who really needs the hassle? But that's when I met Michael in Luxembourg, an officer of the bank with a smooth manner and an Irish lilt. And so it was that I closed the book on my life of singledom with a force and finality to rival the apocalypse. After a couple of months of long distance torture via telephone, email, and the occasional overseas trip, I toted my Irishman back with me to Canada to meet the children.

Now let me make this perfectly clear: my children were angels. I know a lot of mothers say this but I swear in my case it was true. The children never fought with each other and I can count on one hand how many times they argued with me. Okay, maybe two hands, with possibly six fingers on one of them, but in any case, very rarely in all the years of being their mother.

The first night Michael arrived to meet my kids, my son and I had the hugest, most vocal, knockdown, drag-'em-out blowout of an argument imaginable. I thought that the neighbors would end up contacting Social Services, or at the very least bring out a few deck chairs and a bowl of popcorn to watch the spectacle. Alex had decided that he was not going to go to daycare anymore, and while he was the only fifth grader with a moustache, this early physical maturity did not convince me he could stay home alone without accidently maiming himself. Only the month before, he had managed to kill his own pet lizard through complete, abject negligence, and most weeks he couldn't remember to take a shower unless prompted.

But Alex was adamant, and by the end of it all I was in the garden bawling my eyes out with Alex locked in his room like a fifth-grade freedom fighter for human rights. My daughter, Laura, was hiding in her Hello Kitty pup tent kept permanently set up in her room for just such an occasion. Michael came out of the house and sat down beside me on a decorative tree stump.

"I'm sorry," I said, still sobbing. "We're not normally like this. I swear that we aren't." I thought if I were this man I would be charting the first plane back to Luxembourg leaving no forwarding address. You wouldn't see me for dust.

"Really?" he said, as calm as can be. "This is pretty normal for my family. Doesn't faze me much." It was then that I knew I would marry him.

And marry him I did, in a whirlwind romance sparked by our own desire to be together and the threatening storm clouds of Canadian immigration. The ink wasn't dry on the marriage license when we realized we were pregnant with our daughter, Aisling. I called up my ex-husband to share the news. He was already very supportive of Michael and had warned both Alex and Laura that he expected them to show Michael respect. David had always been active in the kids' lives and enough years had gone by for him to see Michael as a valuable addition to the parenting team rather than a threat. Dave's a great ex-husband. I would recommend him to anyone.

"Hi, David, I've got some news," I said, not sure where to start.

"Ya, what's up?" he replied.

"Michael and I are going to have a baby. I'm due in December." I blurted it out, not sure how he would take it. There was a huge, and yes it has to be said, pregnant pause. I held my breath waiting for his response on the other end of the line. Finally he spoke.

"Well, I'm not taking that kid every other weekend too," he said indignantly. I couldn't stop laughing. We had spent so long where my kids were David's kids that he could not conceive of a situation where I would have a child for which he did not share responsibility.

"Uh no," I said, stifling my giggles. "You'd just take Alex and Laura on the weekend as always."

"Okay, all right then," he responded, sounding relieved, and maybe just a little bit disappointed.

I think Michael and I had been married a year when Alex started to have some behavioral issues. Nothing big-time, but with all the change in our lives I thought it best to nip any problems in the proverbial bud. I took him to a social worker down the street who did counseling.

"Tell me, Alex," the social worker said, "how have you been coping with all the change since your mom's marriage and the birth of your new baby sister?"

"Okay," he said. "I like our new house." (We'd had to move from my tiny one-and-a-half-story. Michael couldn't even stand up in our bedroom.)

"And my baby sister is pretty cute." He smiled then. I figured I'd probably overreacted by bringing him there and was about to apologize profusely to the social worker for wasting his time, as he undoubtedly had all sorts of kids on the road to being axe murderers and such. I never should have bothered him with my perfect little boy.

"It's just," Alex said, "I keep waiting for him to go away."

"For whom to go away?" the social worker asked.

"Michael," he replied. "You see, none of my mom's boyfriends has ever lasted this long, so I'm sort of starting to wonder when this one will go. I'm not used to having them around so long."

Right at this moment all the knickknacks and other objects on the social worker's bookshelf started to shake. Later on we would find out it was a small earthquake. I thought it was the physical manifestation of my catastrophic embarrassment. I guess I'd had a few boyfriends in my time. I felt like trailer park trash.

Once we had all composed ourselves for Alex's literal and physical earth-shattering comment, I couldn't help but protest. "But we are married, Alex! Michael is not my boyfriend. He's my husband. We have a child together. He's not going anywhere."

"Are you sure?" Alex asked pointedly. I almost expected him to add on a disciplining "young lady" to the end of that sentence. He was addressing me more as a disappointed dad than a young son.

"Yes," I said, looking him square in the eye. "I'm sure."

"Well, all right then," Alex said. End of discussion. We paid $100 for this revelation, an earthquake, and the opportunity for me to be outed by my son as a total harlot in front of a stranger. Money well spent, don't you think?

Laura had less trouble adjusting to Michael. She was younger, and a girl, and she loved him with an ease that young girls seem to find in their hearts. She had a dad already that she loved, and she had Michael, and nobody ever made her feel like she had to choose between loyalties there. I have both my patient husband and my gracious ex-husband to thank for that. I am forever in both their debts.

But the teenage years were coming. And no matter what Michael claimed to have experienced in his own family back home in Ireland, no one could prepare us for the special kind of hell that was to greet us. There were broken curfews and promises, spots on the face, and spotty school attendance. Alex and his friends would go through eight pizzas from the freezer in an afternoon. Laura brought home boys we didn't like. I often felt as if Michael and I were two shipmates on a schooner in the middle of a hurricane desperately trying to hang on to the rigging and each other.

There were days when I wondered about my emphatic answer to Alex, telling him that Michael wasn't going anywhere. Honestly, these were my own children and I wanted to leave them on the doorstep of gypsies and run. But luckily there are few gypsies in Canada, and both Michael and I stayed and fought the good fight, and in that way he truly earned Alex's and Laura's respect, as well as mine. To Alex's and Laura's credit they never once said, "You are not my father," or some other such retort designed to hurt or undermine. As I said, my kids are angels. They just needed their wings clipped a bit in adolescence.

Of course, we cannot underestimate the contribution of the babies to our success. Aisling was followed by Julia in less than two years, and those two little diapered beings allowed Alex and Laura to see Michael as a father figure, even if he was not *their* father. We often called Aisling and Julia the glue that held our blended family together, and it was true. They connected us all. Plus they were a distraction. No matter how ornery a teenager is being, when a toddler shows up in the middle of an argument dressed in nothing but a pink taffeta tutu, a pair of red rubber boots, and a hippo hat, it's sort of hard for anyone to stay mad. Incidentally, having raised both age groups at the same time, I can tell you that there is not a lot of difference between toddlers and teenagers. They both throw temper tantrums and tend to fall on their face a lot.

Alex and Laura are in their late twenties now. Laura is a mom herself. I have a beautiful baby granddaughter as of last year. I also have two girls at home well into puberty who no longer wear tutus with hippo hats. Their father and I have become shipmates again in the turbulent waters of the teen years, made only more frightening because we know what to expect. And while we have no cute toddlers to distract us from tense moments, these teenagers have a loving older brother and sister who can lend a caring ear and advice as a youthful peer in a way that their mother and father can't.

Michael and I have been married for fifteen years now. I wonder whether Alex is still waiting for him to go away.

We were all together this Thanksgiving, sharing turkey and pulling at crackers, insisting on everyone wearing those ridiculous paper crowns and having their pictures taken for posting on Facebook.

As we prepared for everyone staying overnight, I turned to my eldest daughter, Laura, and said, "Could you go ask your stepfather to bring up some extra pillows from downstairs?"

She looked at me as if I'd burped out loud in church. "What did you call him?" she asked with an eyebrow raised. I could tell her brother had homed in on the conversation as well, as he actually looked up from his *World of Warcraft* computer battle just to glare at me.

"Your stepfather," I said, faltering a little.

"Don't call him that," they both said emphatically, and in unison.

"Well, what am I supposed to call him?" I asked, perplexed.

"He's my Michael," Laura said tenderly. She smiled. Alex made a small nod and returned to the *World of Warcraft*.

And that is when it occurred to me. Never in the fifteen years that we had been married had the children ever called Michael "stepfather." Nor had they used the diminutive "half" to describe their sisters. In fact, I remember a high school boyfriend of Laura's making this mistake once when referring to the unsuspecting child playing blocks on the floor, and Laura showed him the door in a most indignant female Oxy-5 huff. I swear the guy had grass stains on his pants from where she threw him on the front lawn.

Stepfather and *half-sisters* are words that come with emotional and stereotypical baggage that can weigh heavy around the necks of a blended family. Blame pop culture or bad breakups or Disney, but the fact is, the stigma remains. In the end, it doesn't matter what we call each other, as long as we answer.

But what is a "step" anyway, but a person filling in for the role of another when the need and situation arises, like a toddler playing peacemaker, or an adult sibling standing in for a parent, or a Michael being a dad, when your own dad can't be there?

The "step" is not diminutive, it is divine. For these are the roles that we play not because we are expected to, or because we have to, but because we choose to out of love, out of loyalty, and in the case of the teen years, out of sincere and utter terror.

Nobody's going anywhere.

And yes, Alex, I'm still sure.

Part 2 | *Self-Discovery*

IT TAKES A VILLA

• • •

barbara lodge

Since my children were small, I've dreamt of renting a villa in Tuscany. I envisioned my family hiding and seeking in tall sunflower fields, swimming in an infinity pool nestled in the hills, and eating homemade pizza hot and fresh from our wood-fired outdoor pizza oven. Somewhere between that fantasy and reality, my marriage crumbled. Yet, the idyllic Italian dream didn't—it simply morphed into a happily-ever-after-post-divorce-family-vacation with kids, significant others, and all. As this year marks my son's high school graduation and daughter's twenty-first birthday, the timing couldn't be better.

Louise, my partner of nearly four years, is on board with the idea although she periodically questions my motives with inquiries such as "Are you serious?" or, "Have you really thought this through?"

Of course I have.

I've been working overtime for a decade layering good over bad and creating the most intact-broken-family divorce has ever seen. Why? Because children depend upon their mother and father for safety, security, and stability; we owe them at least that much.

Via a little denial of the not-so-easy moments between us, a lot of friendly friendship, and regular weekly dinners, my ex-husband Mark and I have earned ourselves a perfect landing under the Tuscan sun.

Mark and his longtime girlfriend Leyla are late. Perhaps they missed train connections in Rome. Maybe they got lost—this place is hard to find deep in central Italy, high atop a grassy knoll, down a narrow street, up a three-mile driveway, behind a wrought-iron gate. I tend to worry.

When we finally hear the sound of tires crunching along the dirt road, both Gary and Angela race outside and run toward the taxi, laughing, waving, and yelling, "Heya, Dad!" I watch from the veranda, brimming with achievement. It's really true: we are *all* in Italy.

Mark emerges from the backseat with a bottle of Jack Daniels in one hand and two boxes of Cuban cigars in the other. His first words to the kids are, "Hi guys! You can legally drink here—we're gonna get ripped!" He shows off the liquid gold as if it's an Olympic medal, then looks at me directly and offers, by way of reassurance, "Don't worry, Barb, I'm going to teach them some hard lessons about overindulging."

Let it be noted:
1) Mark's a recovering alcoholic/addict who I thought was clean and sober.
2) Our genetically predisposed kids shouldn't drink.
3) Or smoke.
4, 5, and 6) Mark knows these things. He's their father. I'm paying for this damn vacation.

Mark and Leyla (a recovering heroin addict he met in drug and alcohol rehab who's sweet, fit, beautiful, and very close to our daughter's age) choose to stay in the two-story guesthouse instead of the main house with the rest of us. Angela is immediately concerned they feel ostracized. I fear she might be right. Louise thinks they'll enjoy their own space. Gary just wants to get tan.

Anyway, the entire compound is spectacular. Both the main villa and guesthouse are surrounded by gardens of lavender, thyme, rosemary, red roses, electric-blue lobelia, a large grassy yard, and olive trees. It's also so very Italian—constructed of honey-colored stone with a red-tiled roof and terra-cotta floors. The villa, Podere Scopicciolo, was built on the foundation of an 1800s farmhouse, which itself was built on ancient Etruscan land. Our kids are less amazed by its historical significance than by the fact we have a chef and an infinity pool.

Leyla downs a whole bottle of local white wine before dinner while the rest of us play netless water volleyball.

Upstairs in our room, I rant. "Louise! Did you see that? He drinks? Jack Daniels? And he smokes cigars? Leyla drinks too? Who *are* these strangers?? I thought I knew them."

To which Louise responds in her usual Zen-master tone, "You gonna tell them to leave?"

"No."

"Then, there's nothing you can do. He's their father—the other half of their parental unit. You invited him here and he can do what he wants with his kids."

This might be a very long week.

Our first evening together is Father's Day in the States, so I've planned a Happy Father's Day pizza-making celebration in our chef's kitchen with a local Italian professional. I can depend on Mark's easy-talking style, Louise's equanimity, and the kids' pure excitement to carry us through any awkward moments.

The owner of the villa, Gianfranco, enters through the back door to introduce himself and I overhear Mark asking, in a low, almost whispering tone, if he can "*per favore*" get some "*birra*" to supplement the fully stocked fridge.

Wait. What?

Gianfranco obliges and returns with a case of Peroni while I leave the area pretending to look something up in our travel book. The open design of the ground floor with the living room flowing into the kitchen, dining room, and casual eating space is something I was particularly excited about. I hadn't anticipated wanting to slam a heavy wooden door.

I try (and fail) to not watch from the living room as Mark takes a beer, presses it flush against his leg, and steals out into the back-yard. I can't help trembling, given our history, remembering those afternoons ten-years-but-ten-minutes-ago when I saw Mark arrive home from work concealing the neck of a bottle in a brown paper bag, pressing it against that same leg, then disappearing behind a closed closet door.

Did he think I hadn't noticed? Did he care?

I'll leave this one alone. We're not married anymore, and we're on a dream vacation. But still. Discovering a decade after rehab that he's keeping secrets from me, and from the kids, from one house to the next, half a world away, knocks me off my bearings. I'm determined to regain my balance.

Chef Juliana calls us into the kitchen and gives us matching aprons printed with colorful pictures of Italian pastas, vegetables, and spices. We spread flour onto the granite countertops and begin kneading raw dough. The watercolor hills turn pastel pinks as sunbeams stretch far and wide, reaching almost through our open kitchen window. Sun-beams remind me of my father. Perhaps from beyond he's signaling the possibility that matching aprons do not a perfect family make. I have no time to consider his insight; I've got zucchini to chop.

We talk, laugh, taste local cheeses, learn to roll pizza dough, and slice vegetables fresh from the chef's personal garden. Mark worked in a pizza parlor when he was in high school so he impresses us by "tossing" the dough in the air (nearly) like a pro. Angela, sharing her dad's taste for truffles and stinky cheeses, challenges him to a competition of who can build a more epicurean pizza. We are having fun. Together. The rich smells, happy sounds, creativity, and a kitchen overflowing with family are everything I've hoped for. The audacity of the surprise—whiskey bearer is layered over by ricotta, mozzarella, fresh tomato sauce, and truffles.

Dinner's ready and we move outside to the veranda, taking our seats at the rustic wood table. Rolled hay bales dot the land as far as the eye can see and the sun drops behind the horizon, turning the air soft, blue, and forgiving.

The border of a dense forest abuts this golden field and I fixate on the line dividing darkness and light. Earlier in the afternoon, Angela and I were admiring the same view from her bathroom window when we perceived a rustling in the trees. We then heard a thunderous sound, and watched a herd of wild boar dash out of the forest and into the open sunny countryside. As fast as they appeared, they whipped around and disappeared back into the trees. No one believed us. Were these powerful creatures afraid of the light?

The chef provides local wines paired with our pizzas. Since everyone's of age, and Mark's already pouring, I tell the kids that here in Italy their choices are their own and I hope they make good ones.

By the end of dinner, having watched Mark and the kids enjoy themselves to their fullest extent, I find myself bursting with carbs and concern that once we get home, they will have turned into hopeless drunks. Although Louise and I shared our first-ever bottle of champagne with the kids when we arrived in Paris, seeing them drink with their alcoholic father triggers a new kind of double-standard anguish. I picture them each in separate snapshots: my daughter, my son, my ex-husband sitting on a curb somewhere in the middle of the night, dirt-smudged hands, heads downcast in shame, desperate to find the next bottle of grain alcohol, or even a hit of crack. I have no choice at this moment but to throw down my napkin, stand up, and suggest, my voice a tad higher than usual, "Hey, I know, let's go into the backyard."

To which Mark responds, "We're heading right there for cigars and Jack. Join us!"

And everything happens so fast as Mark's young girlfriend teaches my daughter, who teaches me how to take my first-ever shot of whiskey. "You can't sip it, Mom. You open your throat, hold your nose, and swallow."

Well, when in Tuscany . . . I drink that burning liquid because the more I have, the less I feel. I could've stopped their party but, in truth, didn't want to. Voicing my disapproval would've evolved into a family upheaval with me the overreactive party pooper. Too many times at home I've owned that role, being the ruling dictator of our domain. Here, sheltered in the merciful hills of Tuscany, I step down and choose to be part of the "fun," not the target of father/son eye rolls. Plus, if I drink more, there's less left for them.

Louise enjoys a reasonable two shots, tries a singular puff of a Cohiba, and watches us from the sidelines with an expression of concern and love. Mark and Gary roughhouse, acting more like fraternity brothers than father and son. Angela divides her time between fraternity shenanigans and "checking on" Louise and me, making sure we're "still okay." Sooner than later the Jack Daniels is exhausted and to my great relief our party moves inside.

"Okay, goodnight guys! Wow! What a night." I make toward the stairway, feeling more numb than my enthusiastic tone reveals.

"Where you going?" my inebriated son asks. His cheeks are red, his words slurring, and he appears to have shrunk a few inches from his original six-foot-one stature. Angela, it seems, can handle her alcohol and interjects with great conviction and clarity, "You guys should stay. We're going to play poker! And drink beer!"

When in hell did "we" decide that?

Louise and I decline their invitation and resort to our moonlit bedroom, diaphanous white curtains flowing in the breeze. The bathroom floor (where I spend most of the night alone in order to reel and feel and wonder what kind of half-baked-crazy went into this vacation plan) boasts lovely travertine marble from a local quarry.

Every day is new, and on this one we pile in the minivan, headed to Florence. On the Ponte Vecchio Mark buys our daughter a gold bangle bracelet and I buy our son a heavy silver chain. We visit Il Duomo, unanimously declining to climb the steep 463 stairs to the top. During a morning stop for gelato, memories of beer, cigars, whiskey, and upset fade into the sweetness of a double scoop of mango with chocolate sprinkles. That night was an anomaly; *this* is what's real.

Mark and Leyla are going to take the kids to lunch, see the sights, and find the pension he lived in when he was twenty while Louise and I are free to enjoy an afternoon to ourselves. We'll reconvene outside Accademia Gallery in late afternoon to see Michelangelo's *David*.

After visiting a nearby bathroom, I notice the kids still standing where we left them, looking around like confused tourists who've just been dropped in the center of bustling Piazza Duomo. "Where are Dad and Leyla?" I call out, preemptory anger rising as they are nowhere in sight.

"Oh, they went to lunch. They'll meet us later at *David*," Angela says a bit too brightly as Gary studies the ground.

No, they did not.

An urgency to protect my almost-adult children from feelings of hurt and abandonment has me scrambling for words of comfort, but, "Oh I'm sure something important just came up for your dad" doesn't seem to work on their special day in Italy. I am at a loss.

Mark would tell me I don't know the whole story and the kids are fine and would rather be on their own anyway. But, no, I'm not buying that today. Today I see disappointment and confusion in their eyes and I am helpless to fix it.

Louise asks without delay, "What do you guys want to eat?" and relief and love and gratitude for her empathy wash over me like a warm summer rain. Since they have no idea where to eat, Louise suggests Angela find us a cool restaurant that's off the beaten path. Gary insists he'll find a cooler one, and so it goes.

We acknowledge with a silent nod that we'll be forfeiting our day alone. That's what good parents do, after all—spend time with the kids when in Europe. Following Louise's lead, we start to meander. Soon, the kids voice their concern that we'll get lost and will be late meeting their dad at *David* if we don't follow the direct route highlighted in yellow on our map.

"We have all afternoon, and there's really no right or wrong way from here to there," Louise offers.

Louise likes to stroll. My kids and I are strict map followers. But her comment reminds me of the morning she, Angela, and I took an early drive to the nearby town of Casole d'Elsa for coffee while Mark, Leyla, and Gary slept in. As we strolled down the main street, talking about the fact that no souvenirs were for sale and no one spoke English, a life-size alabaster sculpture caught my attention. It depicted a woman kneeling on the ground, cradling a dove with both hands. She held him so gently, so closely, so tenderly.

"Wait! Give me a minute." I crouched next to the sculpture, resting my head on her shoulder as they took a picture and went ahead. I didn't want to leave, could've stayed there for hours. Truth and beauty exuded from this simple piece of stone. I welcomed such sunlit virtues, especially in light of our prior evening of debauchery. Church bells rang as together we wandered down cobblestone streets past children playing kickball and laundry swaying in the breeze. When we slowed to admire a bronze statue of a woman with arms stretching up toward the sky, a disheveled man well into his eighties with wild white hair and plaster-spotted clothes called out and waved to us from his grapevined balcony.

"*Ciao!*"

We waved back and answered "*Ciao*" as I took Angela's hand and picked up our pace. He motioned for us to come up to his "studio."

"Let's go in," Louise suggested.

"Oh no, we'd better not, this could be *very* dangerous," my daughter said. Right then and there I decided we must move beyond our fears of the unknown.

No one in the world knew where we were, yet we ascended the stairs into this stranger's lair. I was more than a little afraid. After scanning the immediate area for weapons and coming up empty, I noticed, to our right and left and in every corner of that place, humans and animals being born from large blocks of alabaster.

"These are just my works in progress," the sculptor said. "Come into my showroom."

My daughter and I, still holding hands, entered the "showroom," and looked at one another in stunned silence. A woman and child, two lovers, a man and dog, two children—each alabaster sculpture represented love's tender embrace.

"Oh, Mama," Angela swooned, "this room is full of love."

I could barely speak the words because such a coincidence would be nearly impossible, "In town we saw a sculpture similar to these. A woman and a dove."

"Ah yes, that one's mine too."

Feeling the sort of chills that accompany indescribable wonder, and marveling at the interconnectedness of all things, I recalled lines from Keats's *Ode on a Grecian Urn*, a favorite back in college, but words I'd rarely thought of for thirty years: "Beauty is truth, and truth beauty. That is all ye need to know on Earth and all ye need to know."

So here in Florence, remembering our potential to find enchantment around any corner, we learn to trust Louise's uncanny sixth navigation sense that delivered us to secret cafés, warm churches, intricate marble mosaics, and our "ultimate" destination. Arriving at the Accademia Gallery early is yet another inexplicable miracle.

When Mark and Leyla show up, they smell and act as if they've been drinking. The kids are so ecstatic to see their dad they throw their arms around him as if he'd just returned from a tour in Iraq. I have trouble tolerating his boozy breath and the fact he abandoned his kids in Piazza Duomo so I step away to get some space, which isn't difficult since the kids are Velcroed to either side of him.

Mark and Leyla will be leaving for Rome in the morning, so on this, their last afternoon at the villa, they invite the kids to lunch. When they return, I try to rustle up a final game of water volleyball in order to determine the ultimate champion. But Leyla goes directly to the guesthouse, Mark falls asleep on a lawn chair, and Gary is avoiding me. While Louise reads in the shade, I ask Angela to tell me about lunch. She looks away, clearly troubled.

"Angela, please. What's wrong?"

"Dad doesn't want you to know. He says you'll get mad."

He doesn't want WHAT?

"Angela, I'd really like to know what you're hiding—I promise I won't be mad at you. What happened?" I worry they've gotten themselves in trouble driving doughnuts, throwing firecrackers, or kicking trash cans. Mark tends to enjoy these behaviors with the kids at home—I'm expected to laugh them off if and when I ever find out. I saw them all get reprimanded by security for causing a ruckus playing tag in Accademia Gallery. I'm not laughing now. "They drank, Mom." She takes my hand as if to calm the storm she can feel brewing. "Dad and Gary pounded beers, but I didn't feel like it. Dad *really* doesn't want you to know. Please, don't tell him I told you."

Mark has been keeping secrets from me since before they were born, and, in the interest of upholding our pre- and post-divorce family unit, I've ignored the obvious and looked the other way.

But now?

He's suggesting they do what he does? He told *my children* to keep secrets from *me? From ME?*

I can't look away any longer.

The sky turns red and orange with dark streaks of violet. Blackish gray clouds whirl up from behind these watercolor hills. The mother of all Italian sunsets forms on the horizon.

Lying in bed that night, I, for once, don't berate myself for divorcing Mark and breaking up our family. Instead I wonder what damage I've caused by putting on a happy face and trying to protect my kids and myself from the truth of *what is*, and the reality of our own pain.

Tears, anger, sadness, and regret that I've pretended so hard and for so long unleash with an unbridled fury that rips off my blinders. Louise holds me through the storm.

Truth is beauty, beauty truth.

She holds me all night, love's tender embrace.

Come the whisperings of dawn, she says, "I'm sorry you're hurting."

And instead of deflecting her kindness by saying, "No, I'm fine, I'm good," I stay silent for what feels like hours. *Yes,* I think to myself, *I am.*

I am hurting.

And I am imperfect, as is my broken family, and this perfect vacation.

Morning sun pours in through the open windows of our villa, and somewhere in the forest a wild boar begins adjusting its eyes to the light.

CIRCLING THE SACRED FIRE

• • •

melanie mock

The roadside monkeys are behind us. So are Delhi, the Ganges, and six hours of crazy driving across the Indian plains, where Tada buses swing past oxcarts and rickety bicycles on a road with no lanes. Using broken English and hand gestures, our guide promises only ninety more minutes until we reach Lansdowne, and I relax, just a little. The long trip from Oregon is nearly over, and my family, crammed into the backseat of a Mahindra Scorpio, has survived.

I relax, that is, until the SUV wends its way up a death-defying path carved into the Himalayan foothills. The one-lane road—shared by cars and trucks, animals and people, buses and jeeps—has no guardrails, except for white gravel marking where one might plummet into a canyon. We do not know the Hindi words for "please slow down," and our attempts at communication seem to suggest "Faster! Faster!" As we swerve to miss a herd of cattle on one side and on the other a precipice leading only to air, my prayer life has never been richer. I send out petitions to preserve my family from destruction, my incantations assuming a sacrilegious edge: "God. Oh Lord, help me."

Finally, we arrive at the Blue Pine Resort, though the name imagines a place more bucolic and restful than this small inn carved into a crumbling hillside. My legs wobble with lingering panic as my stepdaughter Melissa meets us at the front desk, telling us that while we have already covered the road's worst curves, we will need to travel six more miles to reach our final destination: her in-laws' home. For someone with a phobia of heights, the absence of an adventurer's spirit, and now a fear of Indian traffic, this is tough news. I sink into a '70s-era avocado-green chair.

What am I doing here? I think. And, *I don't believe I signed up for this: not now, not when I agreed to this trip, not when I married Melissa's father.*

A year earlier, when my stepdaughter invited us to India, I had been noncommittal about traveling overseas to attend Melissa's marriage ceremony. I wanted her father to go, for sure, but I was less certain about bringing our two six-year-old sons halfway around the world. While I suggested cost would be a major factor in our decision about the trip, this was only a ruse. I had more selfish motivations for staying home: I couldn't imagine a fifteen-hour plane flight with two active boys and worried, too, about their physical health, given what I knew about India and travel, about Delhi belly and malaria and a million other diseases.

But mostly, I was apprehensive about our family's emotional well-being. An overseas trip that involved travel with my husband's ex-wife and her spouse might be problematic; we were friendly but not friends. Our contact with them diminished considerably when my stepchildren became adults, the negotiations of shared custody no longer a thread tying us together.

My sons were not old enough yet to understand the complicated relationships that shaped our family. They adored their older
brother, Ryan, and their sister, whom they called Missy. Melissa had
been dating Rahul for several years by then, so he was also an inte-
gral member of the family. We'd not yet explained to the boys what
divorce meant, or why their older siblings didn't call me "Mom,"
addressing me instead by my first name. There were other significant elements of our family's dynamics my kids didn't notice: That
sometimes, Melissa and Ryan were absent from important holidays
because they were at their mother's house. That sometimes, they
talked about a woman called "Mom," and that woman was not me.
That sometimes, at important events like graduations and weddings,
two other people, named Greg and Diana, showed up as well. That
Diana looked remarkably like their sister. That their dad didn't talk
much to these two friendly people, though Melissa and Ryan did talk
to them. A lot.

Later, when they were older, we would explain to our sons about
their dad's divorce. For months afterward, the boys would panic anytime my husband and I argued, sure their family was also fated for
dissolution. At the time of their sister's wedding, though, Benjamin
and Samuel seemed too young to bear information about divorce
and loss. How do you explain to two kindergarteners that people can
love each other intensely—and then not? How do you differentiate
between run-of-the-mill arguments and those rooted in dysfunction and anger and pain? How do you possibly explain to two small
boys the ways brokenness and loss affect families? Especially since
brokenness was part of my sons' history, too, the loss of their birth
families opening the way for adoption and entry into our lives.

Although my sons were blissfully unaware of their family's odd
dynamics, I was still concerned a trip to India might emotionally
affect them. For my son Samuel Saraubh, a trip to India would be a
homecoming, because three years earlier we had traveled to Mumbai

to adopt him. I wondered whether he would remember his orphanage or ask about the birth mother who left him there when he was one week old. For my son Benjamin Quan, a trip to India would provide other challenges. Adopted from Vietnam when he was seven months old, Benjamin would definitely stand out in India: he looked nothing like us, nor like his brother, and was no doubt the first Vietnamese child ever to attend a wedding at Tarkeshwar Mahadev Temple in Lansdowne.

As I thought about the trip's potential complications for my family, I wanted to balk, to say "no thank you," to send my stepdaughter's dad alone overseas while the boys and I hunkered down in our comfortable Oregon home. But being a stepparent often means discomfort, at least it has for me. Discomfort, even though I got along well with my stepchildren who were thirteen and seventeen when I married their father, nearly seven years after their parents' divorce. Rearranging plans to fit an every-other-weekend custody schedule. Stepping into well-entrenched family traditions that were baffling and mysterious to me. Figuring out whether to sit near (or far) from ex-spouses at ball games and recitals. Splitting holiday time and vacations and rites of passage with another woman I had nothing in common with, and about whom I knew nothing. Nothing, that is, except that she has a history with my spouse, and that together they bore and raised the two children who are now fantastic older siblings to the boys I love more than life itself.

It was for them—my stepdaughter, my sons, my husband— that I finally said yes to India, despite the turmoil and discomfort the trip might bring. And so, as Ron searched for plane tickets we could afford, I planned our journey, concern for my sons and my husband a persistent soundtrack to my preparation. Although I could pack Cipro for infection, force-feed them malaria pills tucked into pudding and ice cream, and buy enough fruit snacks and juice boxes to keep them well fed in India, I could not protect my family from the potential emotional fallout a trip like this might cause, or from the difficult truths about the ways their family had been broken and remade.

By the time we reach the Blue Pine Resort, I am overwhelmed, all the anxieties about my family's well-being compounded by terror that we would die, our car plummeting over one of the surrounding cliffs.

It is not until the next morning that I can begin to see Lansdowne for what it is: a different world entirely from the crowds and heat of Delhi. Dark green forests surround the low-slung buildings of the village, and snowcapped mountains are visible from the town's highest points. Rahul's family has lived here in India's terraced hillsides for generations; his grandfather and uncle were military officers stationed at the Garhwal Rifles cantonment, guarding a remote piece of Indian landscape. Although Rahul grew up in Zambia, and although he and Melissa met in Richmond, Indiana, the small village near Lansdowne is his familial motherland: the place where his widowed father, now married to a Filipina, grew up and still calls home, and thus the place where Rahul and Melissa will reenact the traditions of a Hindu marriage ceremony.

For several days after our harrowing trip from Delhi to the Blue Pine Resort, our family rides through Lansdowne to Rahul's family compound for a traditional henna party, for meals, for the family's wedding reception, for leisurely afternoon visits. The journey never loses its scary edge, especially as our trips often take place at night, or in the fog, or through monsoon rains. On one occasion, our driver is slowed, if only a bit, by clouds so thick he drives with his door open, to ensure we will not plummet over a cliff's edge.

The vehicle convoy making the daily journey includes Melissa's mother and stepfather, her father and me, and our two sons; Melissa is staying with her in-laws. (Her brother hasn't been able to come with us because of work commitments.) If Rahul's family is perplexed by the strange composite of his new in-laws, they never betray their confusion. Instead, we are warmly welcomed to the sprawling home overlooking a cavernous valley—sprawling at least by Lansdowne standards, where poverty, as in most of India, seems endemic. Rahul's aunt and uncle serve a constant stream of good wine, food, and Indian sweets; and for several days we celebrate long into the evening with music, dancing, and conversation.

While my anxieties about the road and my kids' physical health remain, other fears begin to dissipate. My family thrives in India. Ron gets along with his ex-wife and her husband, who sit at an adjacent table every morning for breakfast at the hotel. They join us for hikes with our boys, and allow Samuel and Benjamin to guide them along jungle paths. We all visit the town's open market, and my kids are more intrigued by the shops' candy and cheap toys than by the gaunt women selling spices and the children hanging on to their legs, wearing dirty clothes and plastic shoes. Samuel sees no reminders here of his earlier, hard life in India; if Benjamin feels at all an outsider, he betrays nothing, instead running ahead of us through the market, looking for the cricket bat he hopes to buy.

And at Rahul's family compound, we are all embraced by Rahul's aunts, the boys' cheeks pinched by uncles and cousins who listen to stories about tee ball, the intricate descriptions of base running gaining clarity only when my husband suggests a tenuous connection between Benjamin's tee ball team and India's national sport. The boys—being boys, and with a rapt audience's encouragement—tromp through the flora, capture bugs, follow a blue lizard across the patio. When Benjamin catches another kind of bug, and throws up during the wedding party, Rahul's father tracks down medicine from a nearby pharmacy, closed for the evening; an uncle offers us his bed, where Benjamin sleeps off his contagion while the celebration continues outside; Ron's ex-wife, an Ob-gyn, checks on Benjamin often, offering me advice as a doctor, and as a fellow mother, too.

The wedding takes place on a cool, overcast evening, with a mist hanging over the Lansdowne hills and a sunset, distant over the plains, reflecting pink and orange against low clouds. Beside the temple, red plastic picnic chairs circle a raised fire pit underneath a stone canopy, called a *mandap*, where the priest prepares for the ceremony. Although Hindu weddings are performed in Sanskrit, the priest tells us he will use English as well, so his American visitors might better understand the marriage rites. Melissa and Rahul sit to the left of the priest, Rahul's father and stepmother to the right. Across from the priest, my husband settles in beside his ex-wife, the awkwardness of this sudden familiarity diminished by our week together.

As the priest begins, Rahul's family rearranges the red chairs, providing running commentary, talking on cell phones, making jokes at Rahul's expense. At one point, Rahul's aunt interrupts the priest, explaining that traditionally, the bride's oldest brother must extort money from the groom. Since Melissa's oldest brother isn't with us, the aunt instructs Benjamin and Samuel to twist Rahul's ear three times, demanding money and a promise Rahul will treat his new bride well. The raucous background noise feels unusual compared to the solemnity of American weddings. But the spirited chatter seems more fitting to the joyful aspect of a wedding, as if the hushed congregation at a Christian ceremony were sending a newly married couple to the gallows.

Rahul's *kurta* is tied to Melissa's *sari* and the bride and groom make seven circles around the fire, the priest sanctifying each round with petitions for happiness, well-being, security, and prosperity. After one round, the priest instructs my sons to give their sister fistfuls of rice and she, cupping her hands with Rahul's, throws the rice into the fire. With each subsequent round, Ben and Sam add more rice to Melissa's hand, and then she to the fire. Although this rite is explained in English, I am not entirely sure what is happening, and know so little about Hinduism I cannot visualize the different gods the priest addresses, nor the significance of his prayers.

But then, from the priest, I hear this: that the bride and groom circle the fire as a symbol of holiness and unity, of perfection and peace. My stepdaughter, radiant in a golden sari, takes turns around the fire with her husband. With each pass, she encircles her family as well: her new father- and mother-in-law, ex-patriots living in Zambia; her little brothers, drawn here from Mumbai, from Vietnam; her father and mother, reconciled for this moment. With Rahul, she has drawn us here, knitting our uncommon and broken lives together.

And not only the lives of those sitting here, at the fire, but of those who stand in the shadows, family members we know and have lost: Rahul's mother and sister, my sons' first families. Beyond Melissa and Rahul, I see the faces of my in-laws, laughing, talking, celebrating this union with strangers from distant lands. As Melissa and Rahul circle the fire, we consecrate the birth of something new. Our family radiates outward from here, drawing together people around the world into this sacred space, high in the foothills of the Himalayas.

I LOVE YOU MORE

• • •

kerry cohen

The first time I met Ava, she was sick with a bad cold. Her father, whom I was in love with, had kept her home. Jim and I had been having these daytime trysts. We both worked from home, and so when the kids were at school, I'd go to his house and we'd fuck against the wall, or I'd blow him in his office, or we'd get into bed and roll around for a while, just taking one another in. But this day, Ava was there, in bed. I brought matzo ball soup because it always made me feel better. Jim carried it up to her in her bedroom, and when he came back down we kissed and sat close.

Ava knew nothing about me. Jim and his wife had separated only about five months earlier, so she was just entering this new world, where parents could have boyfriends and girlfriends. This was true for my two sons as well, and Ava's little brother Atticus. But Ava, age seven, was the oldest of the four and by far the most conscious of what was happening to her life.

We heard Ava come down the stairs, and so we moved apart. Ava stomped when she walked, impossible not to hear coming. All three of them—Jim, Ava, and Atticus—were loud people. Their footsteps shook the house. The children had not learned about "inside voices." Even their eating was noisy. They smacked lips, chewed with open mouths. They drank with messy gulps. On this day, though, I didn't know any of that yet. Ava came down to see who had brought her the delicious soup. She thanked me, her eyes wide with fascination at this woman she didn't know. She sat next to me, very close, our legs touching, and ate her soup.

It wasn't until Jim, Ava (now almost nine), and Atticus (four) moved in with me, Ezra (eight), and Griffin (five) that Ava began to tell her mother about me. The kids lived with us every other week, and with their other parent the off weeks. Ava's mother was understandably not thrilled to hear about her ex-husband's love life, but what was much worse was that Ava told her that she liked me a lot better than she liked her own mother.

"I want Kerry to be my mother," she said.

Looking back, I still don't know what to make of Ava's comments to her mother. Was she trying to punish her for divorcing Jim? Amid all the changes—her mother moving into another house, and then her father moving in with us—was she testing how far she could push her mother to see if she would leave for good, now that so much had changed? I can't know. But something was brewing inside Ava, and it had just begun.

I, of course, had my own feelings about divorce. My ex-husband and I had worked hard to stay together. Our oldest son, Ezra, was autistic, and we'd struggled to come to terms with his condition. We'd done counseling. We'd had endless talks. But ultimately, the ways in which we'd gone into our grief about Ezra had pulled us apart. And when we tried to come together, we found we were only friends, not lovers.

Then I met Jim, and I fell wildly in love with him in a way I had not fallen before. The sexual chemistry was very much there, and it was much more than that. We were both writers. We saw the world in similar ways. Our connection was immediate and thorough, reaching from my hair to my toenails. And so I moved out for good, ready to be with Jim.

I hadn't thought about having to help him raise the children from his former marriage.

I hadn't thought about the fact that I'd be away from my own children every other week, which equals half the year, which equals half their childhood lives.

I hadn't thought about the fact that my own children would have to navigate relationships with two other children and an adult that they hadn't asked for.

I hadn't thought about the fact that Jim and I would have radically different parenting styles, his based on having raised two typically developing children, mine on having raised a child on the autism spectrum.

I hadn't thought about how defensive I'd feel, how righteous about what I'd learned from Ezra. How dare the rest of the world, how dare Jim and his ex, not trust what they couldn't know, what only other parents of children with special needs could know. They hadn't *had* to learn what I'd learned, because their children—their goddamned annoying children who hadn't even learned about inside voices!—had developed typically.

I hadn't thought about the fact that I would have to explain again—*again!*—that I had had all those plans too. I too wasn't going to let my children watch more than a half hour of television a day, if at all. I too was going to feed my children only organic food and use only organic products on their precious skin. I too was going to send them to Montessori and protect them from the violent world. But then I had Ezra, sweet, blond-haired, mop-headed, always smiling Ezra. Who came alive once he learned how to use the computer, who communicates through his iPad, who is connected with the digital world much more than he is with ours, and who won't eat anything, and I had to throw away all those plans. And through that process I learned that it turns out none of it matters—not the television, not the organic food, not the chemicals in the air or the violent world. What matters is that they feel loved, that they feel encouraged to be themselves, that they know they are right just as they are.

But I'm getting off track. I'm getting defensive. The point is, I hadn't thought about a lot.

When Jim and his children moved in, for the first time I wasn't sure anymore about being with him. I grew irritated—their endlessly stomping feet, the running through the house, the yelling, the open-mouthed eating. I was horrified by my intolerance, disgusted with myself. Once, fed up and overwhelmed, I left the house, sure I could not be around any of them another second.

But then, things progressed. Atticus fell down the stairs, and I held his soft, sad body as he cried into my shoulder. I said, "I know, I know, baby," into his sweet-smelling hair. Another day, Ava giggled with me about how her father looked in his bathrobe with his hair mussed up, and we found our shared sense of humor.

Ezra preferred his daddy's house. He told me often that he wanted to go to Daddy's house, and I'd tell him how many days, and he'd accept that, just knowing that eventually he'd be going back, that there was some consistency to this new world.

My younger son, Griffin, preferred Mommy's house. He'd always been more attached to me than Ezra was, and I worried more about him in this new situation than I worried about Ezra. So, at bedtime, I focused on Griffin, my small, brown-headed, freckle-faced boy. I lay in his bed with him and I read him books. We snuggled close and I breathed in his scent. Sometimes, after reading, we held one another close, almost like lovers, our faces pressed together. We whispered to each other, "I love you so much," and "I love you more." I needed those times as much as he did. My sweet baby boy Griffin, and Ezra, my truest, wholest loves. Their father and I may have split, we may have changed our relationship to friendship, but my love for my two boys would never transform. I would always love them wholly and absolutely.

But then, these two additional children. They were Jim's, but in this new, odd arrangement, they were also mine. And Ava, always emotionally sharp and intuitive, could feel that my love was uneven. She asked to join us for our bedtime reading. I came up with excuses. I hemmed and hawed. I blamed it on Griffin: he doesn't want you there. And sometimes, wracked with guilt because I *didn't* feel the same way about her that I felt about my own two, I gave in and let her join us. She tried to snuggle close to me the way Griffin was. She laid her small, blonde head on my shoulder; she put her long, gazelle leg over mine. She was awkward, her long nine-year-old body too gawky, all elbows and knees, like trying to fit a puzzle piece where it didn't match. And all I felt was annoyed. This was my time with Griffin, and I didn't want her there.

After too many evenings like this, when I felt too deprived of my time with my son, I started telling her that she couldn't join us. I tried to explain. I said, "Griffin is only with me every other week. Don't you want special time with your mother when you see her?"

She said no, she didn't. She said that it wasn't fair. She said, "How come Griffin gets something and I don't?"

Over the next month, the situation grew worse. She complained to Jim, who brought it up to me once we were settled into bed. We had so few moments alone when the children were there.

"Why can't she just join you?" he said.

"Because I don't want her there," I said. "I want to be alone with Griffin."

"Can't you find a different time to be alone with Griffin?"

"No." I was pissed now. "Can't you take care of your own daughter's neediness?"

We faced each other, fuming, our love for our own children taking over every last spot in our bodies, until we turned away from one another to sleep at separate ends of the bed.

The following week, Jim's ex-wife sent him an email wondering what was happening between Ava and me. Ava had cried to her. She said I was mean, that I kicked her out of the bedroom when I was in there with Griffin, that I wouldn't let her in to read bedtime stories. Jim tried to tell her this was our household business, that it didn't concern her, but she grew incensed. That was *her* daughter who was feeling rejected.

"Maybe Kerry shouldn't have laid it on so thick in the beginning if she was just going to turn on her," I overheard her say to Jim.

Jim and I began to fight. He didn't want his ex-wife involved, but he agreed that his daughter was feeling shunned and I needed to put her feelings first.

"She's *your* daughter," I said. "Why am I responsible for her needs?"

"You're the adult here," he said. "She's just a little girl."

"Yes, a little girl who needs something from her parents."

"She needs it from *you*," he said.

This, on top of all the other problems we had trying to blend our families, the arguments about screen time and the importance of bedtimes, felt like too much. Because, was I responsible to her in that way? Did I have to give her something I didn't yet have, a parental love that was beginning to grow but would never be equal to the love I had for my own two boys? I left the house, enraged, sad, certain we wouldn't make it.

The next week, when the four children came back to the house—Ava and Atticus from their mother's and Ezra and Griffin from their father's—Jim and I were still angry. You could feel the tension in the air. Ava, especially, could feel it. She'd been there before with her parents. Before their divorce, all they did was fight. I don't remember what the argument was that particular night. Something about the kids—it was always about the kids—how one was being favored and another being treated unfairly. In so many ways, Jim and I were worse than the children with this. It's not fair, it's not fair, stop being unfair. Suddenly, Ava began to cry.

"Stop it!" she yelled amid sobs. No inside voice necessary. "Stop fighting! Just stop it!"

I went to her; I sat her on my lap.

"I'm scared!" she said. "I feel scared when you fight!"

"Because of your parents?" I asked. "Because they fought so much?"

She nodded, wiping at her tears. "This is my family now," she said. "I just want my family to be okay."

I held her close, petting her hair. I rubbed my hand down her arm and held her small, thin hand. "You're safe," I said. "Your family *is* okay. Sometimes we argue, but it doesn't mean we're not okay. We are. And we'll get through this."

She closed her eyes, resting against me for a moment. When she got up, feeling better, Jim and I met eyes.

That night, Jim and I lay in bed together and held hands as we talked. We put aside our defenses, our own needs that had taken us through the start of our relationship and had controlled us thus far. Enough of that. There were children here. Small, precious children, who needed us to do what Jim had said: act like adults. Ava needed something. It didn't matter why or why not. We needed to take care of that need.

The truth was, we were going to feel something for our own kids we couldn't fully feel for the other two. That might change over time. We hoped it would. But for now, we could only do our best inside that truth. Griffin and I would have our private story time. Jim would give Ava the attention she needed in the form of special evenings out with Daddy. We would take care of all our precious children, champion the only thing we could: this family we created, imperfect or not.

WAVE POOL

• • •

james bernard frost

It is Saturday, mid-afternoon, and the six of us are driving through a wet swirling storm toward the Great Wolf Lodge, a nature-themed hotel/indoor water park that can't possibly be any good for nature. The vehicle we are driving is a Mazda 5 minivan with manual transmission. I purchased this vehicle about six months after moving myself and my two children in with my girlfriend Kerry and her two children—in the slimy, chaotic wake of a divorce that I hadn't wanted.

The Mazda 5 minivan is the smallest minivan one can buy in America and still stuff six people into. It is also the only minivan in America with a stick shift. I suppose one could call it the least mini-van of all possible minivans, which is the only reason I can think of for purchasing such an impractical sardine can.

In the backseat are, in this order, of these ages, of whose progeny, and with these particular media devices and applications: Atticus, in a booster behind me, age five, mine, with a Kindle Fire playing Plants vs. Zombies; Griffin, age six, not in a booster, behind Kerry, hers, with an iPod currently tuned to Men Without Hats' song "Safety Dance"; Ava, shoehorned into the back bench seat behind Atticus, age nine, mine, on an iPad, purchasing clothes on the application Dream Dresses; and Ezra, smashed into Ava, Kerry's, also age nine, also on an iPad, using the application Scribblenauts to repetitively create and then kill gigantic flying newts.

On many levels, this is not a scenario I had imagined myself to be a part of four years earlier. Before my divorce and before Kerry, my wife and I had been adamantly anti-media—memories of my father as a couch potato, my own video game addiction, and a general disdain of popular culture kept our family away from even having a television in the house.

But with this new relationship came Ezra—a boy on the autism spectrum. And with Ezra came computers and iPads—his preferred means of communicating with the world.

I fought with both his mother and my kids at first, trying to establish rules, shooing my children away from passively observing Ezra's keyboard punching. But after a while it seemed more damaging to have different rules for different kids than to just allow them their games. And so here we are now, each child with his or her own media device. And I have to admit that with all the pain and pressure of post-divorce survival, the heroin drip of children's entertainment sure makes life easy.

Despite the cacophony of electronically generated noises emanating from the rear portion of the minivan, my girlfriend and I are both aware that this drive will be the most pleasant part of our weekend outing, and are trying our best to conduct an adult conversation.

Let's face it: we are terrified of Great Wolf Lodge. When the Living Social deal slipped its way through our spam protection, we had imagined a weekend with other friends and other kids, somehow envisioning ourselves in the South Hot Springs™ sipping wine (it's how they portrayed it on the website), while one of the other dads played lifeguard.

But none of those other parents took the bait, and after we purchased the vouchers and got the kids excited, there was no way out.

So here we are, thirty miles away, with no clue how we are going to deal with Griffin's fear of water, Atticus's lack of fear of it, Ezra's single-mindedness, and Ava's endless distraction. Four kids going in four different directions, a giant water park, and only two parents.

But that isn't even the worst of it—the mathematical impossibility of the parental sheepherding ahead. As we near Grand Mound, Washington—the halfway town on I-5 between Seattle and Portland, where the giant, monstrous Great Wolf Lodge will pop up like Las Vegas rising out of the desert—I've restarted a conversation that Kerry and I have had before.

Let's call it my blonde problem.

Ever since we'd gotten together, once every two or three months I became infatuated with a blonde.

So we are discussing this, with wiper blades beating, zombies munching, Men Without Hats declaring their disdain for friends who don't dance, and Ezra giggling "GIGANTIC FLYING NEWT." It's a story we've discussed so many times that if we had any sense we'd record it and replay it for ourselves so we wouldn't have to go through the torture of talking about it again.

Here's the gist of my recurring narrative: Kerry and I got together, inauspiciously, while I was still separating from my wife. Though we were perfect together in so many ways, I hadn't had the time alone to figure out what I actually wanted in a relationship, or if I even wanted a relationship again. So even though we'd already built a life together, and purchased a minivan, and had a great deal of sex, and shared a passion for writing, and communicated swimmingly well, and had built relationships with each other's kids—even with all that goodness—I still wasn't sure if I wanted it. Because I could imagine myself with this or that blonde. The blondes were always more nature-oriented and therefore more suitable for me than Kerry, who is a dark-haired New Jersey Jew. With this blonde I would somehow be a much-improved person who didn't let his children watch so much television and who lived a healthier lifestyle and who was just somehow less damaged and *less dark.* And with that blonde—well I wouldn't have to commit to that blonde because I'd have a string of blondes. I'd be a very together single dad who took his children on adventures every day, finished a novel a year, worked a steady job, and ran marathons, while maintaining relationships with multiple (and perfectly happy with the duplication) blondes.

And then what I would actually do with this line of reasoning was take what had been a perfectly satisfactory and innocent friendship with a blonde woman, and flirt with her. Then, right before I consummated anything with said blonde, I would freak out and tell Kerry everything and ruin my friendship with the blonde, feel horrible about myself, and make Kerry feel awful and foolish for putting up with me and my blonde fetish.

And so here we are, with Kerry emotionally devastated because I've brought this conversation up yet again, while driving underneath red and blue and yellow water slide tubes to take an exit ramp to the Great Wolf Lodge with our combined four children.

We pull into a Shell station so that I—not a child—can use a restroom.

Ava, Atticus, and Griffin see a Burgerville sign and want fries and shakes.

Ezra says, "GIGANTIC FLYING NEWT!" and giggles.

We arrive at the Great Wolf Lodge and head straight for the water park. My immediate concern as the father of a daughter is Ava's size 7 bikini, which we'd purchased two summers ago in late August when the stores no longer stocked bathing suits. The bikini was the last item on the rack at Old Navy and was not appropriate for any child, but she's been wearing it for two years anyway, and now her size 7 impossibly tiny bikini is even more impossibly tiny.

Since I fear the potential pedophile quotient might be high at the Great Wolf Lodge, I take Ava straight to the Bear Essentials™ Swim Shop and Crocs Store Galore, which likely has the largest children's bathing suit collection in the country, and there we find a surfer girl top with shorts that are more to my fatherly tastes.

While we are gone, the other children, crazily pent-up after the two-hour drive, have all gotten their own bathing suits on and are diving into the wave pool. This goes exactly as Kerry and I had suspected—the children heading off in completely opposite directions. When Ava and I return, Ezra is too far out in the water, Atticus is horizontal in the shallow end being rescued by Kerry, and Griffin is beside the pool crying, not wanting to have anything to do with the water park at all. Kerry, fed-up, screams at me to get Ezra, and after I pull him, very unhappily, back to shore, Kerry decides to take her two upstairs to the room.

And that's really the last time Kerry and I see each other for hours. While Kerry takes her two boys up to the hotel room, Atticus, Ava, and I spend a couple of hours in lines, slowly creeping our way up three flights of stairs before the thirty-second spiral down the water tubes to the water.

Later Kerry takes Griffin, Ava, and Atticus to play MagiQuest®, which involves wandering around tapping wands—each of which costs $19.95—on treasure chests and framed pictures of wizards and video screens strategically placed all over the hotel, while I sit in the hotel and play iPad games next to Ezra. Then I go with Griffin, Ava, and Atticus to the arcade, dropping a $20 bill into the token machine every fifteen minutes for an hour while Ezra lays down some tracks on Garage Band in the bedroom with Kerry.

Eventually, we take the kids out together for a $95 meal of cheese pizza, hamburgers, chicken tenders, and sodas at the Loose Moose

Cottage™, and three helpings of $8 fro-yo that come out of a vending machine featuring a robot arm dispensing toppings. Then we watch the evening program, in which a talking bear and a boy hiding in a hollow tree trunk sing—very creepily—"There's nothing to be afraid of."

Thus the night culminates, after some argument over bedtime and whether or not it is okay to watch the TV, with me passing out on the bed with my clothes on and a wolf tail pinned to my back belt loop.

It is Sunday morning. We survived Saturday, but we now have one more day and one more night here. The MagiQuest® is already old, the water park exhausting, and the arcade too expensive—we don't know how we're going to make it through the day.

None of this is to mention Kerry and I's disquieting midnight argument, in which Kerry informs me that things can't go on like this, that there can't be any more blondes, that if we're going to do this—be a family—she needs to know that I'm committed to her.

Tired and grumpy (but well caffeinated! The Great Wolf Lodge has a Starbucks inside), I take Ezra to the wave pool.

Kerry and I often joke about Ezra that he is our only child who doesn't have special needs. Ezra can be counted on to enjoy certain things, and to enjoy those things without any assistance from a parent. The wave pool will be no exception.

I wrestle Ezra into a lifejacket (he is none too happy about putting it on; he's in a hurry to get into the pool) and once properly secured, he launches into the water without a backward glance or a word to me. I follow. This is going to be a piece of cake—me floating around and looking at the moms in two-pieces, him happily bobbing up and down in the waves.

That's when the lights flicker and the power goes out.

Now fortunately, the Great Wolf Lodge water park is encased in wall-to-wall windows, so we aren't plunged into darkness. And the lights come back on in about fifteen seconds. But the real problem becomes apparent when we are ordered out of the wave pool, and I have to try to explain to Ezra what is going on.

Me: The wave pool is broken, Ezra.

Ezra: The wave pool is broken because?

Me: Because the power went out.

Ezra: The power is out because?

Me: Because there was a power surge, and now they have to make sure everything works.

Ezra: Everything not working because?

Me: Because they need to fix the power.

Ezra: They need to fix the power because?

Me: Because there was a power surge, and they have to make sure everything works.

This endless conversation takes place while lifeguards blow their whistles at us. I have Ezra, resisting, by the upper arm, and I'm trying to pull him to the ladder to get out of the pool. Upon getting out, his pale face goes hot, and I know tears will come next. Ezra's crying always starts without expression, just tears on a blank face.

"Oh no! The wave pool is broken!" Ezra shouts.

Ezra shakes my grip and runs past me to a poolside chair, sitting right next to a mom tending to two children, oblivious to the clothing and towels that have been placed on the seat of the chair to save it. His face is completely red by now, and he rubs his tear-stained cheeks with his fists.

I apologize to the woman. She nods in understanding, though I can't tell whether she really does understand.

These times are the hardest for Ezra, these times when something unexpected happens, when everything is steady and normal and then suddenly it isn't.

"Let's go inside," I say.

"No! No! I want to go to the wave pool," says Ezra, slamming his fists on the armrests.

"Okay, we'll wait," I say.

"When is the wave pool fixed?" asks Ezra.

"I don't know," I say.

"I want the wave pool fixed," says Ezra.

I try to get him thinking about something else—Whooping Hollow™, where the kiddie slides are—but he's stuck.

"Let's go to the slides," I say.

"No! No!" he says.

So we stay there and have our ever-looping conversation, and I watch the moms. We are alike, Ezra and I, fixated on something and unable to stop ourselves.

Eventually, a staff member walks by and I ask him how long it will be. He says that they're running through a cycle and that it usually takes about fifteen minutes to get things running again.

So I tell Ezra it will be fifteen minutes and we have a conversation about that.

Ezra: Fifteen minutes is?

Me: A while.

Ezra: A while is?

Me: In a little bit.

Ezra: A little bit is?

And finally the lifeguards, who have all been pacing back and forth and back and forth beside the pool, doing their rounds like polar bears at the zoo, move into position. I tell Ezra that it is almost time. He makes a break for the water and I have to hold him back. He screams at me, "No! No!" but we see the crest of the first wave starting at the deep end of the pool coming toward us, and the lifeguards blow their whistles, and a whole rush of children and flabby moms and dads go running toward the water. And with them goes Ezra. And me.

There are two types of waves at the wave pool. There are the parallel waves and the diamond waves. The parallel waves are simply horizontal lines running from the deep end of the pool to the shallow. The diamond waves come dually, in a diagonal from the deep left end of the pool and another diagonal from the deep right end of the pool, creating large peaks. They do a five-minute set of parallel waves, take a five-minute break with no waves, do a five-minute set of diamond waves, and then take another break.

We are now in the fourth set of diamond waves, which means I've been in the pool with Ezra for about an hour and ten minutes. My hands are wrinkled to the point of being painful, and I fear that my feet will end up with blisters from the concrete bottom of the pool. In that hour and ten minutes, Ezra has been giggling nonstop.

The five minutes of diamond waves are by far my least favorite time spent in the pool. The current pulls me to the left, and to the right, and back to the left, and I feel nauseous. I keep myself steady in the water, my feet planted on the bottom, but Ezra is floating. He goes back and forth in the water and runs into people: giggling, unaware. When he ends up against someone, I grab his lifejacket and pull him away. I know asking him to be aware of people isn't something he's capable of, so I let him do exactly what he needs to do to be happy.

For a moment, I let myself go too. I duck my head underwater and lift my feet off the bottom and close my eyes and wish I would stop wanting things I don't have anymore.

It is midnight. We have spent over $60 worth of quarters on the game Let's Go Jungle, which involves shooting mutant insects with a machine gun. We have shoveled into our mouths unlimited amounts of robot-generated fro-yo. We have jetted down water tubes with disco lights at night. We have watched the talking bear and creepy boy sing, "There's nothing to be afraid of" one last time. We have let the children watch *SpongeBob SquarePants* until II P.M.

It wasn't easy, but I have let myself be permissive. I have a boy on the autism spectrum in my life.

Kerry and I lie in bed together. The children are asleep in the KidCabin® Suite adjacent. I tell Kerry about the power outage in the water park, but I don't tell it the way I told it before, about how happy Ezra seems, about how free he is in the world. I also don't tell her about the other moms.

What I tell her instead is how I understand now—how I feel for the first time her grief about her son's autism. How much a mother and father must feel like they lose when they have a boy who communicates in a different way: how depressed they must have gotten, how I can understand more how she lost her marriage.

We are eye to eye in the bed, and Kerry wraps her arms around me. In the morning, we will leave the Great Wolf Lodge and head home.

"You need to be less hard on yourself," she says. "I want you to commit, but maybe once you commit the blondes won't be as much a problem as you think."

I know what she is saying without her having to say it, that not all marriages have to be the same, that I need to give up my preconceived notions about monogamy and the exact way marriages are supposed to work.

I feel lighter in that moment.

We are in the diamond waves now. And in them, we need to float.

IN STEP AT THE WEDDING

• • •

mary faith powers

I'm Amanda's *other* mom. She is my only daughter. She came into my life fully formed, walking and talking (a mile a minute, just like her dad) with open arms and a loving heart. A precocious, six-year-old carbon copy of my husband, Jack. I'm lucky, I know. There has never been a moment in the last twenty years that I was anything other than "Mom." Well, almost never.

On our last call with Amanda, she seemed vague to me about her wedding reception. No, she didn't know the exact date or place it was to be held. She had started a new job and was going out of town, leaving all the planning to her mom. She was sure the invitation would have the details. Yes, the invitations would be mailed soon.

I went over the conversation in my head. She'd left the planning to her mom. That would be Sarah, her *real* mom. But wasn't I her mom too? I pushed the thought aside.

When her fiancé proposed, I had never seen Amanda happier. But after the first flush of joy, she grew quiet, struggling with something. Her weight dropped and her skin grew paler, hardly the picture of a happy bride-to-be.

On her last visit, we had sat out on the back porch, swinging slowly, waking up to the day. It was our time together. Normally, wrapped up in quilts in the early morning chill, we talked about dreams and just enjoyed being close. I nudged her shoulder and asked her, "Honey, what's going on? Can you talk about it?"

She started crying. "It's the wedding," she sobbed. "Someone is going to get hurt and it's all my fault!" The ceremony was making her place her two families in slots: Jack and me, and Sarah and Mike. The choice of who to walk her down the aisle was just one of the big concerns. Which dad should she choose? Instead of being a celebration, the wedding had become her nightmare.

The next morning, she announced that she and Nathan had decided to elope and have a wedding reception instead of a big wedding. Her eyes sparkled and I sighed in relief.

It had now been over six weeks since Jack and I had talked to our daughter, unheard of in our history together. I could tell Jack was thinking about the silence too. When my husband starts carving, it is a sure sign that he has something deep on his mind. This project was for Amanda and Nathan, walking staffs, as they had taken up hiking. He had spent hours in our woods finding just the right limbs, planning the designs, and was now working the wood. I could hear him muttering to himself and occasionally cursing. As for me, I bake. Some weird southern gene kicks in when trouble is brewing and urges me to start cooking. There were loaves of bread, several pies, and casseroles in the freezer. A banana pudding stood cooling on the counter.

Each day since Amanda and Nathan's visit, Jack and I had covertly watched for the mail to come. There was some unspoken doubt between us that Amanda might have changed her mind about us attending, our status in her life uncertain. We both listened for the stops and starts of the mail truck coming up our hill. When we heard the sounds of metal hinges creaking open and snapping shut, Jack caught my eye, challenging me with a nod of his head.

When we were first married, we would race each other for the mail, running to see who would open the mailbox first. I think it started as a bet. The loser had to do whatever the winner wanted for the rest of the day, without complaint. Now mind you, in those early days it was usually deliciously advantageous to both of us. Our mail carrier enjoyed coming to our stop. I doubt that any other house on her route displayed so much enthusiasm. "Crazy kids!" she would laugh at us as we came barreling out of the house, screaming, laughing, and struggling over each other. That challenge was back now and we raced, as we used to, although our aging bodies were not quite so fast. Laughing and running, Jack kept me just out of reach of the mailbox, his long arms an unfair advantage. This day he seemed distracted and I opened the mailbox first. "It's here!" I cried. We grinned and hugged each other, then walked hand in hand into the house and opened the invitation together. Of course it was beautiful in sentiment and style. The invitation told us a date, a place, and a time to be there. "You see, now you can relax. I knew it would come." Jack, in his endearing and infuriatingly obtuse memory, had rearranged the players in this little drama of our lives, now pretending he had never doubted and it was only I who was worried about it. *Yeah right.*

I hadn't allowed myself to think much about the wedding reception. With only three weeks to plan, now I was in a rush. I needed a dress and sat down at the computer to begin my search. "Blue dress for other mother of the bride." *There, that should do it.* Oh, there were beautiful dresses to buy, so many shades. Short or long, day or night, all these things mattered. I clicked on a button that said, "Not sure what to wear?" It took me to a wedding etiquette site. *Now, wasn't that helpful?* I thought to myself.

As I read the words on the site, I could feel my cheeks flushing. My stomach dropped as it would on the descent of a tall roller coaster. I sat back in the chair, sensing my world had just shifted, and read with growing horror what the website said.

The website referred to me as a "stepmom." *What?* No, there must be *something* about what I was in there. I wasn't a stepmom. I wasn't "wicked." The more I read the crazier my thoughts got. What did it mean, I'm supposed to stand back? "This is the day for the mother of the bride . . ." So what was I? I covered my eyes and tried to breathe through each wave of emotion. I was humiliated and sad, angry and sad, and finally just sad. *What kind of prize fool have I been, thinking I was simply the other mom?*

Mind you, I consider myself to be a reasonably intelligent person. I think that's why I was so dumbfounded not to have considered how other people would view my relationship with Amanda. The British have a word for it—gobsmacked.

This whole wedding thing was the first time in twenty years I had doubted who I was in Amanda's life. Was I even a mother? Or was I her father's wife and nothing more? This new perception made me . . . smaller, forcing me to review what had been absolute. I looked back over the last twenty years, searching for some clue that would explain my denseness.

I met Jack at work. I was managing the restoration of a historic building in Seattle, The Pearl; he was the electrical engineer. Jack would stride in with a hard hat and an armful of blueprints, a very tall man, well dressed, with a booming voice and a contagious laugh.

Jack began stopping by my desk on his way in and out with a large coffee. He would compliment me on whatever I was wearing that day, and then ask me out. I'd politely say no and he'd tell me, "That's okay, Pretty Lady. I know you will say yes one day."

I learned bits about him on those daily visits. He had been married and had been divorced for three years. His young daughter lived with her mom, now remarried, in St. Louis. He was the oldest of six children. His parents were simple people and they had divorced when he was sixteen, "mainly because there were too many of us and not enough of them," he laughed. He'd grown up in St. Louis and knew it like the back of his hand. Friends he had made in elementary school were still active in his life.

I, as an only child, had no point of reference to understand his world. I have southern roots, born in Georgia. Packing and unpacking were the norm as my family moved from one army base to another. Our constant moves had made me a blend of American everywhere, except for my mouth. The drawl, no matter where I lived, stuck like glue, branding me, especially when I was clearly upset. I learned to keep quiet. Jack was too loud and moved too fast for my taste.

After months of Jack's daily banter, he disappeared. He hadn't mentioned leaving. I found myself looking up at the sound of doors opening with a little too much expectation and too much disappointment. About a week later, he showed up, coffee in hand, with a big grin. "Miss me?" (*Well, dammit all to hell, I did.*) He also brought me a gold charm of the arch of St. Louis. "I just wanted you to know I was thinking about you while I was gone. Now will you go out with me?"

Our first date was Italian. I agreed to "just lunch." In my mind, we had nothing in common. Until his divorce, Jack's roots were deep in St. Louis. I had kept traveling, sticking a pin in a map to find my next home. Yet there was something about Jack and his obstreperous ways that I found charming in spite of myself.

He had moved to Seattle for a fresh start in life. He laughed off the wedding of his ex-wife and best friend. But his bravado went quiet when he talked about Amanda, the pain of leaving her too fresh for him to hide. I looked at him with new eyes then.

As in all great love stories, three months to the day we eloped. We were Nick and Nora Charles. We were Bogie and Bacall. I was wined and dined and unconditionally adored. We fit together in places I had not known were empty. This whirlwind of a man had stopped my wandering ways with who he was and how he loved, both Amanda and me.

On the evening of our wedding day, we called all the families to tell them our news. I'm not sure what Jack told Amanda before he handed me the phone. I'm sure I was nervous when I first heard her voice, my daughter, little and wise. "Can I call you Mom? I hope you like me. Now I have *two* moms and *two* dads. Not every kid is as lucky as me. When can I come? Do you love my dad? Because he's a good guy. I love my daddy and now I love you." I fell. Some cosmic happening that pushed aside every fear of the unknown. She's the one who birthed me, not the other way around. I became her *other* mom on the day I married.

We invited Amanda to our wedding, but Sarah thought she was too young to fly alone. Jack and I did our best to make Amanda part of the celebration anyway. We sent her a "wedding" dress to wear at home on our day. (She reminded me of it recently. Honestly, I had forgotten.)

Because she lived in St. Louis and we in Seattle, we built our new family through phone conversations. We learned about each other by listening and talking, settling into a routine of Sunday calls. We could talk for hours. Sometimes we talked with Sarah and Mike, her *other* dad, too. We learned how Amanda was doing in school, and they would tell us funny things she would say or do. We all loved Amanda and everything fell into place.

I give credit to Sarah. Another woman could have resented our time with Amanda. I think Sarah knew, in some unspoken understanding, that we all would raise Amanda together. There has never been any competition between us. In fact, we jokingly call ourselves "wives-in-law" today.

Amanda had two families, one with her *real* dad and one with her *real* mom, opposite in lifestyles. With Sarah and Mike, Amanda had extended family living close and visiting often. She had weekends filled with celebrations and barbecues, the backyard pool overflowing with kids. Our house was quiet and solitary. There were some moments when the families' viewpoints were opposite too. In a phone call after her first union rally, Amanda instructed us to "buy American" and boycott any store with non-USA goods. Jack and I struggled with the best way to respond. I'm sure when Sarah and Mike heard us talking to Amanda about making prayer beads for trees, there was as much angst on their end. Always respectful of each other's view, I know all four parents did our best to offer Amanda choices, letting her decide her own mind.

Motherhood had not shown up as expected. As an only child, I would tell everyone that I wanted six kids when I grew up, even better a dozen. I dreamt of days with rocking chairs, and first days of school. I looked forward to runny noses, skinned knees, sticky hands, and delighted giggles.

Sometime in my teen years, I started collecting children's books, imagining reading to my little brood as they hung on every word. Of course, there was a loving husband by my side and he spoke little and loved much.

Well, *part* of that came true.

What's that old saying, "When you make plans, God laughs?" While waiting for the doctor to come, freezing in those paper gowns designed to destroy any personal dignity, I imagined hearing the news that I was pregnant. I was filled with hope and planning. *Maybe twins?* His mouth said, "Great news!" yet his eyes reflected my sense of his office, sterile and cold. He told me, as if it was a good thing, that there would be no babies for Jack and me. Those dreams died on that doctor visit. It took a lot longer to let go of the books.

Jack and I bought a home on a lake with a loft for Amanda and decorated it in her favorite color, blue. She and I would talk about all of it on our calls. "Tell me again, Mom. What do you see?" I'd spend the next hour playing, "I'm looking at your sleigh bed with the blue comforter. I see a bookcase, a desk, and lamp. I see the ducks out on the lake and a frog by the dock. There are two skylights for you to see the stars." Over and over, we would tell her what we were seeing, first me, then Jack, and then back to me.

I loved listening to Jack and Amanda. They *understood* each other. He would make her laugh with some odd silliness in a language only those two knew. She would tell us about her day at school, the friends she was making, the stories she was writing. We would sometimes talk for hours, making pictures of each other's lives. It was always the same ending the call. Amanda would start crying. The pain of saying good-bye to Jack brought up his leaving. I know how hard that was for her and I watched the toll it took on Jack. He would withdraw for a time after every call. I could only wait until he processed those decisions again. He would reappear, in an hour or two, pretending he was okay, yet I knew he was wounded.

The day finally came when Amanda was old enough to fly alone. I waited for her at the airport, pacing, watching every movement and Jack watching me. Then there she was, this little Jack in female form, shyly opening her arms to me. Whatever I thought had happened before, it was nothing until she came. Laughing, crying, holding on to this new part of my life, fiercely protective of what she was, my daughter, I breathed her in, knowing that she had changed my life from that moment forward.

Amanda ran up to her loft and made it her own, her stuffed animals placed on the bed in a specific order known only to her, her beloved octopus Squeaks given high prominence. On her shelves, she placed treasures, a feather, a shell. We heard her moving things around a bit. She sang as she worked, filling the rafters with sound.

We marked her height on the walls and sat by the lake. She laughed when Jack chased her and then he chased me. When we ran for the mail, she joined in too. I watched them, cocking their heads at the same moment, laughing exactly the same way and at the same things, eating a dill pickle like corn on the cob. *Forest Gump* moments, we called them. I was constantly amazed at how alike they were. I'm sure there is a study about that somewhere. They had not lived together in years, and yet their habits, mannerisms, and viewpoints were the same.

I confess we pampered her on that first visit. We showered her with everything in us. We couldn't stop hugging each other, talking for hours, playing games at home. We explored the Puget Sound on ferries, watching orcas and dolphins swim next to the boat. We laughed at Jack's hat flying into the water and Amanda's delighted giggles when he picked her up to face the wind. We made space to be alone with each other too: Amanda and Jack, Amanda and me.

When it was time for her to board the plane, Amanda screamed and wept, exposing a wound of absolute abandonment. I witnessed her deepest pain, leaving him. It was Jack's turn to crumble. Both of us shaken, we soothed her with promises of "next time" and "longer."

Our calls had more meaning after that first visit. We could "see" our lives now. She'd ask about the frog on the dock, and the loft, now her space. We'd found "I love you" messages written in her childish hand in unexpected places. We were emptier then, without her.

Amanda's other family grew. She was no longer an only, now an elder. She adored her two siblings and loved helping her mom. She'd talk about the babies as if they were her own. Her innocent words sometimes poured salt in my wounds. I confess, in those moments I envied them, Sarah and Mike giving her what we could not.

Over the years, Amanda's visits grew longer, a week or two, then finally summers. We listened to stories of school, teachers (good and bad), the brother and sister now growing into pests. How hard it was to do it all, chores, babysitting her brother and sister, and keeping up with her homework, math being a subject of "torture." She was so busy with friends and activities after school. Amanda was growing up fast. We realized we were missing a lot and questioned our being so far away.

As Amanda began her middle school years, we made the decision to move. We were still some distance away, but distance to Amanda was now calculated in driving time, not flight schedules. We settled into a new routine, Amanda being with us more often.

Jack and I were able to be part of some of the events in Amanda's life. We were there for the "sweet sixteen" party and her high school graduation. She now drove to us as often as she could. We watched her land her first job, advised on college classes to take, held her when love hurt, and stopped breathing for a while when she found "The One."

Memories flooding me, I closed down the wedding etiquette website and all it implied. I no longer cared what it said I was. No, I did not birth Amanda. I did not have her skinned knees to kiss or have her when she was small enough to rock to sleep. Still, I loved her as my own and she loved me. I knew with certainty, I *am* her mother, other or not. That is the truth to Amanda and me.

Never again would I let someone else define who I was and never was I going to let some outdated tradition tell me how to be. If etiquette demanded I stand in the back, it simply did not matter to me.

When the frantic phone call came from Amanda, she had missed us so.

Everything was crazy, she said. She was working so much and there was so much to do. "Oh, Mom, I need you . . ."

I bought the damn dress.

The reception was lovely. The *real* mom and the *other* dad, the *real* dad and *me*. We danced and laughed and congratulated each other. It didn't matter Who or What or How or When. We simply were Amanda's family, with two moms and two dads.

FINDING MY FAMILY

• • •

alaina smith

When I was a kid in the 1970s and '80s, people used to say that children of divorced parents were victims of broken homes. That if a mom and dad separated, their house might fall down. These days, parents divorce and remarry all the time, so they say families are blended—as if shuffled into a new form like strawberries mixed into a frozen daiquiri. Unfortunately, unlike dealing with a kitchen blender, there's no manual for negotiating the resulting frothy mess.

During my teen years, nearly all of my friends had families in distress. Some friends had their fathers leave their lives, while others were dealing with fathers who, although still around, were abusive. Most parents we knew lived apart, or if they were together, they were unhappy. On the rare occasion when I'd meet someone with an original set of contentedly married parents, I'd think skeptically, *Huh. That's weird.*

Being an overachiever, I was off the charts on the family-upheaval scale before I even hit high school. Between the time I was nine and thirteen, my parents divorced, Dad moved out, Mom remarried, Mom and I moved twice, Dad remarried, my dad and stepmom had a baby, and they moved across the country. It was as if I'd stepped onto a merry-go-round spinning at top speed; looking out at my life, I was dizzy and disoriented by the familiar images turned into a confusing blur. Puberty did not help.

My parents were similar people, both introverts, and I was no different. When they each remarried, they picked people with personalities from the other end of the spectrum—adventurous, easygoing, social people who also happened to be phenomenal cooks. I ate a lot of macaroni with store-bought tomato sauce in elementary school. Not that I'm complaining; I like pasta. It's just that now I prefer linguine with my husband's garlic Alfredo sauce, tossed with sautéed mushrooms and served with Pugliese bread. Apparently, if I learned nothing else, I learned to marry someone who loves to cook.

As I tried to adjust to new stepparents who were such opposites of my mom and dad, I struggled to reconcile the differences between my changed reality and my expectations about how things were supposed to work.

One of my earliest tests came at the wedding reception of my mom and stepdad. My new stepfather had fourteen nieces and nephews, so I inherited a rowdy band of step-cousins. In my house, you didn't break the rules, but these kids weren't from my house, and they made their own rules. A few of them urged me to join them in sneaking out to decorate my mom's car with shaving cream and toilet paper to display the happy couple's just-married status. I agreed, thrilled to be included as one of the gang, but also too scared to say no. I started to help, but the more I envisioned my mom's reaction, the more anxious I got. I drew the line at helping with the toilet paper decorations. I was already nauseated with stress, and knew I'd be in big trouble when Mom found out. I was right. Mom was furious. Fortunately, my new stepdad thought it was funny. Between fits of laughter, he urged Mom to take it easy on me, and she did.

My stepmom, too, was a revelation. Before she and my father married and moved to New York, my stepmom lived in Austin, Texas. When I was eleven, Dad and I went to visit her there. We did fun things that I'd never done before, like getting pizza delivered (how decadent!) and staying up late to watch *Saturday Night Live* (how grown-up!). I was impressed by how cool she was, and whether we were playing my favorite board game, CLUE, or going out to trendy restaurants, she made me feel as if we were just two popular girls, hanging out and doing what popular girls did. She encouraged Dad to be adventurous and try new things, like expensive beer, high-quality coffee, and spicy Mexican food. I ate the spicy Mexican food, too, and discovered my mouth could catch fire. I didn't know what to think at first, but over time I grew to enjoy it.

Having new parents not only meant an avalanche of new experiences, it also meant I transitioned from only child to sibling. When I was thirteen, my stepmom gave birth to my half-brother, Dylan. Unfortunately, I had no idea how to relate to my new baby brother, and as I stumbled through my teen years, our relationship didn't make any progress. I didn't know how to communicate with little kids—they didn't make sense, and they wouldn't listen to reason. Few things could fluster me faster than children. The babysitting jobs I reluctantly took varied between uncomfortable and disastrous, and by age fifteen I was relieved to get a work permit so I could make money as an office assistant. Dylan and I were separated by nine states, thirteen years, and my own confusion.

When I did travel across the country to see my brother, dad, and stepmom, I was no better at being a sister. I was a self-focused teenager, uncomfortable with kids and intensely missing my friends, while Dylan was a little boy testing his limits, sitting through a

Mom-appointed "time-out" for tormenting one of the family cats. I was more likely to curl up on the couch with a horrified look on my face than try to offer sisterly guidance on the proper treatment of pets.

Whether I was in Oregon with my mom and stepdad or in New York with my dad, stepmom, and brother, I often felt out of place and misunderstood. I didn't fit anymore. I wasn't angry with my parents for splitting, and I knew they were happier in their new lives. Still, I had a hard time relating to them, especially as I transitioned away from childhood and into adolescence. My family changes were by no means tragic, but teen years are their own tragedy. I struggled to find my balance.

My coping method was selective isolation. Shutting myself into a separate universe bordered by my closed bedroom door, I cut myself off from everything but my lifeline—the beige, spiral-corded, landline telephone that connected me to the family who fit me best: my friends. Friendships were my true home, and my friend Katy was often at its center.

Katy was like me in many ways; we were *A* students, fellow band members, good girls who still wanted to have fun. I loved going over to her house, just four miles away. Whereas at my house I lived as a bedroom hermit, at Katy's we might be anywhere—watching TV on the couch in her family room, making cookies in her kitchen, or chatting in patio chairs on the back deck. At Katy's, I always enjoyed myself, relaxing in a way that I didn't at home.

I loved everything about Katy's place. I loved the fact that the front door was periodically repainted; rich colors like plum, forest green, and burgundy rotated places through the years. I loved being allowed to eat Red Vines candy from the basketball-sized, clear-plastic container in the kitchen. I loved sitting down to the delicious, nutritious, protein-laden dinners that her mom made us. Most of all, I loved feeling like part of her family. At Katy's, life made sense.

I knew Katy's home life wasn't perfect, but when I was there, I preferred to pretend that everything was as wonderful as I romanticized it to be. I especially admired Katy's mother. She could breeze into the house in her stylish suit and whip up a mouthwatering meal like *boeuf bourguignon* or *coq au vin*. She was a successful career woman, a gourmet cook, and, like me, an overachiever. I was intimidated but captivated by her, and I desperately wanted to impress her—I wanted to be her "other daughter." Katy's mom represented an ideal that no other mom could compete with, because ideals aren't realities. I didn't have to experience any tough times or mother/daughter arguments at Katy's. Instead I could enjoy the best of what her family had to offer. At home, I was unhappy and desperate to distance myself, and occasionally disappearing into another family was a great escape.

Spending time at Katy's house offered the added benefit of seeing her little sister, Heather, who was three years younger. Heather looked up to her big sister and usually wanted to do whatever Katy did. When Katy and I had to make a home video for a Spanish class assignment, we coerced Heather into being our "production assistant" (i.e., slave). We gathered in Katy's kitchen to record our Spanish-language television commercial advertising "Explosivo," the fictional breakfast cereal we'd invented for the occasion. We put Heather in charge of the cue cards. As she struggled to lift the oversized poster-board cards into the air, her tiny frame mostly lost behind the white space, Katy yelled at her to raise them higher. Katy and I spent the afternoon frequently breaking into laughter, ruining our takes. Torturing a little sister was just what I needed sometimes.

In truth, I adored Heather. I envied Katy and Heather's close relationship, and I imagined being a sister would be great fun. Although I spent my teens actually being a sister, the term was more technical than practical, as Dylan and I rarely saw each other. Circumstances allowed me to avoid adapting until I was ready, until he became a young adult and we could talk at a more relatable level. It would take until his late teens for us to really connect.

In the process of avoiding his young life, I know I missed out. I don't know much about his childhood, except for a few random facts, for example that he was obsessed with cheese and cheese-adjacent foods. Shopping for birthday cards for him, I have to put back all the ones that say, "Remember that time when we were kids and you used to . . . [insert charming childhood anecdote here]." Card shopping is hard anyway; delusional card companies who still believe it's 1950 rarely make cards that fit modern families. Still, each time I shop, I do my best to find something for my brother that might present me as the cool older sister I always wanted to be—as Katy got to be with Heather—and I give thanks that as he's gotten older, we've become friends. Dylan has grown into a man I am proud to call my brother; he is smart, big-hearted, and fun to be with, and the emotional distance I once felt has melted away. As an adult, I can appreciate him and my parents more than I ever could as a struggling adolescent.

These days having four parents and a brother feels as normal as it once felt strange. In reaching out to others, I discovered that a sense of family is something I can choose to create, not something decided for me. Katy and her family came into my life as I struggled to find my way, and nearly thirty years later, we still have a relationship—but now I also have deeper relationships with my own parents and sibling. With the help of biology, marriage, and friendship, I've blended a family as sweet and satisfying as a frozen strawberry daiquiri.

Part 3 | *Evolution*

TALES OF A CONFUSED APOSTROPHE

• • •

melissa hart

May 1981—The woman named Annie races up the street and squeals her Miata to a stop outside my mother's disintegrating ranch house. At the front door, she pumps my hand in her large fleshy one, then reaches into a paper bag for a hardbound copy of *Little Women*. "This was my favorite at your age," she tells me. I am smitten.

She bounds into the living room with its mismatched cat-pee couches and dumps a bag of tennis balls on the weary carpet. "Bounce 'em," she tells my little brother and sister. "We only want the ones with lots of spring."

My mother appears in the kitchen doorway, her cheeks pink from mashing hot spuds in mayonnaise and mustard.

"Got that potato salad ready?" Annie strides over and kisses her on one flushed cheek. Then she reaches to the top of the doorjamb for one of the cigarettes Mom hides so that she won't feel quite so tempted, but also not quite so deprived. I suspect Annie's been here before, maybe even last weekend when we had to stay with our father.

Mom spots my question across the room. "Annie's come to teach us to play tennis."

Annie is lithe and powerful on the court. My siblings chase errant balls. My mother practices her serve, over and over, until she receives a nod of approval. On the grass under a pair of sprawling oaks, we eat potato salad and hard-boiled eggs and apples. My siblings and I drink the lemonade we've squeezed from backyard fruit. Annie and my mother split a Budweiser, chuckling as snowy foam from the cracked open can cools their faces.

That first Mother's Day, I make Annie a card so that our celebratory crepes around the table on Sunday morning don't feel so awkward. My fifth-grade teacher taught us to fill a sturdy piece of paper with crayoned colors, then cover them with black Crayola so that we could scratch words and patterns into it, revealing the rainbow beneath. The heart is easy; it's the apostrophe that confounds me. Annie is nobody's mother, but she's holding my mom's hand under the table, and yesterday, she took us all to Penney's to buy bags of new clothes.

In the end, bewilderment trumps grammar. "For Annie," I carve block letters into the black shellac. "Happy Mothers Day."

May 1982—We don't know what to call Annie. She's lived with my mother for months now.

The year before, my siblings and I fretted over what to call our father's new wife. Not Mother, and certainly not Mom. Dad suggested Mama Elsa, a saccharine affectation that turned my stomach. In the end, we just called her Elsa.

Now, my little sister and I look down at our blank rectangles of construction paper, Magic Markers in our hands. We've been at Mom's for a whole Saturday—for once, we're easy with each other, relaxed. "Annie's kind of our stepmother." I tap the blueberry-scented pen against my teeth while my sister huffs the one that smells like black licorice. "But they're not married."

"I heard her telling those women at the barbecue yesterday that she didn't want kids." My sister shrugs. "Maybe we shouldn't mention Mother's Day."

"But . . ." I think of how, at Easter, Annie taught us to batik hard-boiled eggs, how she chased me around the house with one that had broken open while boiling—a hideous mess of cooked white that scared me but also made me fall on the carpet in hysterical laughter. I remembered how, two weekends later, she spent a whole day tie-dying T-shirts with us, and then—since we had lots of dye—my brother's underwear and a pair of my mother's, too. "Happy Friend's Day," I write on my pink paper, then crumple it up.

In the end, my little brother, wise in spite of his developmental delay, solves the problem. In his scrawled first grader's hand, he writes, "Happy Day, A-Mom."

A-Mom. I inscribe it on the first page of a book I've bought her—a biography of Louisa May Alcott. When my mother sees the inscription, she gets quiet and I can't tell from the shine in her eyes whether she's happy or pissed.

The afternoon Annie chased me around the house with the egg, adding her laughter to mine, Mom grew taciturn and went into her office and shut the door. My mother and I never laugh that way together, but we cry almost every night because of the courtroom's decision to separate us.

That Sunday night, Annie stays at home while Mom drives us back down the Pacific Coast Highway to our dad's house. When we stop for ice cream in Malibu, I buy her a vanilla cone with the last of my allowance for cleaning the chicken coop. "Happy Mother's Day," I tell her again and pray that my sister won't reveal how my teacher made us write essays for the community Mother of the Year contest.

"I have three mothers," I'd said to Mrs. Jansta.

The woman had blinked at me, baffled. "Well, write about the mother you live with."

I'd written about Elsa and won, and now my stepmother and I would ride on a float together in the town's Fourth of July parade. "If Mom finds out," I whisper to my sister outside Swensen's, "she'll kill me."

She finds out.

I live . . . barely.

May 1985—My mother decides to rent a one-bedroom apartment in the city where my siblings and I live with our father. "I never see you anymore," she complained when she arrived Friday evening to pick up my sister and brother, and I declined the invitation to spend the weekend with her ninety miles away from my Saturday track meets and Sundays spent trolling Venice Beach with my friends.

Her new apartment lurks half a mile from my high school; it's dingy and uninspired. "Smells like mold." I throw my sleeping bag and backpack down in the bare living room. But secretly, I am thrilled to have my mother in the same town. "Now I can come here after school, like normal kids."

My mother runs a finger through her graying brown bangs. "Your father might not like that."

"Dad doesn't give a damn what we do." He doesn't; he's busy bopping his secretary, a girl five years older than I with dreams of being an ice dancer. But Annie misses my mother. Mom has a free-lance job; she can travel back and forth up the Pacific Coast Highway whenever she wants. Her girlfriend has a nine-to-fiver five days a week. She feels abandoned.

"Annie misses me on weeknights," my mother tells me after a couple of weeks in the apartment. "When you said you could come over after school, I didn't realize you meant nine in the evening. I had no idea you'd be so busy."

I seethe. My friends had come over that night to hook up the cable and eat pizza. I showed my mother off to them—her relaxed demeanor so different from that of my stepmother with a temperament rigid as her aerobicized abs. "Can't you just stay?" I beg.

But my mother packs up the apartment in two VW busloads. Before she drives off with the second, she holds me tight against her. "Maybe you could come and live with us."

I picture the tiny high school in the town where she lives and squirm away, my chest tight with rage.

That second Sunday in May, I don't make Annie a card. I deliberately hand my mother a cheap Hallmark and a potted daisy over scrambled egg and bacon crepes. "The flower was supposed to be for your apartment," I tell her, "but now that you've given it up, I guess you can just plant it outside your house."

She does, but she forgets to water it. It dies.

May 1989—At UC Santa Cruz, I could be absolved from the dilemma that confounds me the second Sunday in May. No one expects a college freshman to think of anyone but herself right before finals. But I've spent a semester sitting in the front row of Women's and Gender Studies 101. Proudly, I walk to the bookstore and buy a blank card on recycled paper. I write a note, carefully inking the apostrophe on the right side of the S so that my salutation reads, "Happy Mothers' Day, Mom and Annie."

I am the only child of lesbians that I know. In high school, I'd hid the fact from my classmates with their unpredictable homophobic jokes spat out between Polish slurs and observations on dumb blondes. In college, I'm out and proud. I wear a rainbow pin on my banana slug T-shirt. Into every conversation, I work phrases that begin, "My two moms . . ."

Daisy, the blonde goddess from my class, told the class she'd like to be me. I'd like to be Daisy. I allowed myself to think I'd like to sleep with her too—those long golden limbs, that good-natured, upturned smile. But when I got to the part in my daydream about our actual intercourse, I blanched and went out with the hippie-guy pianist from our class instead.

I put the Mothers' Day card into a shoebox with a copy of *The Autobiography of Alice B. Toklas.* I add a couple of rainbow pins. My enviable sophistication propels me down the long hill from campus on my bike, past the homeless guys on the mall, to the post office.

I remember at the last minute that I've bought Elsa nothing. I duck into Bookshop Santa Cruz and grab a stuffed toy slug and another card. I forget about the apostrophe and have to scribble over it, turning it into a random gastropod oozing just after the *S.*

"Happy Mother's Day," I write and feel traitorous.

May 1990—After an earthquake demolishes downtown Santa Cruz and my roommate flees our condemned house, I transfer out and move in with my mothers. My boyfriend moves in, as well, tiptoeing past their bedroom at midnight after his shift at the group home to collapse onto my single futon. Through the heater vents, we hear my moms talking in low, anxious voices. We don't consider how—if we can hear them talking—they can hear us making love.

For the first time in eleven years, I get to live with my mother. I am overjoyed. But she's managing a group home; we communicate mainly through a notebook left open on the bathroom counter. Annie's home evenings. She locks herself in her room, and I have the house to myself until my boyfriend arrives.

I miss my mother. Annie grows increasingly silent and glowering. At last, scrubbing cookie dough off the telephone, she speaks. "I lived with a bunch of people after college." She looks over the counter at me, and her brown eyes are harsh and angry. "I don't want to live with a bunch of people now."

I am dense. It takes her two tries to explain that she's asking me to leave. The second time, she says it bluntly. Heartbroken, I enroll at UC Santa Barbara. I pack up the futon, my boyfriend, and our cat. That year, I buy a generic card, scribble my name, leave it on my mother's desk, and leave.

I will never live with her again.

May 1996—I get my first real job as a teacher in the spring, after subbing all year. My class is full of special-needs students. In her post-college years, Annie worked at the state hospital with developmentally delayed adults. Now she is between jobs, so on Saturday evening after Mom's chicken-fried steak and mashed potatoes and peach cobbler, she and I hunch together at the dining room table. She's helping me program an electronic voice box for one of my kids, who is mute.

"He needs to be able to communicate his basic needs," she tells me. "Food, water, the bathroom. And his emotions. Record things like 'I feel happy,' 'I feel sad.' Also . . ." Her mouth turns up and her eyes sparkle with the wickedness that must still entice my mother in her less menopausal moments. "You need to give your student an emotional outlet button."

I study the little black box on the belt that my third grader will wear around his waist. I touch the line drawings of a cup, a frowning mouth. "What do you mean?"

"Kids need to be able to vent," Annie tells me, "even if they can't talk. For adults at the hospital, I used to program in their favorite curse word or angry phrase." She mimics the computer's neutral voice. "Go to hell, loser."

111

"My guy's only nine," I tell her. "He'll get suspended from school if he curses."

We settle on "Eat my shorts." My student's a fan of *The Simpsons*; the term will appeal to him and appease my principal. Over and over, Annie and I push the button on the voice box that she's marked with a hand-drawn picture of shorts dangling near an open mouth. "Eat my shorts! Eat my shorts!"

By the tenth repetition, we are dying, falling against each other in hysterical laughter. I accidentally knock my shot glass of apricot brandy to the ground. It shatters.

In the kitchen, my mother looks up from washing dishes. Her mouth is a thin, hard line. "That glass was your great-grandmother's." She turns off the water and disappears into her office.

I spend the night. The next morning, I tuck the Tracy Chapman CD and my card for Annie back into my duffel bag and set out the cookbook and stainless steel compost bucket I've bought for my mother. There's a card inside the bucket with a gift certificate for Starbucks.

My sister is off at college, but my little brother has made Mom and A-Mom his traditional homemade cards. Separately, they've taken him to JCPenney to pick out fuzzy socks for my mother, and a leather glove for Annie who's lately traded tennis for the more sedentary sport of golf.

Annie doesn't seem to notice my lack of a gift. But my mom sifts through wrapping paper and rereads cards, and then frowns at me.

"Actually," I say with my face on fire, "the compost bucket and gift card are for both of you."

In the bathroom, I sit on the toilet seat cover with my head in my hands. I long for an emotional outlet button—a line drawing of two mothers. When I push it, a mechanical voice will say, "What the hell do you want from me?"

May 2000—For once, the second Sunday in May presents a different conundrum. My grandmother has moved next door, and she has stage four uterine cancer. "Could've been prevented," Annie whispers to me in the E.R. one night. "She had symptoms, but she wouldn't go to the doctor."

I know this. I adore my grandmother, my mother's mother. After her diagnosis, I cry and cry. My mother does not, to the best of my knowledge, but she makes barbecued chicken and a pineapple upside-down cake, her mom's favorite. For Mother's Day brunch, she ties a cheery red kerchief over my grandma's naked head and helps her out to the sun porch. Annie pours flutes of champagne and tells jokes.

Annie is good in a crisis. She is the reason that I can move eight hundred miles away after my grandmother's death. She will take care of my mother.

I don't send my stepmother a card anymore. She and my father have relocated across the country, and she's busy with her dogs and her friends and her own aging mother. This year, I've purchased a card-making kit—one of those Klutz packs from the toy store—and picked out beautiful paper from the stationery store for three cards. My grandmother gets one with seashells. I create an Asian-themed card for my mother who's discovered Pema Chödrön. For Annie, I do Art Deco.

Annie looks at the blue and white angular patterns for an instant, and then, distracted by my grandmother's coughing, sets it down on the coffee table. Later, she puts a half-drunk glass of Ensure-vodka smoothie—the only thing we can get the patient to consume—on top of the card. I watch the circle of water spread and dissolve the paper.

May 2007—I promised, years ago, to return to Mom each Mother's Day from my new hometown—a promise I kept exactly one year. My brother lives with my mother and Annie now; they are a family unit with their own habits, eccentricities, their own celebrations.

I feel shut out, a dissociation that rankles because I asked for it.

My sister has a baby. The family gathers together at her condominium to celebrate with a catered champagne and bagel brunch. I am not invited. "We didn't think you could come," my sister says into the phone. "You're so far away."

No one voices the rest of the story—that I've been trying to adopt my own child for two years. All focus is riveted on the new baby boy. I send a Harry and David gift basket, pears enough for all. My sister claims the apostrophe.

May 2012—We fling ourselves to different parts of the world. Annie spends the month back east with her oldest niece who's just birthed a girl. This niece is the closest thing she has to a daughter, she says, and she wants to be of help.

Sadness engulfs me. Eight hundred miles south of me, my mother drives down to my sister's condo for brunch the second Sunday in May, and my husband takes our daughter and me to Portland overnight. We've sent his mother her favorite chocolate-covered almonds, my mother more pears.

My mother and Annie could marry now—a window of opportunity in San Francisco, Massachusetts, New York, but they do not. "Hell no," my mother says.

"Hell no," Annie echoes.

In the end, I send my mother's partner nothing but a text. "Happy Day." I punch in the numbers in Pioneer Square as my daughter plays on the brick steps surrounded by the beautiful old buildings.

Annie doesn't reply. I think I might boycott the holiday in the future, or turn it over to my child with her charming finger-painted cards and wobbly I Love Yous. "Let's focus on Christmas Eve, instead," I tell my husband.

It's the one night a year on which my family comes together around a big round table at the strip-mall Chinese restaurant near my mom's town to share eggrolls and moo-shu pork and Mai Tais. There are no expectations beyond Annie's insistence that she pay for the meal. We read our astrological characteristics from the paper menu and laugh at our sorry attempts to use chopsticks. For one night, we are intact and healthy and relatively happy. On the way home, we sing carols, then fall into bed intoxicated by grace and absolved from apostrophes.

IT'S A MOM THING

• • •

cynthia whitcomb

I was a forty-year-old single mom with two kids when I got
a letter postmarked "Houston" from my high school sweetheart that
said, "My divorce was final today and I think I've been in love with
you my whole life." This was somewhat stunning news. I was a free-
lance television writer who had two weeks previously bought a ranch
in Wyoming and moved there with Nick, eight, and Molly, five,
knowing no one in the state of Wyoming.

There followed a heated, interstate romance. He brought his little boys to meet us on his oldest son Jake's fifth birthday. Sam, his
youngest, was three-and-a-half.

Let's start by admitting the trickiest thing about being a stepparent. Most parenting skills translate. The tough one is the process
of coming to love someone else's child as if he or she were your
own. With your own kids, you love them with every cell before they

even see light and draw their first squalling breath. That little bump inside you when they kick to get you to stop playing that country music? Love. You're totally gone by the time they clamp onto your breast and you realize you never knew what unconditional love felt like before that little head was cradled to you. This is not exclusive to mothers. Fathers who hold that little bundle on day one go through the same chemical, spiritual, emotional miracle.

With stepkids, even when they are adorable three-year-olds, you look at them and know that one day they will frown up at you and say the dreaded words, "You're not my mother and I don't have to do what you say!"

Jake was eighteen months older than Sam, dark-haired, small for his age, and the quiet one. Sam was the freckle-faced redhead with blue eyes, big for his age and outgoing—the alpha toddler. They were both crazy smart. In their pictures from that time the only way to tell which one was older is that Jake was thinner and had more hair. Otherwise it was a coin toss. They were adorable. How hard could this be, right?

The first tactic that worked with Sam was the "sick box," which engaged his attention and gave us something in common. My grandmother raised six kids before the television era. Someone once asked her how she had time for six children and she answered, "One takes up all your time. Six can't take up any more." She created the sick box. It was a cigar box filled with tiny toys, mostly Cracker Jacks prizes from back in the days they had real toys and not just paper stickers. When children were home sick, they'd get the box and could arrange the little toys on the bedspread and entertain themselves. My mother continued the tradition when we were kids. And I had made one partly of those tiny, hand-me-down toys from my mom's childhood and mine, added to over the years until there were several hundred tiny toys that fit into a kid-sized shoebox.

Sam was as far from sick as humanly possible, but I offered to let him play with the sick box and he went from suspicious to happy in seconds. He played with it for more than an hour and the second day of our acquaintance he came up to me right after breakfast and said, "Can I play with your little toys?" Score one for my maternal lineage.

I tried to come up with fun things for us all to do together that would win them over and help the four kids to bond. Hiking. Fishing. Barbecue. Fireworks. On the ranch, we could see all manner of wildlife on a daily basis: deer, elk, moose, skunks, foxes, eagles, and badgers. One day I looked up from the deck and saw Sam on the path in front of the house chasing a huge porcupine, arms open to hug the "doggie." His dad grabbed him before he could get hold of it and spared us all a night of grief.

Other than the sick box, all my manufactured attempts at bonding didn't seem to be working for Sam, so I got more creative. We hunted for bones in the woods and took them to the local rock-and-bone guy, hoping we had found dinosaurs and bears, only to find out the bones belonged to cows and coyotes. Still, the kids would try to assemble them into some sort of recognizable creature. Here a jaw with teeth, there a rib. They were into it, and Sam was one of the gang, bonding with my kids, especially Nick who was a good big-brother-type boy, kind and inclusive.

But my arm around Sam's little shoulders would be shrugged off. When he chose a chair at the table it would be next to anyone other than me, even a girl like Molly. I didn't take this personally. I understood that his rejection of me as a mom was, in his kid mind, an act of loyalty to his real mom. But I didn't give up either.

Although Sam had no interest in bonding with me, he wasn't without his own system of comfort and companionship. He was already inseparably bonded to a soft, white marshmallow of a stuffed Puffalump cow named Cary, who, in spite of being a cow, was also somehow a "him." Sam could not go anywhere without Cary, and going to bed without him would have been a tragedy, except it had never yet happened in his short life.

It was not too surprising that Sam had some trust issues. When his mother took the boys from their home in Houston on a long car ride to Portland, Oregon, they were told that they were going on vacation. Several weeks later, after asking one too many times when they were going home to Daddy, they were finally told that they were never going "home." This was their home now. And Daddy was no longer the guy they could run and jump in bed with anytime a thunderstorm shook the house. He was now a Disneyland Dad who saw them one weekend a month, and he sent them little toys and suckers in the mail.

And now this summer in Wyoming, things were changing again. Here was this new mom in the picture. Who, in a few months, was about to officially become their stepmother.

On the twenty-third anniversary of our first date, we were married in our old hometown. As soon as we could work it out, we moved to Portland, Oregon, to be near the boys. Disneyland Dad turned into Dad with whom they slept over every Wednesday night and every other weekend. And Dad's new wife got serious about figuring out how to be their extra mom.

Jake was easier to love. He was the underdog, for one thing. Sam was fast with a punch. Jake would often be the one getting hit and not hitting back, having learned that if you hit the baby you're going to get it, but if the baby hits you nothing's going to happen to him.

Jake was also the wry, sardonic, funny kid. You'd find him wandering around the house singing quietly to himself, and if you passed close by, you'd hear the revised oldie "*I am so beautiful to me.*" If the kids saw an explosion in a movie, Jake would say, "Don't try this at home. Try it at your friend's home." Or if drugs or alcohol or sex came up in conversation, Jake might say, "There's a time and a place for everything. It's called college." Another kid asked him where he got his T-shirt, and he instantly answered, "'Nam."

Once when my husband was out of town and all four kids were with me, Jake, six, wandered in, having woken from a nightmare, and I let him climb in and sleep on Dad's side of the bed for the rest of the night. Weeks later when his dad was scolding him for something, Jake said, "Oh yeah? Well, I slept with your wife." We laughed so hard we forgot what the scolding was for. You get the idea. He was the funny kid whose hair always looks Harry Potter—rumpled and whose homework papers always end up on the floor of the car with dirty shoeprints on them.

Sam was funny sometimes, too, of course, though not always intentionally. At the ranch when he was three years old he came running to me to whisper that he'd "burped a poo." And I knew what to do. At a restaurant when he was five or six he asked to be excused to go to the restroom. Five minutes after he came back, he asked to go again. I said, "But you just went."

He replied, "I know but last time I only did the F word."

I had a bad moment. "What's the F word?"

He whispered, "Fart."

I let him know that *fart* was not the F word. At least he was getting his letters, right? When he had learned to read, once from the backseat he yelled, "You just passed a sign that said 'Do not pass.'" It made him happy to prove me wrong.

Sam was named for his mom, was a redhead like her, and had gotten the message, stated or subliminal, that he'd better be loyal to his one and only mother. Jake, named for his father, took after Dad in looks as well. So an invisible line was drawn in the sand between Sam and me. One I was determined to obliterate.

Jake was faster to warm up to three new family members. He had no problem calling me "Mom" like my other kids. Come to think of it, he may have thought it was my name, the way you can have two friends named Mike. Sam was not going for it. Now almost five, he was growing into that redheaded, freckle-faced kid in children's books who is always full of mischief.

Sometimes Sam would suddenly pitch a screaming fit over something minor. I needed to figure out a solution to this. He was too old for it to be the Terrible Twos (or as my sister Laura calls them, the Theatrical Twos), but not too old to have flashbacks. And too big for me to try to wrestle him out of trying to punch the other three kids if they were within arm's reach when he'd start to rage. After a few weeks, I discovered it was low blood sugar, a thing his dad also suffered from.

I experimented by putting him in a chair and telling him he could not get out of it until he drank a glass of juice. He'd finally take it, staring murderously at me, gulp down the juice like a gunslinger in a bar, and amazingly within thirty seconds the storm would be over, he'd hand me the empty glass, I'd let him out of jail, and he'd trot off to play happily, seemingly with no memory of the raging fury, now all smiles with his freckles still wet with tears. Sometimes in stepmothering you get lucky. And sometimes you fail.

Once, flying back from the ranch with all four kids, when their dad had gone home early to work, we were in a small airport and Sam started in on a temper tantrum. I left the older three kids at the gate, and made Sam go with me to return the rental car. I put him in the backseat, went around to the other side and put my carry-on bag beside him, then returned the car. As we were walking back, and he was trying to think of some way to push my buttons, he came up with a doozy.

"You hit me with a suitcase," he said.

"I did not hit you. The bag didn't even touch you."

"You hit me with a suitcase."

He kept repeating this, making sure I understood his intention was to publicize my abuse and report my cruelty nationally. And he

got to me. Just his calmly repeating this over and over. "You hit me."
By the time we got to the gate I wanted to. I was furious. I sat him
down with the other three and had to take a walk and call his father
to be able to let it go.

So we had our ups and downs, Sam and I. And sometimes I liked
Sam and sometimes I needed a timeout. In my own room. With the
door closed. And some F words. I needed to find a way to love Sam
as I did the other three kids. I wanted to feel love. To be filled with it
like biblical grace. But we can't control our feelings. They just come
and go with minds of their own. What finally answered this dilemma
for me and helped me become the loving mother I needed to be was
that small creature that looked a lot like a dirty marshmallow pillow.
Cary the Cow.

One afternoon I took the four kids to Toys-R-Us to spend their
allowance and buy some mom-sanity-saving Slip'N Slide—type water
stuff to get us through the summer weather. They were determined
to each find something they could buy with their $5. An exercise in
math and maturity. Totally educational.

The kids ran around manically (or maybe I mean maniacally) and
after an hour I managed to corral them through the checkout line
and into the van, grateful that Oregon has no sales tax and when
something says $4.99 a kid can buy it for $5 and get a penny back in
change.

When we got home, and it was time for bed, the sound of a kid
scream followed by sobs scared me. As a mom you develop the ability
to differentiate between play screams and scary screams. This was a
scary scream. I ran up the stairs and found little Sam sobbing into
his pillow. But this was nothing a glass of juice could fix. I could only
make out one strangled word: "Cary!"

He had taken Cary the Cow to Toys-R-Us, as he took Cary everywhere. But somehow in the glamorous world of new toys towering to

the ceiling in rainbow plastic splendor, the dingy, once-white cloth cow was abandoned on the floor and not remembered until now.

Crap. Toys-R-Us closed at 9. It was 8:52 and we lived 30 minutes away. Thank God, I didn't hesitate long enough to do the math. I was off and running the second I got the picture. I hollered, "I'll be right back!" and left Sam sobbing and the other kids and my husband bewildered.

I broke a few speeding laws, but still got to Toys-R-Us too late. The sign was dark and the parking lot empty. Inside, work-lights burned as employees cleaned up. I pounded on the glass doors pantomiming a toy emergency. A janitor took pity on me and opened the door. I said, "I'll just be one second" as I raced through the store, scanning every aisle. No little marshmallow cow anywhere. I went to the spot where Sam had been playing with the Power Rangers Action Figures. It was dairy-free.

Finally, in a corner I found a shopping cart filled with trash, and squashed at the bottom, bits of white cloth cow poked through the metal mesh. I scrabbled through cardboard and sticky trash and finally pulled the little bovine out of the jaws of impending death. I was so happy and relieved to see him, I hugged him myself and hollered, "Thank you" as I ran out.

When I bounded up the stairs to the boys' room, Sam was not asleep, but he was no longer sobbing. He was a sweaty, tear-damp, sad little rag doll of a four-year-old boy lying limp and exhausted in bed. He saw me and then his eyes fell on the sad little rag doll of a cow. "Cary!" Sam buried his face in soft, white cow tummy.

And I felt it. I choked up and loved the hell out of that little boy. Here's the thing about love: It's a verb, not an emotion. You love as an action. You just do it. And when you do, the feeling will follow.

The Cary Rescue was a turning point. Not long after that night Sam started calling me "Mom." We still had our ups and downs, but we were thereafter on hugging terms and having two moms started to seem like the most normal thing in the world. Because you know what? Even small children understand that strangers don't run out in the middle of the night to rescue beloved cows. It's a mom thing.

THE BEST AND HARDEST THINGS

• • •

kezia willingham

Becoming a stepmother has been both one of the best, and one of the hardest, experiences of my life. It's not because my stepson is particularly hard to parent. It's not because I don't like the additional responsibility, or because we don't get along. Rather, the hardest part about being a stepmother, for me, is not being my stepson's actual mother.

My husband's son Mario is smart, funny, and keenly observant. He has a witty sense of humor and a genuine interest in the world around him. He is sensitive and kind. At ten, he falls in age right in between my fifteen-year-old daughter and his four-year-old half-brother. When the kids are getting along, they make a wacky, clever, sweet trio of children who range in color from pale white to nutmeg brown. My happiest moments have been spent with them as we sit around the house cracking jokes or explore new parks in the city.

The three of them are amazing children—my favorite people in the world to hang out with.

Not getting to see Mario every day is a challenge. Things happen in his life that I have no control over, such as last spring when he told me, "My Mom is getting a new job soon. She's going to work from 6 P.M. to 2 A.M."

"Who's going to be watching you while she's gone?"

"I can stay by myself. I'll go to bed early."

Wow. That's really sad.

If he were my child, he wouldn't be left alone all night long. In my house, on school nights, the kids are generally in bed by 9:00 P.M. after a story. My husband Antonio provides childcare while I'm at work during the day. We would not leave the kids alone for six or eight hours at a stretch—ever. Hearing Mario explain that he would be left home alone for most of the night on a regular basis made me cringe and left a sick feeling in my gut.

"You can come stay with us during the week," I offered.

"But then I would have to change schools," he replied.

I knew that Mario would not choose to come live in our house and that we couldn't file for custody, for financial reasons and my husband's precarious legal status.

The man who makes peanut butter sandwiches and cares for our children every day is a convicted felon. Now, to many people, that fact alone would raise red flags. However, while my husband clearly made a mistake that has affected the rest of his life, he is not what you imagine when you think of a criminal.

Antonio originally came to this country from his native Honduras in order to help raise his five younger siblings after his father died. He is actually quite passive and shy. He likes to avoid conflict and make people happy. In our five years of marriage, I don't think he's ever once raised his voice to the children or me. If either of us has a quick temper, it's me. The thing that most attracted me to Antonio when I met him was his devotion to Mario. Whenever he brought Mario to preschool, they would come in holding hands, and Mario's face always lit up when Antonio came to pick him up afterwards. Mario still enjoys his time with his father. As a stay-at-home dad, Antonio does most of the housework, prepares dinner every evening during the week, and volunteers at our youngest son's preschool.

A decade ago, before Antonio and I met, he was dating Cindy, Mario's mom, a recent immigrant like him. He was passionately in love with her. She became pregnant with Mario about a year after they started living together. She stayed home with the baby at first and Antonio worked three jobs to support them, but she found the demands of a young child unsatisfying so she went to work. Not long after, she decided that she did not want to live with Antonio anymore either. She was young and living in a country full of opportunities and relative social freedom. She started dating other men, yet would always go back to Antonio. They were caught in an on again, off again relationship. However, Antonio, a practicing Catholic, believed in the traditional family and wanted to raise Mario with her.

One night after they'd broken up yet again, he went to see Cindy and found her in the arms of another man. Mario was with one of his aunts. Antonio lost control and leapt through an open window, picked up a kitchen knife, and threatened the man, insisting that he stay away from Cindy. The man wrestled him to the ground and chased Antonio out of the apartment. Cindy called the police and Antonio willingly turned himself in the next day. His lawyer advised him to plead guilty to felony charges of domestic violence and residential burglary, and he lost his three jobs when he was incarcerated for six months. At the time, Antonio didn't realize that because he is not a US citizen, he was giving up any right to remain in this country.

This history has impacted where we can live, where my husband can volunteer, and has prohibited Antonio from filing for custody. Ultimately, it may be the very thing that removes him from this country permanently. It is the reason that he cannot become a Lawful Permanent Resident.

So while I might believe that Mario would be better off living in my home, I know the courts would say otherwise. While I've wanted Mario to feel safe and have as normal a childhood as possible, I know that my power is limited in that regard.

It has been a struggle from the beginning. When Mario was five years old, he often told me, "I hate my mom because she hates me."

Those days, it was not uncommon for him to curl up in a fetal position, wailing, when it was time to go back home. Of course, I didn't know all of what went on at Cindy's, but I suspected that part of the problem was the unpredictability of his visits. One day his mother would call and tell Antonio to pick him up; another she would call and state that it was time for Mario to come home, as in that minute. It didn't matter where we were or what we were doing.

Because of our concerns over Mario's well-being, Antonio and I consulted an attorney at a free neighborhood legal clinic. One winter night we sat in a tiny cluttered back room of a community center as the lawyer explained why it would not be a good idea to file for legal visitation or custodial rights. "With your felonies," she said, looking at my husband, "a judge will not be inclined to give you unsupervised access to your son. You might end up with one hour of supervised visitation with him a week. Judges do not take felony domestic violence charges lightly."

We left that meeting with heavy hearts and decided to make the best of the visitation situation as it was: undefined, casual, and sporadic.

The erratic nature of Mario's visits left us all with a perpetual feeling of uncertainty. When would he come next? How long would he stay? Antonio was reluctant to set boundaries with Cindy. She threatened to call the police if he didn't do what she wanted. Getting arrested would mean getting deported and having no contact with any of his children. Alternatively, he didn't ever want to tell Mario, his own son, he could not come over.

I couldn't get over the manipulative nature of Cindy's threats. I'd married Antonio in part to keep him in Mario's life, but I didn't want my personal values to be overlooked. And my personal values were strongly influenced by the needs of my children, all three of them. Mario was stuck right in the middle of his parents' conflict. For instance, his mother would tell him that his father loved the new baby more than him. Or Antonio would say negative things about Cindy in front of Mario. I felt powerless witnessing the effects of their relationship on his emotional health.

My role as a mother has always been very important to me, and I believe that children need basic things in order to grow and develop in a healthy manner: food, love, guidance, and a sense of predictability and structure in their world. I'd worked in early childhood settings for most of my career, and I knew that a sense of routine is critical in establishing an emotionally safe environment for young children. Mario had no routine at all. He was often emotional, angry and sad, and prone to outbursts of screaming and rage. Cindy and Antonio might not have seen why a schedule would help his development, but I could.

From the beginning this was always a source of conflict between Antonio and me, but it came to a crisis when our baby turned one year old. I was about to return to work after a year of unpaid maternity leave. During that year, I had separated from Antonio for four months and returned to my hometown in Oregon. When I was called back to work in Seattle, I had to decide whether to stay in Oregon as a single mother or return to Seattle and make my marriage work. One of the hardest things in our marriage had been feeling as if my needs were second to Cindy's and Antonio's. After much deliberation, I decided to give my marriage another try. I knew that I wanted to keep my family together, even if it was hard. But I also knew that if I moved back to Seattle, back to Antonio, things would have to change. Faced with the prospect of returning to work full-time, I couldn't go along with the erratic visitation routine any longer and I told Antonio so.

"It's not good for Mario to never know when he is coming over, or when he's going to leave. It's hard for my daughter because she never knows what's going on. And I don't want our son growing up like this. All three of our children's lives are affected by Cindy's moods and desires. You need to change the way you do things. She needs to understand that a schedule will work best for everyone. It's not just you and her anymore. There are five people involved now." I felt like a jerk for asserting myself, but being "nice" wasn't getting any of us anywhere.

Antonio pushed back. "I want my son to be here when he wants to. I want him to know I care about him. And you know she will get mad if I say no when she wants Mario to come over, and then she'll call the police. I went to jail before and I don't want to go back."

I held my ground. "It isn't good for him to see you controlled by her all the time. Someone needs to stand up to her. I will not live like this any longer. I refuse. If you want her to control your life, then you need to move out and get your own apartment."

Today, after five years of marriage, I am proud to say that while we still lack a formal schedule, Cindy has learned to ask, not demand, that Mario come over. It took years to get to this point because I had to take on both Cindy and my husband. In the process, I consulted a social worker, police officers, and the lawyer at the legal clinic. All of them explained that the worst thing Antonio could do was continue violating the restraining order by allowing contact with Cindy. Finally, after about nine months of negotiation, Cindy agreed to start arranging Mario's visitation directly with me. This has diminished all of her threats and spontaneous demands, and Antonio learned it did not mean the end of his relationship with his son.

Cindy and I communicate primarily via text messaging, leaving a trail of exactly what was said. This way, she has direct contact with our household without violating the no-contact order. Every communication is documented in case she follows through with threats to call the police.

There were so many times when I thought it would be so much easier if I were Mario's mom. If he were my son, I would get to set the rules. He wouldn't have to go back and forth between two different homes. He would, at least, have a normal routine. He would have a brother and sister to grow up with, and two parents who lived in the same house.

But I am not his mom. He has a mother. No matter how much I might want to be his mom, I never will be. I didn't carry him for nine months and give birth to him. I might not agree with many of Cindy's choices, but I have to respect her role as his mother. She didn't abandon him. She is not a drug addict. I believe she loves him, but sometimes her unresolved issues with his father interfere with her parenting. I have to accept my role as a caring adult in his life who tries to be a positive influence.

At ten years old, Mario never says he hates his mom anymore. He does not crumple into a fetal position when it's time to go back to her house. The wailing has stopped. In contrast, he seems happy most of the time. He does well in school. I am amazed when I think about the difference between who he was at five and who he is now.

In our home, the kids are in bed by 10:00 P.M. on weekends. They do not play video games or watch TV all day long. I try to get them out to the park at least once a day when it's not rainy. Their dad often takes them to the soccer field in the evenings.

I still sometimes wish that I were Mario's mom. But at the same time, I've seen his connection to his mother strengthen over the years. I believe she is a better parent today than she once was. I am sincerely proud of the progress *all* of us have made.

As a stepmom, you do not always get recognition for the behind-the-scenes work that you do. You might not get to sign your stepchild up for soccer or swimming or decide which school he will attend. You might feel that it would be best for him to stay in your home, but it's not within your power to make it so because you may not have legal rights.

Yet there are rewards: a hug from your stepson, the way his eyes light up when you walk in the door after work, the conversations you share about life. Watching him laugh and play and run with his siblings. Answering his many questions about the world. Enjoying his company so much that you want him to stay longer than the couple of days he is with you.

With all of our challenges, we take it one day at a time. I try to savor the best moments in the midst of the hardest. To challenge myself to appreciate what we have as a family instead of what we don't. To acknowledge that stepmother is one of the hardest roles I've experienced in life, but at the same time, it is one of the most rewarding.

DISPATCHES FROM NEVERLAND

• • •

jessica page morrell

I come from a large family of blurters and big mouths. We offer unsolicited opinions and advice and hold forth on topics idle and large. We talk and sometimes shout over each other. We don't listen much as we bluster along, can be especially shrill when it comes to politics, and hold grudges long and hard.

Most of my growing-up years were spent in a small northern town. Flanked by countryside, lakes, and forest, it was a place of endless summers, long silent months of snow, and night skies like a magic show. I was a reader and a make-believe girl, carving kingdoms and homes from leaves and ferns, clothespins and old bedsheets, paper scraps and dreams. But mostly I was an outdoors girl, adventuring on my red Schwinn, swimming every afternoon in summer until the steamy dog days of August, and ice-skating every day in winter. Along with my sisters and brother and a gang of neighborhood kids,

I played into the grassy twilight while fireflies twinkled like fairies in the night. Mostly I roamed and imagined. The white pine forests and singing waters were my haven, my Neverland. It was a green and magical place far from grown-ups, far from cares.

This yesterday self has always dwelt in me.

Because we had six kids in my family, we owned a big, five-bedroom house. When I was fourteen, to beat the scrambling, the low-wage jobs, the one-pound of hamburger stretched to feed a family of eight, we moved to another town in southern Wisconsin. During those years I read a lot and as the oldest daughter was the responsible one. This meant I cooked dinner every night, then did the dishes, and watched over my younger siblings. I resented it. Eight loads of laundry every Saturday. Changing six beds. Cleaning the whole house before I was free to join my friends at a football game.

I had dreams, but no real plans for my future, so life swept me along. I married young, had a daughter, Jennifer, but divorced when she was two-and-a-half. Her father left the state when she was three, remarried, had another daughter, never contacting Jennifer or paying child support. Jennifer and I spent lots of time outdoors and for two years lived in the far North in a tiny cabin. But I wanted a family, a sense of belonging, and most of all, a father for Jennifer. I settled on Richard when she was eight.

He had a whistling-aloud confidence and some fine qualities, but we had big disagreements about money and raising my daughter. One of our first arguments came when he wanted to leave Jennifer alone at night. When I explained that I'd never leave an eight-year-old alone because it wasn't safe, he chimed in with his sister Suzie's child-raising methods. If it was good enough for his niece and nephews, it was good enough for Jennifer.

It didn't take long before I was battling against standards that I would never adopt, stunned that I was part of an extended family that pretty much drove me nuts, who were in denial about most parts of their lives.

I wanted better for my daughter. I tried to keep our arguments secret and laid down rules: She would not be belittled or criticized unfairly. As she approached adolescence Richard was not to comment on her changing-into-a-woman body. My rules made him angry since he knew best, since his family knew how to have a good time. Their goods times were fueled by booze. Lots of it. Meanwhile, he insinuated to my daughter that he was the better person, the wiser parent.

Exhausted by constant emotional abuse, battles I would never win, or strategies we would never negotiate, Richard and I separated when Jennifer was sixteen and a junior in high school. Jennifer moved out during her senior year since I couldn't tolerate her rage toward me and she couldn't tolerate my rage at her stepfather. She continued to visit Richard, and she rarely visited me. During those times my guilt was a mountain. I went to therapy, wept, howled, and pounded pillows. My parents were not speaking to me over my second divorce and their insistence I go back to Richard, and I felt like a wolf alone in a frozen wilderness cut off from my pack.

When I was first divorced for the second time I hoped to meet a man with small children, another tribe, but as time went on I decided I never wanted to be part of a blended or dysfunctional family again.

Now picture all this as background to a late blooming of the heart. To be exact, I met my current love, Jon, when I was fifty-eight. Falling in love at fifty-eight was precious and combined the teenage thrill of backseat sex with the terror of falling backwards into a bottomless canyon. We were merging at a fragile time in our lives. I'd been in a car accident that resulted in a head injury, a time of shadows and dark rooms, a long recovery that had drained me and devastated my finances. I was still unsteady, trying to regain my rhythms. Jon had also been through health problems, a bad divorce, and coping with his mother's decline.

However, a year later we were not only cohabitating but had bought a newly built house and were hanging curtains, laying rugs, and planting trees and flowers. The house smelled like paint and wood shavings, a fresh beginning and a drastic change for me since I'd lived alone for twenty-six years.

Jon had also been married twice. It's surprising how fragile the human heart can be in later decades, how deep the scars from love's disappointments. He was bitter and I was untrusting after years of bad dates and bad boyfriends. But we somehow came together with our two squeezed hearts.

They say that opposites attract—I say opposites have lots to argue about. Our differences stem from our childhoods and the vastly different ways we were raised. My parents were beyond strict, they were the law, and we were taught to be workers. On the other hand, Jon's mother doted on him, would call him three times a day when he went away to college. Growing up he had few rules, obligations, or chores, things I consider normal child-raising.

When we met Jon's hobbies were games and television. His sedentary ways, along with a steady diet of pizza, French fries, and cheeseburgers, suggested to me a cardiac incident by age sixty. Our biggest differences were our diets and lifestyles, and I believe they came from an indoor childhood versus an outdoor childhood. I'm a make-mine-organic foodie. I eat my vegetables. He has avoided them all his life.

Although Jon holds a respectable government job and we share similar values, his lifestyle seemed like a warped Neverland. Not my childhood version where sunlight shimmers through the trees casting the world in emerald. Instead, it's a place where you never grow up, never eat broccoli, your freezer is stocked with pizza and sausage biscuits, you drink soda by the quart, stay up until all hours playing computer games, sprawl on the couch for marathon ninja-warrior-TV-watching on weekends, and don't bother with housework or exercise.

Opposites. But he makes me laugh, he's wizard smart, and no one has ever understood or loved me so thoroughly.

And then there is Jon's adult son, Patrick. His Neverland is a more extreme version of his dad's. Patrick is a giant. He's over six feet and well over three hundred pounds. He's been prone to depression since adolescence, diagnosed with attention-deficit disorder, most days sleeps past noon, and spends most of his time gaming and watching television. His main game is Magic: The Gathering and he has a genius for it, but even his father admits he's making about a dollar an hour playing it.

Patrick dropped out of school at fourteen, and his father helped him with a correspondence course so he could eventually graduate. He has tried various medications for depression, but refuses to try them anymore. During the first year I knew him, he usually answered in a few syllables or single sentences.

Back to being a blurter. The first time I met Patrick he was twenty and Jon asked me what I thought of his son. The first words out of my mouth were, "Well, he's morbidly obese." Jon's whole body recoiled. He needed me to see past his son's physical self and recognize how Patrick occupied a huge place in his heart. I didn't recognize the extent of Jon's ongoing concern and sadness at all he'd missed during his son's growing-up years since he and his wife divorced when Patrick was two. He needed me to understand their past and how he'd tried to be a good dad, even though they lived fifty miles apart and he didn't share custody. He still saw the small, fragile boy in Patrick where I saw a misfit, a hulking man-child.

To say Patrick feels alien to me is an understatement. He is the largest human I've ever met. Sometimes it feels as if a bear has lumbered into our midst when he's around. Jon and I had a fateful discussion as we were planning to move in together. Jon asked me about Patrick coming to live with us in case he'd succumb to depression. I answered with words that came out too fast, but were straight from the heart. "If your son living with us is a deal breaker, then we shouldn't move in together. You should start making other plans, because I will never live with your son, no matter the circumstances. And the truth is that Patrick might suffer from depression at times, but he's also the laziest person I know." The silence on his end of the phone was as hollow as nightfall on a frozen mountaintop.

I knew that I was asking him to choose, that I was suggesting that he not rescue Patrick if he fell. The next day Jon admitted that since I worked at home, it would be difficult for me to have Patrick around. My relief was enormous.

After my stance about Patrick never living with us, a year of screwups on my part and a simmering resentment about Patrick's behaviors and habits followed.

In the beginning of our relationship Jon would often reference television shows, movies, and chess games played three decades ago. I'm talking blow by blow, or I guess move by move. He'd also describe Patrick's exploits at Magic, a game I don't understand but that seems to require strategy and imagination. These conversations not only didn't interest me, but I could not imagine games and television as a substitute for hiking and rivers, concerts and theater, and dinner parties. When Patrick visited, he and Jon would plunk down on the couch for hours, channel surfing and chatting about TV shows and Magic while I cooked dinner and took care of things, my resentment simmering. During those times it felt as if my heart was shrinking.

It also made me crazy that Patrick didn't return his dad's phone calls, or stay in touch. Or he seemed to call when he wanted something like staying at our house during a Magic tournament. It worried me how much Jon worried about Patrick and deeply missed his son's company.

Of course some of this behavior was to be expected, as a young man spends more time with his friends and has less in common with his father. But being the blabbermouth, I started making suggestions. Then I became shrill because I saw Patrick's problems mirroring mistakes in my own life, in my daughter's life, and in Jon's life. We had all made our biggest missteps in our early twenties. I was certain that with my helpful input, these dreaded misfires could be avoided. That Patrick might shift toward a hopeful future.

Then came two flashpoints. Patrick's mother had left him alone most of his childhood with a TV and frozen food. I sensed a deep, haunting aloneness in him. A few years before, she wanted him to learn how to cook. She suggested to Jon that I teach him. Jon was excited about the plan. I was doubtful, as someone who has cooked professionally. I know the hazards of the kitchen. You might guess that his fumbling, enormous presence in a normal-size kitchen was a near-disaster. At the exact frazzled moment I was finishing four side dishes and pulling a sizzling ham out of the oven for a holiday gathering, Patrick thrust his smartphone into my face to show me an online cartoon. I almost dropped the hot pan on my feet. Also, though it sounds unkind, simply trying to maneuver around his bulk was difficult.

I drew another line after this incident: Patrick's mother isn't allowed to make suggestions about me and their adult son. Since Patrick is now going on twenty-three I am not the person to remedy any part of him. I let him know I care about his happiness, and that I adore his father. But I've been a fixer and a caretaker since I was about seven and this one isn't up to me.

Flashpoint two was after a diatribe about how Patrick should attend community college. Jon said, "No matter what you say, I will never harden my heart toward my son." And I was tossed back in time, back into the thick of the arguments with Richard. Finally ashamed at my words, no matter the intentions, I realized that Jon's and Patrick's upbringings would always be different from my own and I needed to stop criticizing or comparing. My roaming childhood was possible because of an intact family and small towns nestled in green countryside. Theirs had a lot to do with divorce and mothers with worse mental health problems than mine.

As for the Cinderella parts of my childhood that, well, sucked, I didn't need to replicate them. I didn't need to cook or care for them as is always expected in my family. What I wanted most was for them to spend time together, to know each other as men. For all of us the past is done. And I freaking need to stop resenting people who don't work as hard as I do.

I learned I had projected my fears about younger generations onto Patrick. All those kids who never venture into nature; never smell a piney forest; who hunch for hours in front of electronic devices, never hearing birdcalls or noticing colors that aren't on a screen.

More understanding dawned. My situation and its problems had grown too burdensome: the years of recovering from my accident and chronic pain, the legal mess that resulted, the wearying years of taking care of my family, of coping with my mother as she became more difficult due to dementia and with my siblings who didn't want to acknowledge her condition. Add in concern about my daughter and supporting writers by the hundreds. All this has sapped me of generosity.

By the time Patrick came into my life I felt used up. And in any step-parenting situation, even when an adult child is involved, generosity of heart is necessary.

This realization has been enormous. I'm learning to appreciate the good stuff. Patrick is kind, compassionate, and well-meaning. And funny.

My family has holiday traditions that bind us together. Patrick has attended a few, but in a house filled with kids and people he doesn't know, he isn't comfortable. Near Christmas we invited him for dinner along with Jon's father and stepmother. I cooked. We exchanged gifts. As I was preparing for the day, I was apprehensive, fretting about how we have so little in common. The meal didn't turn out to my standards, but our guests were gracious, the conversation easy. It was a glowing, family kind of day. At my suggestion Jon and I had searched out the perfect wok and cookbooks for Patrick, along with a cooler just the right size for his road trips to Magic tournaments. As usual, his dad gave him clothes because Patrick is uncomfortable in stores, and I gave him a toaster oven.

Patrick appreciated his gifts, was smiling and chatting and almost gregarious. When he stepped into the night to join his friends, carrying gifts and leftovers, it was as if a giant sigh was released. Then we all remarked how much better he was doing as Jon beamed.

These days, things are better all around. Oddly, it started because Patrick's mother suffered a serious illness and he started helping her. From all accounts she's a difficult woman, but her illness changed their dynamic. He cleaned out her house, stuffed full of things from a lifetime of hoarding, moved her into an apartment, and moved into his childhood home with two friends. They pay rent. He's living with his dogs again and so has that responsibility. He also started working part-time as a driver for a medical company. Mostly he's just happier. He eats better. My hopes are that he will become healthier and more intellectually engaged.

Meanwhile, Jon loves my cooking and also eats better and walks more. I worry less about his cholesterol. We have started traveling, building memories, and enjoying my grandchildren whom he regards as his own.

Recently, Jon phoned Patrick several times to ask if he was joining us for a holiday meal. Patrick didn't phone back. After a few weeks I mentioned that I was annoyed since I was trying to figure out the menu and seating. Jon replied that he too was frustrated and Patrick needed to be accountable. I said, "Raising adult children is hard. You just don't have a lot of input in their lives." I was remembering the times I'd wanted my daughter to change her ways or beliefs.

He answered, "Patrick has always been hard. I notice that your daughter is stubborn, but she eventually comes around to reason. Whenever I've wanted something from him he slows down, then stops. Like an ox." I had to laugh. I will never share their particular Neverland, will never spend hours at poker tables or Magic tournaments. Will never want a mostly indoor life. However, in that moment I realized Jon and I were not arguing about parenthood, but commiserating together about it.

OFFICIAL FAMILY

• • •

sue sanders

I stood in my ivory silk wedding dress clutching a bouquet of peonies and glanced down at my six-year-old daughter. She was standing frozen next to me, holding a basket filled with rose petals. Smiling, I squeezed Lizzie's hand and looked over at Jeff. We were finally about to become, according to Lizzie, an "official family."

We'd been an unofficial one the previous few years, after I'd met Jeff when Lizzie was four. Not many years before that, I assumed my family would be a traditional one, which was odd since I've never been a conventional person. I met the man who'd become my first husband in college and we were together eighteen years. Eschewing the typical post-college path of entry-level job and power suits with shoulder pads (it was the '80s), I instead set out with John on another route, traveling the world while cobbling together whatever jobs we could. I taught kindergarten in Paris, was an extra in an Australian television commercial, and harvested apples in New Zealand.

After several years ping-ponging around the world, we unpacked our bags for good in New York. I assumed that we'd live happily ever after, as our parents seemed to after they'd married. Both sets of our parents met after college and had been together since the early 1960s. To us, their relationships appeared as solid as the bedrock our Manhattan tenement was built on. I assumed our lives would be similar. (It took me years to learn looks can be as deceiving as a Hollywood movie set: what appears strong and sturdy is often just an empty-backed facade.)

After we'd been together thirteen years, John had his first psychotic episode. "Psychotic episode"—how I hate that phrase. It makes mental illness sound like an inane sitcom instead of the nightmare it can be. I spent the final five years of our marriage fruitlessly trying to make him better. I took him to doctors, collecting diagnoses as if they were baseball cards: depression, major depression with psychotic features, bipolar disorder. Each diagnosis seemed a little scarier than the previous one. His doctors told us that bipolar disorder, while not curable, was treatable, like diabetes—as long as John took his pills. But he didn't like taking them and often stopped once they started working.

During a prolonged "better," we got pregnant. I just *knew* a baby would help John stay well—if he wouldn't take his pills for himself or for me, of course he would for his child. But I was wrong. Eventually I left with our daughter. I'd tried—I spent five years counting his pills, begging him to take them. I made countless excuses to friends—and to myself—for missing their children's birthday parties because John had gone off his medicine yet again. I watched him ignore our daughter as she held her arms open wide for a hug. One morning, after a prolonged manic episode—he had been up for days—I woke to find all the pictures of my family turned over. I finally realized nothing would change unless I did—and that our relationship was over. I gave it my all until I gave up.

So I became a single mom. And, as is the case with many single moms of young children, my daughter's social life became mine. Lizzie and I dug in the sandbox with red plastic shovels, jumped into piles of crunchy fall leaves in the park, and went on countless playdates, her friends' mothers my main link to the adult world. But, after a year, it felt like something was missing from my life: extended conversations with people over the age of three. I missed adult company, specifically adult male company. So I started dating and soon met the man who'd one day become my second husband.

Jeff and I met online, flirting and getting to know one another remotely. When Jeff and I met in person, we very early knew we had something. What, at that point, we weren't quite sure. But when Lizzie and Jeff finally met, we knew—deep inside before we'd even admit it out loud—that we'd found a family. As time passed and our relationship deepened, it all seemed easy and natural, something I hadn't experienced since before John got sick, or perhaps ever. I'd tried for so long to make my marriage work by myself that I never realized how exhausting it was until it was over. Because John had been so sick, even when we were together I was practically a single parent to Lizzie. Diapers, feeding, bathing all fell to me. Being in a healthy relationship with a rational man felt . . . good. This was a new and unusual sensation. At first I was certain something was wrong, that I was missing a slew of wildly fluttering red flags. But I relaxed and trusted my gut. Jeff actually *wanted* to parent. He checked out a stack of parenting books from the library and, late at night while Lizzie slept under her red kitty comforter, we discussed them. Although we tried to take things slow for Lizzie's sake, it was as if we'd been thrown into a perpetual motion machine, and our relationship kept moving ahead on its own. So, a little over a year after we met, we moved in together.

Lizzie finally had an unswerving relationship with a "father." Not with her biological dad, whose illness often made him an inconsistent presence in Lizzie's life, but with Jeff, who chose to be there for her. And as they grew closer, he became the father she'd never really had. Sometimes I'd stand near the doorway to Lizzie's room, tucked around the corner out of sight, and I'd listen as Lizzie demanded to hear her favorite story again, one that Jeff had invented. Jeff would sigh theatrically and say, "Okay, but this is the *last* time." And then, lowering his voice, he'd begin:

"Once upon a time, I didn't have a family. I was sad because I really wanted one so I searched the world, looking. I went to the post office and asked if they had any families. 'Just stamps,' the mailman said. So I left, sad. I went to the pizzeria to get a cheese slice. I asked if they had any families. 'No families, just pizza,' the pizza woman said. So I ordered a slice and ate it unhappily. I went to the grocery store and asked if they had a family. 'We had one last week, but we're fresh out. We do have lovely red apples, though,' the grocer said. So I glumly bought some. On the way home, the apples tumbled out of the bag and I started to cry. A nice woman stopped and helped me pick them up. Her little blonde daughter asked why I was crying. I told her I didn't have a family. She said if her mom said it was okay, I could be part of theirs. It was. And that's how I found my family."

"Again!" Lizzie would squeal. I smiled from the doorway of Lizzie's room as I watched her snuggle into the crook of Jeff's arm and giggle. And Jeff told the story again.

While Jeff is an unwavering presence in Lizzie's life, through the years there's been a less steadfast one: John. Visitation is infrequent and always arranged by his mother. She and I are close. Though John isn't able to be a consistent presence in Lizzie's life, I want to be sure that his parents are. Tom and Nancy have helped us both emotionally and financially. When I finally left John, Lizzie and I briefly moved into their comfortable suburban Dutch Colonial. At night, after Lizzie splashed in their tub, had Grandma read her several stories, and was tucked into one of the twin beds in the guest room, Tom poured me a glass of Pinot Noir and we planned how to get John back into the hospital. Tom and Nancy had met and liked Jeff, and came to our wedding. But it's got to be difficult for them. Is it awkward to see Lizzie treat Jeff as the father he is to her? Does it hurt seeing Lizzie run to claim Jeff's hand and hug him, something she's never done with John?

A month or so after John and I separated, when he'd been discharged from the hospital, he came with his parents to my apartment for a visit. As we walked to a nearby restaurant, Lizzie offered John a Tic Tac she'd wrapped in aluminum foil, saying, "Here, Daddy, medicine to make you better." John shooed it away, as if it was a pesky fly. Lizzie grabbed my hand and I held hers tightly, telling her how thoughtful she was. I asked if she wanted me to hold Daddy's "medicine" until later. She gave it to me. That was one of the last times I remember her calling John "Daddy."

Jeff—whom Lizzie calls "Jeff" to his face and "my dad" with her friends—and I talk about just about everything. Lizzie is, and has always been, part of the conversation. She knows John's sickness makes him act the way he does and that any emotion she experiences is okay. But I'm not sure how much she understands. Jeff tells Lizzie if she's excited to see John, that's fine with him, his feelings won't be hurt. He loves her so much he's got lots of love to spare. And that if she's not excited, that's okay too. But sometimes I wonder what she really thinks. Years go by without hearing from John at all. Then he'll call, casually, as if he just saw her that morning, saying, "Lizzie, it's Dad." I can see her body tense in anticipation over what might come next. The conversation always seems slightly off-kilter. He'll ask, many times in a row, if she wants a guitar. When she politely says no thank you, she really likes playing the piano and the saxophone, he ignores her and tells her she should play guitar. She can join a band! And when John is not taking his medication, it's far worse: she gets packages from him, manila envelopes plastered with dozens and dozens of stamps, filled with broken CDs and essays about his drunken exploits. Jeff and I have to preview them before we hand anything to Lizzie. We give her whatever we can and store the rest away.

Jeff is the counterweight to this. He's seen Lizzie grow from a pre-schooler who skipped to the playground often wearing a frilly tulle skirt, sparkly red shoes, and a tiara, to a twelve-year-old who loves to read fantasy, is writing her own novel, and is an ardent environmentalist. She's determined to get the snow leopard off the endangered species list one day. Jeff knows the minutiae of her life. He knows the names of her friends, including that of her very first crush. He can sense, without a word from her, if it's been a bad day in middle school, and he's helped her sort through being on the receiving end of mean-girl drama. When she was little, he listened patiently to countless knock-knock jokes, even laughing at the ones that left us slightly baffled. (Sample: "Knock knock." "Who's there?" "Elephant!" "Elephant, who?" "Elephant face—ha ha ha ha ha!")

Last year, John and his mom visited us in our new city and we invited them to our house for dinner. John left the table many times to go outside and smoke. Lizzie, although polite to him, hovered near Jeff and was quiet much of the meal. After dinner, we drove John and his mom to their hotel, and on the way home, we talked. Jeff asked, "So, sweetie, how did it feel to see John?"

"Okay, but weird," Lizzie said.

"What do you mean?" he inquired, voice neutral.

Lizzie paused for a minute, lost in thought, and replied, "Think of my life as a box. My friends and loving family are in the box and John is outside it."

Jeff and I exchanged a glance. Sometimes it was hard to read Lizzie, to know what she was thinking about John. But she obviously had been sorting through her feelings on her own. I reached over and rubbed Jeff's shoulder, then twisted in my seat to grab Lizzie's hand. I blinked back a few tears, so grateful for my "official" family.

THE ANGEL STEPS DOWN

• • •

elizabeth king gerlach

A tinny version of "Silver Bells" piped through the speakers at the big-box store as our family meandered down the aisles of lights, inflatable snowmen, and cinnamon-scented pinecones.

"I don't understand why people put angels on top of a Christmas tree. That's stupid and it sucks." My stepson Michael flexed his new junior high vocabulary, looking up at the long row of lighted angels in satin skirts. The intensity of his declaration took me aback, although I tried hard not to show my feelings. Instead of launching into my to-each-his-own lecture or a boring, grown-up opinion about the beauty and peaceful countenance of angels, I simply shrugged and held my breath and tongue.

"Wish we could get *this* star." He was eyeing a big plastic star on a shelf, a little too high for him to reach. I glanced up. *Gaudy, tacky, plastic,* and *cheap* were the first words that sprang to mind. I banished those initial reactions and chose silence. His gaze hung on the star for a while, but eventually he unlocked from his innocent wish and moved on down the aisle toward the lighted reindeer, then off to electronics.

On this early December day, almost an entire year since the last Christmas, I doubted that my normally sweet and amiable eleven-year-old stepson remembered that a simple crochet doll, one that I consider to be our Christmas angel, held the place of honor atop our tree and had for over twenty years.

Long before we became a blended family, she looked over my children and me.

A friend who was living in Colombia sent this doll as a gift one Christmas when she and I were in our early twenties. She was spending a year there teaching, traveling, and living the adventurous life. I was a new mom whose life had recently been turned upside down when my oldest son received a diagnosis of autism. Why my friend sent me this particular gift was a mystery, but the little doll reminded me of the young Virgin Mary, humble and beautiful. She gave me great comfort when I felt overwhelmed and frightened. She eventually found her calling watching over us from the top of our Christmas tree. Every holiday I'd lovingly placed her there.

The doll saw much from her perspective. She witnessed the first Christmas after my divorce when Nick and Ben didn't have their dad there. She saw me the year the boys went with their dad to California to be with his extended family, and I sat alone and sad, wondering why my life had turned out this way. She saw eight long years of me being single, cutting and putting up the tree myself, struggling with the lights, and trying hard to make everything just right. All those years when having a son with a disability took all of my courage and strength, and I wondered if I'd always be alone.

Then Scott and his two young boys, Michael and James, came into our lives—a miracle to be sure. It's not easy to find a man with a heart big enough to embrace a stepson with a lifelong disability as severe as autism. Autism affects just about every area of a family's life. My son has been my greatest teacher, and I treasure, respect, and embrace him and the special presence he brings to me and to the world. But there is no denying the daily challenges.

Inevitably, our marriage and the blending of our families caused a lot of change and struggle for everyone. That first year and every year until adulthood, the boys were shuffled and shuttled from one house to the next, making sure that each child got time at the home of the other parent. Schedules were set months in advance as to who would "have them" on Thanksgiving or Christmas Eve or Day.

That's just the way life is with blended families. You have to be willing to plan, coordinate, and then go with the flow when things fall completely apart, which happens a lot.

We had to work extra hard to promote family time. Facilitating group experiences that work for children from four to fourteen is not a simple feat. No matter what, though, we would carve out some special time to all be together during the holidays, and find and decorate the "perfect" Christmas tree.

Since we live in Oregon, Christmas tree country, we naturally began the blended family holiday tradition of dragging everyone out in the rain and mud to choose and cut our own tree. My second son, Ben, has the kind of temperament that could care less what kind of tree we choose just as long as he gets to be the one to wield the saw and cut it down. He was used to doing the job alone, but in the new family, everyone wanted a turn. Perhaps the Christmas angel was there, offering Ben a temporary halo, but he was gracious enough to give everyone a turn with the saw. The little boys were mostly frustrated, and they gave up after a couple of tries. I think Ben was proud that year to carry the tree with his new stepdad and hoist it on top of the car. I was proud that my teenage boy was turning into a man with a sense about what really mattered.

That first year we got the same kind of tree my boys and I had always gotten, a bushy Scotch pine. But the subsequent year one of my stepsons innocently asked, "Why can't we get a noble fir, you know, like the kind we get at Mom's?"

You would think he'd asked to change religions.

"We *always* get a Scotch pine," exclaimed Nick. "No, no, this just won't do!" He grabbed his hair at the roots and spun in circles.

Any small change in routine can throw him into endless loops of worry. Routine and tradition are sacrosanct. Something as seemingly insignificant as switching from a pine to a fir, in his mind, might precipitate the end of the world inwardly, and present outwardly as unhappiness and resistance.

He melted down right there at the tree farm faster than a marshmallow in hot chocolate. Instead of staying with the family, I struggled to get my screaming son into the semiprivacy of the minivan and wait out the storm with him there.

But, autism or not, we got the noble fir in the name of fairness. Later, after the tree was decorated, the Christmas angel didn't seem to mind the change a bit, and as the actual day of Christmas neared, Nick decided that the tree wasn't so bad after all. From then on, as with every small victory, he was fine with either kind of tree.

If only the angel could have accompanied us on all our many outings to the tree farms. She could have provided me with some much-needed female companionship as well as more patience. There was the year the usual tree farm we'd been going to for years was closed. Nick was unconvinced that any other tree farm would do. We drove around for a long time in order to find another; he didn't even get out of the car that year.

Another year, my husband's younger son, James, wanted his own tree, for him alone to decorate. We couldn't afford to spring for two trees. Moreover, I argued the issue of unity. Didn't one Christmas tree in a common area bring the family together? What was the point of two? Should we get one for every room of the house? Scott wondered if I really needed to make a federal case out of James's request. Was I being too controlling?

As parents, the times we weigh the prevailing issues between our guilt and good sense are too many to count. This comes with the territory of parenting and I believe the challenges are magnified when step-parenting. Accommodations are one more opportunity to find a balance in the blend.

Perhaps the angel was there again that year because I had an idea for a compromise. I gathered as many branches from the tree farm slash pile as I could, and when we got home, Scott lashed them together and stuck them in a bucket. We decorated the makeshift tree with twinkly lights and ornaments. James would grudgingly come to be satisfied by this. To this day, over ten years later, he still loves the beauty of lights and color, and has holiday lights strung in his bedroom year-round.

Now it was Michael wanting something that only he wanted—something that was his idea. Michael was in the middle in our step-family. How difficult the difference must have been for him to be the oldest at his mom's house and placed squarely in the middle at ours. He usually went along with the program in an easygoing way. So when he told me that morning in the store that angels on trees sucked, I knew his opinion wasn't directed at our angel. He would never have said that to me. As with most kids, he saw something he wanted in the moment and threw an idea out there with the hope that it would stick.

I looked long and hard at that star. Twenty dollars for a plastic star with LED lights that somehow changed color in slow motion that would surely break in a year or two? "I don't think so," I said to myself as I moved on to the lighted outdoor reindeer that I'd been wanting for several years. Maybe we could eventually collect a herd.

Our finances had been tight for the five years we'd been together, and many little luxuries got put aside in the name of prudence. But we had recently made the move to a bigger house since the six of us were busting out the seams of my old house. At our new house, as with so many things, the old lights wouldn't work and/or there weren't enough of them. We were here to buy lights and maybe a reindeer, and that's all.

My husband was in the next aisle looking at more icicle lights. Every year Scott dutifully goes out, usually in the pouring Oregon rain, to hang the outdoor lights. This action is just one more way he shows how much he loves all of us. He was busy picking out lights, gutter hooks, timers, and the like when he asked me about the reindeer. I hesitated. It wasn't just the money. I thought of the little brown crochet angel, packed away somewhere in the attic and biding her time until decorating day, the rightful queen of the treetop. She had been with me all those years and held all those memories. *My* memories.

Then something inside me shifted. I let go of the bottled-up feelings and the words gushed out. "Nope, we'll have to wait another year with the reindeer. There's something we need to buy instead. I'm not sure why but we have to."

I led Scott over to the other aisle. That plastic star was calling me back like a beacon. Scott looked at the star, then back at me, and said, "What? Waste of money. What are you thinking? It's like a disco ball from the 1970s!" He is the tasteful, understated sort.

"I'll explain it to you when we get home." I put the star in the cart and kept the purchase a secret until the time came to decorate the tree.

Tree trimming holds many time-honored traditions as well as the occasional disaster. Nick insists we play the same CD year after year. The boys vie for who gets to hang the primo ornaments and argue about why eggnog doesn't taste like eggs. We usually have a fancy dinner. One year we had a fondue feast and dipped apples, bread, and sausages in cheesy goodness, followed by chocolate fondue with fruit and cake for dessert. Another year, we cooked a goose, just like the Cratchit family in *A Christmas Carol*. Ben was attending culinary school at the community college and he prepared the meal. The goose turned out great. We can't say the same for the gravy, which, ten different pans and a pound of flour later, turned out to be a gelatinous mess. (Luckily, Ben did master gravy and graduated with a degree in Culinary Arts.) There was also the year that our new cat decided to go after the singing bird ornament in the tree. Everything, including the cat and the angel, took a swan dive to the floor. There is rarely a dull moment around here.

So the year I brought out the new star, my son Nick almost ruined that evening with his stubborn refusal to accept a new change. "What about the angel? She goes on the top. *The angel is supposed to go on the top of the tree.* This absolutely, positively won't do!"

Everyone sighed, knowing that this just couldn't be easy.

"Michael chose this star," I said. "It's very beautiful and colorful. You'll see. Sometimes we have to let other people choose. Now is one of those times."

Michael's face beamed—a star unto itself. Nick charged off into his room. We all carried on without him, wishing he could be flexible in the moment, but understanding that he needed some time to get used to the star.

Scott carefully attached the new 1970s multicolored disco beacon atop the tree. We turned off all the lights and stepped back to see the splendor. The star *was* beautiful. Eventually, Nick sneaked back into the living room, relaxed about the new addition, and watched the starlight slowly change from red to blue to green.

I would miss the crochet angel that had looked over all these boys and me, but my heart knew the time had come for her to step down. This was, yet again, a moment for change and compromise. The angel doll quietly settled into a new spot on the piano near the holiday village, happy, perhaps, to watch our crazy lives unfold from a new perspective.

The simple choice to let go of something old and precious often opens the door to new possibilities. I fancied the little angel approved. The plastic star was our own Christmas miracle, one that united us. A star whose LED glow I hope will last a long, long time.

Part 4 | *Acceptance*

MY SECRET FATHER

• • •

gigi rosenberg

My mother didn't want me to love him. She wanted me to be rid of him, the bad man, my father.

"Just think of it as if I'd been artificially inseminated," she told me as she washed dishes at our bright yellow kitchen sink when I was a teenager. As if deciding he didn't exist would make him disappear.

After my parents divorced when I was a year old, I was the only living thing that passed between them.

When I was two, my mother said I told her, "I want a man who will wear a hat and drive the car." Shortly after, she met Marvin. Six weeks later she married him.

A few years later, an angry argument erupted over the phone on one of the rare occasions my parents spoke. My mother and Marvin were trying to convince my father to "give me up" so Marvin could adopt me.

I lay on my bed listening to their muffled voices downstairs yelling about me. When the call ended, my mother told me that my father wouldn't give me up. Further proof of his selfishness, she said. It was as if he were an obstruction to a greater happiness, not just for me but for our whole family.

What was the matter with my father anyway? The only complaint I remember was that he never had enough money. Yet if I acted in a way my mother didn't like, if I was moody or impatient, she'd say, "You must have gotten that from Bob." Not "your father" and certainly not "your daddy"—just "Bob."

My mother told me she met my father in the 1950s at the Henry Street Settlement House on New York City's Lower East Side. She taught ceramics to the neighborhood kids there. "He walked into the art room one day with a broken sculpture, and I helped him repair it," she said.

My father insisted they'd met at a party.

Either way, he was good-looking and funny, and she loved his artwork.

My mother was pretty and independent. My father liked women who could take care of themselves.

A few years after my parents married, when my mother knew it wasn't going to last, she decided she wanted a baby. My father shook his head, unenthusiastic.

"Babies are expensive," he said.

"Don't worry. The baby won't cost you a dime," she said. "I'll pay for everything." A woman ahead of her time, my mother didn't need a husband to have a baby.

After the delivery at Mount Sinai Hospital, after my father had seen me and then left, the hospital presented her with a $300 bill. Apparently my parents had never discussed how they would pay for the delivery. My mother called a close friend who had a wealthy husband and asked to borrow $300 cash so she could take me home.

Years later my father told me that when their marriage was breaking up, not over but on its way to collapse, he thought about disappearing for good. Then one day, walking home, he saw my mother
shopping at a fruit stand with me in a stroller. When I spotted him,
he said, my eyes lit up and my arms flailed, happy to see him. "After
that, I couldn't disappear," he said.

Most Sundays after the divorce my father rode the Long Island
Rail Road from Penn Station to Little Neck. I waited on the platform
with my mother and a stomachache. My father snatched my hand as if
rescuing me from an evil witch, and my mother snapped, "She needs
a new winter coat," as if this was the least he could do.

At my father's house I drank "Black Cows" made from Coca-Cola
and milk. Soda was forbidden at my mother's house. My father took
me to the zoo, we rode the Central Park carousel, and he always
bought me Cracker Jacks because I liked the prize.

At my mother's house, we lied to everyone, saying that Marvin was
my father. But I didn't call him Dad. I called him Marvin. When my
sister and brother were born to my mother and Marvin, they didn't
call him Dad either.

"Why do you call your dad Marvin?" family friends asked us.

"Because that's his name," I answered, and nobody questioned us
further.

Close family friends knew that Marvin wasn't my real father. But
we never talked about it. *Keep your father secret* was the code I lived by.
I feared his existence would confirm my badness and make me an
outcast in my family and odd among my friends.

My father insisted that I use his last name, Shore, not my stepfather's name, Rosenberg. Then, in third grade a friend asked, "Why
do you have a different last name than your mother?" In the 1960s
in Queens, among those neat sidewalks and modest houses, all my
friends had the same last name as their mothers. Nobody I knew had
divorced parents.

"The school made a mistake," I said. "That's my middle name."
I didn't want to be different. I didn't want to visit a man my mother
hated. I wanted to forget about him.

"I want to use the name Rosenberg," I begged my mother. "I want
the same last name as you."

"We just won't tell him," she said and directed the secretary at my
school, P.S. 94, to change my records. Relieved at how much a lie
could do, I buried my secret father deeper. When friends asked why I
couldn't play on the weekend, I said, "I'm visiting an uncle in the city."

I traveled between those two worlds like a spy unable to speak of
one to the other. When my mother picked me up at the station after
a weekend with my father, I felt stiff and icy, and it took a day for me
to melt back into life with my other family.

My mother never told me I had to visit my father, but somehow
I knew the visits were nonnegotiable—a burden I was born to. Some
Sundays I held my nose on the phone and told him I had caught a
cold and couldn't make it.

One day, sitting across from me on the train as the trees of Bay-
side, Queens, whizzed by, he asked, "What are you reading?" and
extended his hand to see the book I had brought.

In my bedroom that morning, minutes before we'd left for the
station, I had frantically erased my name from my schoolbook, *All-
of-a-Kind Family*. I had written it in pencil in the neat printed box with
the names of all the previous owners of the book.

My body froze. My heart beat in my ears. My mother and I had
lied. But I was the one to be caught.

He opened the book. I watched his face as he scanned the list of
names. The last one, poorly erased, was Marjorie Rosenberg.

He said nothing.

The trees blurred the windows. I wanted to run like the train, disappear like the trees, forget this man and these visits. I wanted to be
the fatherless daughter my mother wanted.

Instead I pulled myself inside, made myself small and tight. Maybe he yelled at my mother about it later. After that he mailed me letters addressed to *Gigi Shore c/o Rosenberg*. But he refused to write *Gigi Rosenberg*.

When people said, "You look like your father," referring to my stepfather, I felt hot and irritable, as if they were tapping on a door I wanted kept locked. I smiled a small smile and said nothing or changed the subject, distracting them from the scent of the secret.

I wanted to love what my mother loved. I wanted to hate what she hated. Now that I'm a mother, I know this is normal, especially in a young child. To want to emulate your mother is innate. But what if your beloved mother hates the man you came from? It was an unsolvable riddle.

My mother told me that when she and my father divorced, she refused alimony, which I imagine came as a relief to my artist father. Perhaps she thought that if he didn't support her, he wouldn't be able to claim me. She would have refused child support too, she said, but it was mandatory. My father sent her $25 a week, in a check, made out to me.

Once, as my father and I walked by a mailbox at Penn Station, he took an envelope out of his pocket and showed it to me. He'd addressed it to me in his sprawling script, so I reached for it. But before I could grab it, he opened the mailbox slot and dropped it inside, and the metal door of the mailbox slammed shut. That gesture said it all. *This is yours, but it is not yours.*

My father remarried and had a son with his new wife, so on visits with them I slept on the Castro Convertible in the living room. At night he read to me from an illustrated copy of *The Wind in the Willows* about the adventures of Mole, Rat, and Toad, a threesome I found incredibly boring but that he loved reading to me. I fell asleep watching the green dial light of the dusty radio, longing to be home with my mother and the family that felt like mine.

How could I not love him? He was my father.

He could be brooding and impatient, but he was also kind and warm, and I knew he loved me. He was my only parent who played games with me like gin rummy and Monopoly. We watched *The Wizard of Oz* together and sang along to "Seventy-Six Trombones" from his recording of *The Music Man*.

When I brought an apple pie that I had made at home from scratch, he sliced into it after dinner, and we discovered that all the fruit had slid to one side of the pie. I was mortified that my pie was half-empty. My father said matter-of-factly, "Oh, it's just a shifting of the fruit," as if it happened every day, and I didn't feel so bad about my baking mishap.

In high school I moved to Boston with my mother and family, and the weekend visits with my father ended. My mother told me that his child support checks ended then too. In the divorce agreement, my mother had agreed to stay within a certain distance of New York City. When we moved to Boston, farther away than allowed, they never discussed it. His checks just stopped, and I guess they called a silent truce.

There were years when I didn't see him.

Over the next thirty years, things slowly shifted. My father came to Boston for my wedding. He liked my husband. My husband liked him. I had a daughter, whom he loved ferociously. During an extended hospital stay when it looked as if he might not live, he told me that my brother (the son he'd had after me) and I were the best things that had ever happened to him.

Over time, I realized I was a brooder too. I noticed we liked the same books. He mailed me Mark Helprin's *Ellis Island and Other Stories* and Nicole Krauss's *The History of Love*. My father was incredibly supportive of my endeavors and believed in me with an unshakable faith. I appreciated how honestly he talked about his life as a painter, accepting both the productive times and the fallow times.

A few weeks before my mother died, my father called me while I was visiting her, and I put her on the phone. They talked like old friends. After the call my mother said, "He still has such a nice voice. He was so good-looking and such a talented artist."

A month after my mother died, after my siblings and I had scattered her ashes off the Oregon coast, along with those of my stepfather, who had died the year before, I received a chilly email from my sister.

My mother had decided not to divide our inheritance equally but instead to leave the bulk of it to my sister and brother, the two children she had had with my stepfather and whom I grew up with. She'd never told me about her decision; in fact, in the few conversations we'd had before she died, she had intimated that it would all be divided equally among the three of us.

The news came as a body blow.

I called my sister seconds after reading her email and said naively that I thought there was a typo in it. "No, there isn't a typo," she said. Then she told me she had to wake up early and couldn't talk.

But before she hung up, she listed the reasons she thought my mother made the decision and one of them was, "You have a father. Mom thought you might get something from him."

You have a father.

This was the first time anyone in my family ever uttered those words. Yes, I have a father. Whom my mother wanted me to be rid of. Who we all pretended did not exist. But it was too late to say any of this. My mother, my accomplice, was dead. I couldn't ask her why, after all those years of keeping me in and my father out, she excluded me too. I had done everything she wanted. I had visited him, kept him secret, never crossed over.

Or had I? He was my father. Erasing him would have been erasing myself too.

On my first visit to New York City after my mother died, I realized there was something I wanted.

I told my father, who was turning eighty-eight years old, that for his birthday we were going to have a photograph taken. He agreed, but I wasn't sure he understood why I wanted to fuss with a professional photographer. A snapshot seemed easier.

Yet when I arrived at his apartment on East Ninety-Third Street, he was already waiting on the sidewalk for me, clutching the cane he now used to walk.

When Erica, the photographer, arrived, she hailed a cab, my father slowly lowered himself into it, and we whisked him to Central Park. Erica seated us on a bench on Fifth Avenue on this cold, sunny February day. I had warned Erica that my father could be moody, but he liked her immediately, and the three of us fell into an easy rapport.

My father and I sat on the bench close together, affectionate in a way I'd never been with my stepfather. I leaned against him; he leaned into me. The three of us—Erica and my father and I—fell into a timeless space. If people walked by, we didn't see them. If taxis honked, we didn't hear them. She posed us, and we happily complied, sometimes smiling, sometimes not, a few times laughing hard, and once tears welled in my eyes as my father and I held each other in the silence of New York City, the city of my childhood and of my sometimes-secret visits with him for more than fifty years.

I'm glad I have this photograph.

"You have a father," my sister said. As though I had planned it that way. Yes, I have a father. That's why I wanted this photograph. Not a snapshot but a formal black-and-white portrait. He existed. I existed. He was my father. Here is the proof.

My mother didn't want me to love him. She wanted me to be rid of him, the bad man, my father.

CINDY AND ME

• • •

jennifer margulis

I was carrying my eighteen-month-old on my back, walking to the library, when "DAD CELL" popped up on my phone. "It's your dad," my seventy-something father said in a tight voice when I flipped the phone open (despite years of using a cell phone with caller ID, my father starts every conversation by telling me it's him). Through the static of a bad connection my father and I exchanged pleasantries.

"Cindy's been institutionalized," my father said finally, his voice strangely jocose. "She had a nervous breakdown."

"For real?" My breath caught in my throat. I stopped walking. My brain whirred like a machine, clicking pieces of my childhood into place that I hadn't thought about in over twenty years.

I was ten years old the first time I met Cindy. My father and I were living, just the two of us, in an oversized Victorian in a suburb of Boston. I didn't know it then but my parents were in the midst of getting divorced.

A professor of biology at Boston University, my mother, along with my three older brothers, was still in Pasadena, California, where she was on sabbatical at Cal Tech. My mom had taken all four of us to Pasadena with her, but she was so busy doing research on micro-organisms that she didn't know that boys ran up and kissed me on the lips on the playground. She wasn't home when my older brothers' friends played music so loud it made the floors vibrate. These older boys who scared and thrilled me taught me how to skateboard and offered me bong hits. I started wetting my bed at night, sleeping in damp sheets because I was too ashamed to tell. I called my dad and begged him to let me come home early. I was doing so poorly in school and seemed so sad that my mother let me go.

After I flew back to Boston by myself, my father and I settled into an easy routine. I felt safe in the quiet of our house and knew it was a privilege to be home. Not wanting to give my father any reason to send me back to California, I was careful to clean up after myself, put my napkin in my lap at dinner, and help unload the groceries without being asked. My father was kind and attentive. When he announced one morning after I had been home alone with him for a few months that his graduate student, named Cindy, was coming over, I couldn't wait. "She has a motorcycle," he added. "She says she'll take you for a ride."

A motorcycle! I put on an old helmet and zoomed around the house, going "vroom vroom," willing Cindy to show up soon.

"Cindy has a dog," my dad said, smiling at how happy I was racing around in circles like a much younger kid, the morning sun filtering in through our stained-glass windows.

Cindy arrived, on foot, two hours late. Her motorcycle had broken down en route. I was crushed that she came without it. But I couldn't hold it against her when she was finally standing on our green wraparound porch and I was yanking the front door open to let her in. Cindy was tall and blonde and pretty. She had a fetching smile and laugh lines around her eyes. She promised she would bring Street next time, the tiny white dog she had found cowering and starving on the streets of Sicily who only responded to commands in Italian (*Vieni qui!* for "Come here!" *Siedi!* for "Sit"). Cindy also promised she would take me bicycle riding, since the motorcycle was too dangerous. She said she liked math and could help me with my math homework. She asked me lots of questions. I fell instantly in love.

My mother and my brother Zach returned from Pasadena. My oldest brother left for college and my second brother decided to move back to California to attend computer school. There were loud muffled arguments behind closed doors. My mother announced she was going back to Cal Tech. They fought over one of her colleagues, a man named Ken Nelson. I didn't know why but I knew I hated him, and that Ken Nelson, whoever he was, was driving my parents apart. My father told her if she left again she shouldn't bother coming back. One day I noticed that the twin bed in the spare room had been slept in. Then one morning my parents called my brother and me into the living room.

"We've grown apart," my father explained in a strained voice.

My mother nodded and smiled. "We still love you," she said. "It's not your fault."

"We're getting a divorce."

Zach burst into tears. I felt proud not to be the one crying. I didn't know the word *divorce*.

At first my brother and I spent half our time in Boston, at my mom's Back Bay apartment, and half our time in Newton, where my elementary school was. Zach went to a private school in West Roxbury and carpooled from the city, but I had to take the T every morning and walk from the station. I was so tall that the conductor didn't believe I was only ten. When he insisted I pay the full fare I burst into tears.

I don't know if my father had an affair with Cindy before he and my mother split up. But I do know that after he was no longer Cindy's chemistry professor, my father started openly dating her. He wanted her to move in with us. Cindy told my father that Street would have to come too and that my father would have to buy her a piano. A dog! And a piano! When I was seven I'd written a series of saccharine stories about a little girl who was dying for a pet but whose mother was allergic to cats and whose father disliked dogs. I'd wanted to take piano lessons after studying piano at summer camp. My father told me I probably wouldn't stay with it, and then he would have wasted his money for nothing.

But now I would have Cindy and Street and a piano! I couldn't have been happier. My mother spent most of her time peering under a microscope at spirochetes in her laboratory at Boston University and flying overseas to give lectures about the origin of eukaryotic cells. She would bring Zach and me to work with her sometimes. Though I loved goofing around with her graduate students, we were stuck in her office for hours. She always had "just one more thing" to take care of. Then, when we were finally leaving, she would stop to chatter enthusiastically with every person she saw in the hall. She liked to show off her children to her colleagues, though we shook their hands limply and stared at them sullenly, too hungry and frustrated to remember to be polite. Long past dinnertime, my brother and I would be tugging on her purse and pulling at her clothes, trying physically to usher our mother out the door.

I knew Cindy wouldn't be like that. She was some fifteen years younger than my mom, she seemed genuinely interested in my life, and she had a dog I could love and care for with the ferocity of a lonely little girl.

Cindy moved in. She taught me to tell Street, *Andiamo!* ("Let's go") to get her to poop when I took her outside. She helped me figure out a clothing allowance so I could use my babysitting money to buy my own clothes, and she invited me to bicycle beside her when she went for long runs.

One day I came home from school and Cindy was standing at the sink scrubbing the fireplace andirons with steel wool.

"Are they dirty?" I asked, perplexed.

"No," she said in an oddly shrill voice. "I'm just. Really mad. At my mother."

My father was in the dining room getting ready for his weekly poker game. "Is Cindy all right?" I whispered to him, hoping I was out of earshot.

He shrugged, then smiled. "A lot of people have problems with their moms."

Two weeks later we went for a bike ride. I pedaled hard on my beloved blue Raleigh, the wind blowing back my thick brown hair, the sun warm on my shoulders.

"You shouldn't be standing up," Cindy scolded. "Downshift. Downshift! If you have to work this hard, you'll never last the distance." Had I been working too hard? I don't remember if we successfully completed the twelve-mile round-trip ride. I only remember the feeling, all afternoon, that I was doing something wrong.

Cindy kept her promise to help me with my math homework. We sat at the kitchen table and I chattered about how Stephanie Koontz had skipped ahead to eighth-grade honors. I always loved how concrete math was, how there was only one right answer, how I could memorize the rules and apply them. Math, unlike my seventh-grade friends, was predictable. Cindy ordered me to concentrate. But no matter how hard I looked at the numbers, they weren't making any sense.

"It's easy, you're just not trying," she scoffed.

I closed the book harder than I should have. "Thanks for your help," I said sarcastically, taking the stairs to my room two at a time.

My father cooked. I cleaned the kitchen. One night, when my brother was at my mom's house in the city and it was just the three of us, Cindy took off her glasses to better scrutinize how I sponged the table.

"You missed a spot," she pointed.

"Did I?" I pretended to be confused. The love affair was over. I set my shoulders. I had enough problems of my own without Cindy criticizing me.

"Come over here and see," she commanded. I walked as slowly as I could back to the table. "See those streaks? You didn't do a good job."

I took the sponge she thrust into my hands and went back over the table again, purposefully missing spots this time, mangling the sponge as I squeezed the dirty water into the sink.

Every compliment was a veiled insult. "You're going running with us. I'm so surprised you've actually kept it up," she told me one chilly autumn afternoon. I outpaced them both that day but never went running with my father and Cindy again. "I can't believe my jeans actually fit you when I'm so much taller and thinner than you are. Sure, you can borrow them!" when I needed an outfit for a middle school dance.

"Why does Cindy always give me such a hard time?" I asked my father one day during a rare moment when Cindy wasn't around.

"She doesn't," he dismissed. "Cindy loves you. You're just jealous."

"Jealous?" I was in seventh grade. Late one night a boyfriend climbed in through the window and turned on the light in my room while Cindy and my father slept, oblivious, just down the hall. Another time Becca Steinberg bought some pot and we smoked it in Ordway Park, right across the street from my house. I loved my French teacher but hated the kids in the class. My biology teacher was having a baby. Jenny Trueblood mailed letters to her friends by addressing them to herself and putting their return address on unstamped envelopes. My father didn't know any of this. He had no idea what I was feeling, what I was doing, or even whom I spent my time with. The only feeling I could ever talk to him about was my anger at my mother for being so absent.

"Of my relationship with Cindy," my father insisted, "you don't like that when I'm with her it takes time away from me being with you."

That wasn't true. Cindy wasn't robbing me of my father, she was helping give me the space I wanted to grow up. She had brought music and a pet into our lives. Even as she berated and belittled me, I loved that Cindy could give my dad a hard time about things and he would change his mind. Though I felt as if my father was immovable with me, he listened to her. So much so that when Street died Cindy got another dog, a Jack Russell Terrier she let me name Tosh. My father was the one having growing pains during my adolescence. Attentive to me as a child, he wasn't sure how to behave toward me as I was becoming a young adult. He stopped saying goodnight to me, tried to order me to bed because he didn't want me to stay up later than he did, and freaked out so much about me going on dates that I lied about what I was doing. Though there were things I was happy to do with my dad, like accompanying him on his training-for-the-Boston-Marathon runs on my Raleigh, I knew I would rather be on the roof kissing Mark McGuire than spending time with my father.

I started acting so surly and things got so bad among Cindy, me, and my father that we went to a family therapy session with a sharp-tongued New Yorker whom I instantly trusted and liked. My father slid down in his chair looking smaller and more vulnerable than I'd ever seen him. Cindy looked pale and stricken, like she wanted to bolt from the room. I felt my back straighten. "Can you hear what your daughter is telling you?" the therapist chided. "You need to stop putting her in the middle of your relationship, and blaming her for things she's not responsible for. That's called triangulation and it's not a healthy family dynamic. You are the grown-ups but you're acting like children. Leave her out of your arguments from now on."

Junior high ended. Cindy's bullying, directed more at my father than at me, escalated. Tosh and Cindy moved out. I asked my dad later why they broke up but neither of us could remember if there was a precipitating event. I never heard from Cindy again.

"She struggled with mental health issues," my father said on the phone.

"She did?" My voice was both indignant and elated. Something heavy unclenched inside me. I felt so strangely happy that I giggled. "I never knew that," I said. "You said the tension between us was my fault."

"Did I?" my father considered. Maybe I was imagining it but I thought I could hear regret in his voice. "Cindy was really insecure," he admitted, being uncharacteristically candid. "You know she had that affair with Marshall Smith, my poker buddy. Even after they broke up she would call him in the middle of the night threatening to kill herself. He told me she was diagnosed with something . . . what's it called . . . Borderline Personality Disorder, I think that's what it was. I'm sure she felt threatened by you." His voice was tight and uncomfortable. "That certainly wasn't your fault."

I was now the age that my father and mother were when they were newly divorced, rejoining the dating scene, living through their second adolescences, involved in emotionally turbulent relationships with new partners who came in and out of their lives. My husband James's dad married four times and divorced three. Though my father didn't live with another woman again until he married for the third time when I was twenty-one, Cindy was one of many girlfriends he had over the years.

Both children of divorce, James and I had married reluctantly. We wanted something more than a flimsy commitment that could be easily discarded. With the naiveté of young lovers, we promised each other that our marriage would mean more than our parents', that we would work through every argument without giving up on each other, that our children would never have to navigate the tangled world of stepparents.

My father and I hung up. I flipped the phone closed and tucked it into my coat pocket. My daughter kicked her legs impatiently. She couldn't wait to get to story time, when she picked out her own little rug, sat on it all by herself for all of three minutes, and then snuggled into my lap.

LOVE PERSEVERES

. . .

shannon bardwell

Fifteen days after Anne's sixteenth birthday, her mother walked out. I'm sure Anne felt as if a bullet had exploded inside her. She and her father spent the next year clinging and grieving. Now, whenever life gets hard, I think about that girl on her sixteenth birthday and how, two weeks later, her mother disappeared.

All I can do is love her, really love her. It's the only thing that can come anywhere close to healing her heart. That and trying to give her all the time and space she needs.

When I came into her father's life I was full of my own bullet holes and not anxious to take on another family's responsibilities. I was finally free after twenty-five years of a not-so-good marriage and thought I would stay that way. One bad marriage is enough for anybody. "Let's just have a Friday night date and have our own lives and houses and everyone will be happy," I suggested to Sam.

He didn't see it that way. Sam's the kind of guy that needs a wife, a companion, a lover, a partner, a helpmate. He said he was not interested in a Friday night date. In fact, he didn't want to date at all. He wanted to marry and make us a family.

"It's not that easy," I protested.

But the more I got to know Sam, the more I grew to love him. We wrangled back and forth about marriage and commitment. He was sure; I wanted to think and pray about it. At fifty-two I had been married most of my adult life and I wanted some time off.

He said, "At our ages, we might not have time."

I prayed some more. We went to church a lot.

Then there was Sam's daughter. By then Anne had turned seventeen and would be a senior in high school. Soon she'd graduate and be on her own.

Early in my first marriage I had wanted my own children. My then-husband and I had talked about it: what they would look like, how many there would be, whether they'd be boys or girls. Then one day he stopped talking about children.

"Tell me! I want you to say it," I demanded.

"I don't want any children," he said.

Eventually the dream of having my own children died, along with the marriage.

So with Sam I might have a daughter, a grown, smart, beautiful daughter. She could take care of herself; after she went to college she could come home or I'd go visit. We could have lunch and talk and go shopping.

I was soon to learn that grown-up daughters still need parenting. Cars cost more than dolls, college is further away than the corner coffee shop, and wounds from a mother's abandonment are far worse than scraped pinky fingers.

All this I would learn after my honeymoon.

When Sam and I came home, I moved into another woman's house. Sam cleaned out a closet and a dresser for me. I moved my clothes in and brought along my favorite coffee cup.

The house was crowded; there was no room for anything of mine. It looked as it had when Anne's mother left, even though Sam claimed Anne's mother had taken half their stuff and then returned for half again. "That just couldn't be," I said as I surveyed the rooms. "She might have to come back and take another half."

There wasn't an inch of space that wasn't occupied. I cried one day because I couldn't find the light switches, they were all blocked by furniture. Sam and Anne knew where they were, but I stumbled in the dark trying to turn the lights on. The kitchen was fully equipped, but not as I would have arranged it. Why wouldn't the cutlery be in the top drawer next to the dishwasher?

Anne wanted everything just as it was right down to the tabby cat clock that hung on the kitchen wall. I didn't understand. Anne would be leaving soon. Why did it matter whether the cat clock was on the wall or not?

Sam said the clock hadn't worked in years.

Anne cried, "Leave it there."

I cried, "It's got to go."

Sam stood there wringing his hands.

I had been living in my own house alone. Overnight I was in Oz with two roommates. One was the man I loved and had committed my life to. The other was a teenager who was struggling. As much as I had vowed to love her father, I had vowed to love her too. I was beginning to see exactly what that meant.

At first it was strange to go to the refrigerator and look inside. My mother always said, "Don't go into people's refrigerators." That thought lingered with me even though technically, I guess, it was now my refrigerator.

At times I felt as uncomfortable with my new stepdaughter as I did with that refrigerator. At night I wondered, *Do I go downstairs in my PJs?* It was like walking in front of a stranger wearing your pajamas, only these strangers were now my family.

Every night we'd gather around the TV for a favorite sitcom. Anne and Sam would whoop and holler and talk all at the same time. It was *The Office*, *Project Runway*, or endless reruns of *The Golden Girls*. I hadn't owned a TV in years. My evenings had been spent reading a book or listening to the radio. My nerves were fraying, but I was scared to leave the room for fear of isolating myself from the family, so I stayed night after night.

Soon I made an appointment with a marriage and family counselor because I needed someone to give me permission to leave the room.

Other times Sam and Anne would share memories of Anne's childhood, vacations, or talk of relatives. I had nothing at all to contribute. When I was alone with Sam I would whimper, "I don't have any memories. I tell my memories and Anne says, 'That's nice.'"

Sam was kind. He would hold me and say, "We are making memories now. Memories take time."

One day I found a box of old Polaroid photos stored under the stairway. I searched those photographs as if I was looking for Waldo, learning everything I could about life before me. Then I went through them again, studying the backgrounds, trying to figure out where each photo was taken. I saw that tabby cat clock.

I also listened to their stories and asked questions. "What did you do on your thirteenth birthday?" "What was your favorite part about Disney World?" I made their memories mine.

Sam would say to me, "Remember . . ."

"Yes," I would say and finish out the family story as if I had been right there.

Sometimes I'd look across the field behind our house and visualize a younger Anne playing. I could see a four-year-old in her

Halloween costume. She was ten and it was her birthday. She was thirteen picking out pumpkins at the pumpkin patch.

Anne came and went. Sometimes when she was home I would suspend whatever I was doing and we would sit down, one-on-one, and talk. Those talks would last an hour or two; we'd go deep. I was amazed at how open Anne would be. I'd listen, and occasionally I'd offer a little guidance.

As time and care healed my wounds, Anne's started to heal as well. Sometimes I wished I hadn't cried about light switches and tabby cat clocks, but in doing so Anne saw we could all be wounded and a little bit crazy at times.

One day I said, "Anne, I know the year with your dad after the divorce was a special time."

I thought she would agree that the memories were special, but her eyes welled up and she said, "It was a really sad time."

Not until that moment did I fully realize how sad and lonely Anne had been as Sam filled the pantry with thirty cans of chicken noodle soup and half a dozen jars of peanut butter, learned what tampons to buy and how to wash and iron her school uniforms, and talked to other parents about PTA meetings and girls' social clubs.

Every latent motherly instinct inside me made me want to grab Anne and hug her, but I knew she wasn't ready for hugs, not from me. "I'm not a hugger," she always said, so I kept still.

"I'm so sorry," I said.

Other times our conversations were light and fun. We talked about hairstyles and clothing.

"Anne, I can't believe I'm going to tell you this, but I am because my mother used to tell me the same thing. That blue skirt you were wearing yesterday is a bit too short. I mean . . . when you bend over . . . well . . . you shouldn't."

"I know," she said. "I washed it and it shrunk."

Her excuses sounded like mine did at that age. I giggled inside thinking now I was on the mother side.

The light moments were good and welcomed because none of us were having an easy time of it. Anne threw temper tantrums with her father. Afterwards she screamed, "I'm going to my mother's!" The door slammed and she peeled off down the driveway.

My heart hurt for her. I prayed she'd be safe and knew she'd be back. For all our faults, we were her safe place.

Sometimes Anne would stamp her foot at her dad and say, "You keep pretending we're a family, but we're not!" She was right. We were finding our way. Who knew what a stepfamily even looked like?

After Anne left for college I hung up a framed verse we'd been given as a wedding gift. "Love is patient and kind, it always protects, always trusts, always hopes, and always perseveres. Love never fails."

I stared at the verse and thought Sam loved like that, without reservation. He loved and did not withdraw.

I wasn't used to an unconditional kind of love. It's hard to love someone when you don't feel safe. Sam made us feel safe. I wanted that love with Anne.

When Anne came home on weekends and fall breaks, a month for Christmases, spring breaks, and every summer, I started by saying out loud, "I love you." At first it was awkward and I got eye rolls or grins or sly smiles. Sometimes I said it when I didn't feel it. I figured if I said it the feelings would follow. They did.

Then, as I slowly moved into roles of decision-making and discipline, mostly regarding finances, I'd tell Anne, "I promise you I will always do what's best for you. You may not like it and it may not be what you want, but I will always do what's best for you." I said it again and again and I meant it even though the repetition was exhausting.

There were calls in the middle of the night from who-knew-where. "I'm stranded. Can I use the credit card?"

"Yes!" I'd scream over a crackling phone line.

"I've locked the keys in the car," at college of course.

"I'm on my way."

"Can you help me move my stuff to the dorm?"

"Yes."

"Do you think Dad would let me . . .?"

"Probably not."

Anne's major was architecture, so Sam and I made many trips to the lumberyard and then to the school to deliver school supplies. Some parents got to deliver number two pencils. We got to deliver 4×8 sheets of plywood.

Responding to Anne's needs made me feel "motherly." I knew that I would never get the Mother's Day card and that was okay. I wanted more. I wanted Anne's trust. I wanted Anne's heart.

Sometimes I reminded Anne, "I'm the best stepmother you will ever have!"

She would grin and say, "Good, I don't think I can go through this again."

"Not to worry, dear one. I'm not going anywhere," I assured her.

As much as I hated the sound of "step," conjuring up Cinderella and her wicked stepmother, it felt unfair to call myself anything else. I didn't give birth to Anne. It was Anne's mother who raised her for most of her life and contributed the most to whom she became. I thought to myself, *Children—people—know if you really love them or not. They know if you'll be there for them . . . they know.* And so I sat tall in the chair of stepmother.

WAITING AT WINDOWS

• • •

deb stone

In March 1989, my coworker Eli invited me to accompany him and his two adult daughters, MacKenzie and Sammie, for a day of skiing. His wife, the girls' mother, had died unexpectedly six months earlier. I was too worried about falling on my ass to consider how his daughters felt about my intrusion into their world so soon after their mother passed. I was twenty-nine, the same age as Mac-Kenzie, and only eight years older than Sammie.

Five months later, Eli and I moved in together. We discussed that he would stepparent my six-year-old sons, but it didn't occur to me that I'd be a stepmother to his daughters. I introduced them as "Eli's daughters" rather than my stepdaughters, and they introduced me to their friends as "Debbie". Who knew how they explained it outside my earshot? I never asked.

MacKenzie worked as a deputy sheriff in another town. Because she lived some distance away, we saw her infrequently. She had many of the qualities I admired about Eli: honesty, loyalty, and responsibility. She was slow to warm to me, but never impolite. I sensed that she had planned to spend more time with Eli after her mother passed away, but suddenly my twins and I monopolized his time.

Sammie was as gregarious as MacKenzie was reserved. She and her husband Daryl lived nearby with their two blond, blue-eyed children, Maverick, who was two-and-a-half, and four-month-old Sabrina. Their third child, Jenna, was born in 1990, a chubby-cheeked baby whose dark hair stood up like a lawn that needed mowing. I loved Eli's daughters and grandchildren, not in the way that I loved my own sons whom I'd birthed and raised, but because they belonged to Eli.

At first, Sammie was a delightful stepdaughter. Her ready laugh and spontaneous spirit lit up any room. It was a surprise to me when my relationship with her turned sour within months. She and Daryl were often unemployed and borrowed money from Eli and me. At first, I didn't mind, but time after time they didn't pay us back. Although I enjoyed babysitting the step-grandchildren, I resented it when Sammie began dropping them off for a couple of hours, then disappearing for days. She had no telephone. If I drove to their apartment, no one answered my knock. When they finally showed up and I confronted Sammie, she screamed and swore, loaded the kids in the old Camaro that Eli had given her, and sped away.

"You need to *do* something," I said to Eli.

His jaw clenched or his face flinched, but he said nothing. She was his daughter and he would handle it his way: silent avoidance. Sometimes I'd scream and swear until Eli said, "Debbie, enough." I'd comment that he was contributing to her crappy parenting, but he wouldn't respond. Meanwhile, my sons needed help with homework and rides to baseball or Boy Scouts. There was no time to argue for long.

In August 1992, Sammie moved out, leaving Daryl with the three children. He couldn't manage them alone, and asked Eli and me to keep them for a couple of months.

"Not without some parameters," I said.

He and Sammie signed guardianship papers so we could put the kids on our medical insurance and enroll them in preschool. The plan was that one of the parents would get his or her life in order, and the kids would move home.

We filled those early summer days with visits to the zoo, the science museum, and trips to Saturday market. The little ones traipsed along to Scott and Matthew's soccer games, and buckled up in the backseat of the van while I drove the twins to Boy Scouts and swimming lessons. I enjoyed the step-grandchildren, yet was also aware that Eli and I were stand-ins for parents whom the children loved and missed. They often cried for Mommy at bedtime, and they missed rough-and-tumble play with Daryl crawling after them on all fours like a ferocious beast as they giggled and screamed to get out of his grasp. On days when Sammie planned to visit, Maverick, Sabrina, and Jenna stood with their noses pressed to the picture window watching for her to arrive. My own mother had walked away when I was five. I hadn't seen her again until I was an adult, so I knew how it felt to wait for a mother who never arrives. Sometimes, after waiting fifteen minutes, I'd load the kids in the car and drive to the park. We would arrive home to an angry note from Sammie: *Where were you? I came for my visit!*

Too bad, I thought. *Should have shown up on time.* If she was going to mother these children, she was going to have to figure things out. For the kids' sake, I hoped it was soon. Maverick was often withdrawn, and little Jenna wandered around saying, "Mommy?" Sabrina asked, "Where does Mommy sleep? 'Cause we don't have the 'partment now."

"She'll get a house soon," I would say, "and you'll go live with her. Remember the plan?"

Everything changed the day four-year-old Sabrina made a comment that her daddy's peepee had put bad milk in her mouth. I was horrified. I called Eli at work and told him I was calling Children's Services Division. The receptionist on the phone told me to call the police. A detective scheduled a forensic interview at the child abuse center. The physician recommended counseling for all three children and the only therapist we could find for sexually abused preschool-age children was forty miles east. We took the trip once a week, with three fifty-minute appointments back to back, and then drove home again in time for my twin sons to get off the bus from school.

Daryl was forbidden to visit once he'd been indicted. Sammie didn't believe the allegations and snuck the children to see him, so her visits were cancelled. She was furious and blamed me, but I didn't care. She was an adult. I couldn't do all the things I needed to do for the kids and support her too. I needed to ramp up my emotional reserve; we were going to be a family of seven indefinitely. Some days I felt angry, some days sad. Often, I was overwhelmed. I learned to cook casseroles; seven is nearly twice as many mouths to feed as four. We bought a minivan. In time, our family learned to move as one. We would be moving amoeba-style through the mall, and Eli or I would say "Duck line" and the five kids would fall behind us into a line that could snake through any crowd.

Attachment grows in the everyday doing of things, the please-pass-the-potatoes, kissing-bumped-elbows, tucking-in-at-bedtime kinds of things. Untangling snarls after shampoo. Teaching the tying of laces in shoes. One evening, the five children were gathered around for a story, and I pulled one of my almost-too-large-for-laps sons onto my lap and said, "I remember the day you were born . . ." Sabrina squealed, "Do me! Do me!" so I pulled her on my lap next and said, "I remember the day I met you . . ." A year passed.

By then, there were no labels like "my kids" or "step-grandkids" in my mind, just children I loved.

When Sabrina saw Daryl at the defense table for the first time in fourteen months, her face lit up in a big smile. She lifted her shiny red shoe up on the ledge where witnesses set their notes, and played with the buckle while she told everyone what her daddy had done. The trial lasted a week. The jury convicted Daryl of six counts of sexual abuse against Maverick and Sabrina. He was sentenced to twenty-six years and three months in prison.

After the trial, Maverick needed more one-on-one adult attention. He went to live with his birth father (he had a different father than the girls) but when that didn't work out, he went to live with Eli's older daughter, MacKenzie. Sammie worked on and off, but never managed to take on the role of mom. She would promise the kids, "I'm getting an apartment. You'll come and live with me soon." But she continued to be the visiting mom, the holiday mom. I fixed the meals, did the laundry, helped with homework, took them to the doctor, drove them to counseling, did all the daily things mothers and stepmothers do. By the time the kids were in elementary school, they were calling me Mom. Sammie was furious.

"Look, Sammie," I said, "they know you're their mom, but I'm doing the work moms do. We can both be Mom. It's not a big deal."

A decade passed. By then, Sabrina and Jenna were in junior high. Sammie visited on and off. She'd show up at the girls' middle school to bring a cupcake. I tried to explain that middle school was different. She couldn't just walk into a classroom as in elementary school.

"They're *my* daughters," she said.

By high school, the girls had begun lying and stealing. Keeping secrets. Acting in ways that seemed out of character for whom they had always been. I thought it was because they were teenagers, until the day Jenna screamed, "You won't let us go live with our mom."

"She doesn't have a place to live," I said.

"She would get one if you let her have us."

I felt sick to my stomach. I loved the girls. I'd been mothering them for over a dozen years. Kissed boo-boos. Cleaned up puke. Taken them to Disneyland and Mexico. How could I let them go? I didn't think it would work out, but in my heart I knew I needed to offer Sammie the chance. When I talked to Eli and his elder daughter, MacKenzie, they disagreed.

"This is Sabrina and Jenna's home," Eli said.

I knew what it meant to wait for the chance to go home with your mom and never have the day come. I called Sammie.

"Get an apartment by the end of this month. The girls are coming home. If you can't make it happen, *you're* going to tell them."

It took her a week. I should have wondered how she was able to pay the first and last months' rent. Instead, I held my head in my hands and wondered if I had been the problem all along. Maybe they could have gone home sooner. Had I been selfish because I loved them and didn't want them to leave?

"Don't be absurd," Eli said. "She didn't have money for gas or food during visits. How could you know she'd find a way to get an apartment?"

Sammie and I sat at my dining room table with Sabrina and Jenna to tell them that they would be moving in with their mother at spring break. I went to Jenna's room that evening to tell her goodnight and she had already packed. I went to my room and cried.

Within weeks of moving in with Sammie, the girls were running around unsupervised. They complained that Sammie refused to buy their school supplies and hygiene items. Still, they didn't want to come home. I could have helped pay for things but didn't. I felt sorry for the girls, but I wanted them to realize why they'd lived with us all those years. Jenna failed all her classes the first trimester at the new high school.

"If you can't keep your grades up, you're coming home," I said. "You're a junior in high school. There's no time to waste." By the end of fall term, she was still failing. I drove to Sammie's to help Jenna pack. Sammie was furious. Eli and I were still the legal guardians so I was adamant. Sabrina had turned eighteen and moved in with her boyfriend. She had six months left in her senior year.

"Come home, Sabrina," I said.

"I want to do it on my own," she said.

"I'm worried about you finishing school."

"Don't worry about me, Mom. I'll finish, I promise." She looked worried. "I want to tell you something but I don't want you to be mad at me for me not telling sooner. You know that trip Mommy and Jenna took to visit Chico State? Mommy was teaching Jenna how to harvest marijuana. They brought two crates of it back to Oregon to sell. And Mommy's using meth."

I felt the blood rush out of my face, my heart pounding in my throat. I understood the implications. Sammie had been using Jenna to distribute pot to other students. How could I have missed this? When Jenna got home from school, I interrogated her. She sat angry and mute with tears streaming down her face.

"Did I waste my life," I yelled, "so you could become a dreg and a loser like your mom?"

When yelling didn't wear her down, I insisted she get in the hot tub with me. We huddled in separate corners, me hurling words at her through rising steam, trying to make her crack, trying to make her admit what was true. Maybe she felt more vulnerable in the star-draped night; maybe the bubbling hot water broke her down. More likely, she just wore down. Finally, she admitted she and Sammie had driven weed from California to Oregon. The good stuff that had gone chronic and brought top-dollar prices. Six or seven crates at a time with one to two pounds in each crate.

That was it: I was done with Sammie. I told Jenna there would be no more visits. Within days, Jenna ran away. A week later, the police picked her up and hauled her in to the juvenile holding cell.

I brought her home and laid out more limits. She glared silently. Jenna knew how to bide her time.

I called the Canby Police Department to report the drug dealing. The officer showed up at my office to take the report. "We have a Neighborhood Watch person in the apartment below," he said. "He would have noticed."

"The girls say a couple pounds are kept in each flip-top crate in the master bedroom."

"They probably meant ounces," he said.

"Pounds," I said. "*Pounds.* Do you understand how many Ziplocs a crate holds?"

The police checked Sammie's apartment a few days later. By then, she'd left the state.

Jenna was two months short of eighteen. I was worried that she was going to be arrested for drug dealing. Eli and I could be liable for her legal fees. I filed a petition to remove myself as guardian. The judge admonished Jenna to follow my guidance, attend school, and have no contact with Sammie, but he refused my request to be removed as her guardian.

That night, Jenna slipped out her bedroom window and ran away through the dark woods, dropping out of high school a month before graduation. The police took a report but said they had insufficient staff to search for runaways who were practically eighteen. On Jenna's birthday, I sat in her bedroom and cried.

I wanted Sammie to pay for what she'd done to her children and for her betrayal of my trust. I used Google search to ferret out information about the manufacturing operation in Chico: names, dates of birth, and addresses of the growers. Since the local police seemed uninterested, I called the drug task force. A week later, police seized one hundred pot plants in a raid of the property of one of the growers. He wasn't home but police arrested another man who lived on the property. The police also seized methamphetamine, packaging materials, scales, stolen property, and guns. Still, nobody picked up Sammie for questioning.

The police requested a photograph of Jenna so they could identify her if she turned up hurt or deceased. Spring turned to summer turned to fall. Christmas came and went. Six months, and still no word from Jenna. Sabrina had graduated and was working at the mall. Maverick had joined the army.

That January, the telephone rang. It was one of Sammie's drug-dealing friends. Sammie was in the hospital. She was going to undergo brain surgery. Would we come?

When a doctor is going to cut a hole the size of a golf ball in your stepdaughter's skull and flake away the layers of tumor that have adhered to her brain, you want to be there. You want one last chance to look her in the eye and say "I love you" even if she is a fuck-up. We drove over immediately. As Eli and I listened to the neurosurgeon explaining that the twelve-hour surgery might leave Sammie blind or paralyzed, Jenna walked in.

"Hi, Mom," she said.

I wanted to rush over and throw my arms around her, but my legs suddenly felt as heavy as stone. I stood there with my heart pounding, snuffling back tears. Eighteen-year-old Jenna, gone from us for nine months, strode over and gave me a hug. Tears streamed down my face. I suddenly understood the Biblical story of the prodigal son. I didn't care what had happened between us. I was relieved to see Jenna. I wanted Sammie to live.

The neurosurgeon surveyed the group, then turned to Sammie and said, "Ready?"

The orderlies wheeled Sammie to the operating room. The rest of us gathered in the waiting area: Eli and me, MacKenzie, Sabrina and Jenna, and the drug-dealer friend, making jokes, working jigsaw puzzles, staring at our phones. Maverick was stationed in Iraq and couldn't be with us. Minutes turned to hours. The clock crept past midnight. Still Sammie was in surgery.

The hours that pass while you wait to hear if someone you love will live or die pass with a particular kind of acuity. There is something about trauma that converts love from an idea that says *I see you,* to a force that says, *Whatever it takes, I'm here for you.*

The neurosurgeon came out about 1:00 A.M. He had removed a large section of tumor, but couldn't get it all. He'd picked away at the bits attached to her optic nerves and pituitary. She was probably going to have vision loss and memory deficits. She might need surgery again. In the weeks that followed, I applied for Sammie to get Social Security disability. Drove her to doctors' appointments and follow-up exams. Moved her into an adult foster home. Sammie wasn't happy. She wanted her old life back. For a long time after that first surgery, I wrestled with my feelings about Sammie. Now she would never take responsibility for what she'd done. *It's water under the bridge,* I thought. *She doesn't remember it now.* The neurosurgeon had said that the tumor had been growing for years. Maybe it explained why things had always been so hard for Sammie, why her judgment had always been poor.

Then, news we'd been dreading: the tumor was back. The risks of surgery would be greater this time, but if she didn't have it, the prognosis was grim. Sammie spent a month in the hospital recovering. This time, the effects of surgery were more severe. She lost all sight in one eye. She couldn't learn her room number or remember what had occurred minutes earlier. Hospital staff served her meals, and minutes later, she would ask for lunch, not remembering she'd just eaten. She didn't remember having visitors. She was like the child forever waiting at the window for someone to come. I wondered how much of the past she could recall.

I'd been visiting her every day for three weeks when one afternoon I arrived and spotted her tied in a chair across from the nurses' station. I could hear her calling, "Can somebody let me up?"

"Hey, Sammie," I called to her. "You look tired. Ready for a nap?"

She nodded as she struggled to stand, impeded by the garment that held her tight to the chair. I untied the strings and helped her out of the restraint. She clambered into bed, lay down, and waited for me to tuck the blankets around her shoulders.

"Comfy?"

"Yes."

I reached up to the zipper of the canopy net that enclosed her hospital bed. The Posey unit looked like a giant mosquito net over a tent frame. It was designed to provide a safe environment for patients at risk of escape.

"I don't like it when you zip me in," Sammie said.

"I know, Sweetie. Pretend you're camping. It's a special tent."

I gave her a hug just as the nurse walked in.

"I love you," I said.

"Love you, too."

"You guys seem so close," the nurse remarked.

Sammie and I burst out laughing. Her laughter burbling out at the same time as mine confirmed that Sammie remembered how bad things had been between us.

These days, we're copacetic. I understand that Sammie's behavior isn't willful. Maybe it never was. Maybe the tumor was always lurking in the background, short-circuiting her intentions to be a good mom. It feels good to give her the benefit of the doubt. My twin sons and Sammie's three children are grown, but Eli and I adopted other children. We have one left at home.

Sammie lives in a memory care facility now. She hates living there, and sees me as one of her lifelines. I take her for outings and coordinate visits with one of her friends. The brain tumor didn't turn her into a dutiful stepdaughter. She sometimes tantrums when she's frustrated, but there's no point being angry.

"When my youngest is a teenager," I say, "I'm sending him to live with you. You owe me big-time."

Sammie grins.

"And as soon as he's grown," I tell her, "I'm getting stoned. I bet you could hook me up."

We both crack up. It's good to hear her laugh.

HALF-AMERICAN TO HALF-CHINESE: TRANSLATION THROUGH MARRIAGE

• • •

emma kate tsai

I stared at the photograph. I didn't want to like her. She had curly hair. I didn't know Chinese women had curly hair. My hair was as straight as a horse's mane, just like my father's. We all had it—me, my brother Elliott, and my identical twin sister Addie—his Chinese hair, not my mother's Caucasian limp brown hair.

The woman in the photograph wore a full face of makeup that went with her outfit, an ensemble that whispered high fashion—subtle, classic. Even at ten, I could tell the difference between my mom's Walmart tube tops and stretch pants and the photograph woman's designer threads, asymmetrical hem, intricate beading, leggings paired with a tunic, and four-inch heels.

She stood against a professional photographer's backdrop of dark blue with a polite smile. Never had I seen such a look on my mother's face. In every single picture of my mother, she was talking, laughing, smirking, or flirting. My mother had attitude. The photograph woman looked not only authentically stylish but sweet.

"If I married this woman," my father answered, "she'd be your stepmother." School was over for the day—I was in the fifth grade—and it was my turn to sit up front. I had asked my father for the definitions of *in-law* and *stepfamily* after a class discussion about relationship terms. It was then that he pulled the photograph out of his wallet to show me what *stepmother* would mean for me.

If he *married* her? Who *was* she? What was her name? Did my father have a girlfriend? Did they hold hands? How old was she? Had he taken the picture himself or had she given it to him? I stared straight ahead and didn't ask a word. Addie and Elliott whispered to each other in the backseat. As I shifted against the sticky plastic upholstery, I wished I were with them, further away from the beautiful stranger now pocketed.

My parents divorced when I was two. I have no memory of them together, only two pictures of them, a professionally shot portrait of the couple from their college days, and a blurry black-and-white photograph of their courthouse wedding. The way my mother tells it, my father didn't understand a word of English the first three months they were dating. "But he looked like a Chinese Elvis. I had never seen such a handsome Chinese man." Elliott was a wedding night conception. Addie and I came twenty months later.

My father, whom I call Baba ("Dad" in Chinese), claims the only reason they got married was that he had sex with her. "I was on my way to meet my Chinese girlfriend, Linda, but I ran into your mother. Right thing to do, marry girl you have sex with." Of course he never mentions my mother's stark beauty, her full lips, her contagious laugh, her watercolor-blue eyes, her perfect skin. What earned her seventeen marriage proposals, or at least that's how my mother tells it. And no matter how many times Mom stood us up or let the sun set on our backpacks as we waited on the elementary school curb, we could never stay mad at her for long. Not even when she holed herself up in her dark bedroom rather than take us to the park, and gave as her replacement a pizza coupon and a tiny knob-dial television set. "I want privacy. Don't even think about knocking unless it's an emergency. Someone better be dying or bleeding," she'd say. Not even when her dire warnings showed a certain joyfulness. We couldn't wait to be with her.

Baba knew how to turn the smile on for the camera, but it faded along with the flash. Mostly he gave demands and discipline. "Go study now." "*Tao yan.*" "Dinner for eating, not talking." "Go to sleep now." He spoke in few words, maybe because he was saving up for those semiregular shouted lectures. I likened him to a college football coach, pointing his finger in my face and sprinkling me with his saliva. That is, just before he slapped my hand what seemed like a hundred times—for forgetting my jacket at school, for bringing home a B+, for misplacing the remote control, for talking on the phone longer than three minutes. But, he was Chinese. It was "cultural." That's what teachers and counselors told us, friends and parents of friends, and Mom. To spank was Chinese. To lecture was Chinese. To shout was Chinese. To set rules was Chinese. To demand perfection was Chinese.

Baba wasn't always a tyrant. Did that make him part American? He walked between my sister and me in parking lots from car to store, holding our hands until we reached the door. I quizzed him on what I saw that I didn't understand. "Why do they put rice in salt shakers?" "Why did that guy have a breakdown in that movie?" "What does N mean on that stick in the car?" And he answered every question, eager to make me smarter. When Baba mowed the lawn, he propped me up in the oak tree in front of our house, stopping to kiss my hands whenever he took a break. He woke me up that way too, taking both my hands in his and kissing them all over. If a woman was in our house, in his bed, in our car, at the dining room table, maybe I'd lose the charm and have nothing left but the fear.

The woman's name was Ines. Soon after the photograph emerged from my father's pocket, Baba told us he was going out on a date. It was the first time he had ever hired a babysitter. He'd been seeing Ines and my inquisitiveness brought this new relationship and the photograph to light. When I was at Mom's, I always imagined Baba doing what he did when we were there: cooking *gai lan*—lion's head— and rice, washing the dishes, taking a call from his mother, or some old friend, in Taiwan, shouting, *"Wa cai,"* and slapping his thigh. I was wrong to think he was alone. He was with her. Stupid pretty Chinese woman.

The cute, lipsticked sixteen-year-old who babysat us ordered a pizza, let us watch *Teen Witch* on cable, and entertained our interrogation about boyfriends and freedom. "What's he like?" "Does he kiss you on the mouth?" "What happens to your lipstick?" "How do you get a driver's license?" "Does that mean you can do whatever you want?"

I should have felt like a kid in a candy store to get a night off from my dad. No studying *and* I could talk and watch TV and eat American food. But, I kept thinking about the photograph. In between answers to our questions, I looked at the door. I'd pretend to get a glass of water so I could peek out the kitchen window into the driveway. When Kim, or whatever her name was—we never saw her again—sent us to bed around ten, my father still wasn't home. I stared at the ceiling and wondered if he would ever speak English again if he married the photograph woman.

What would another Chinese person in our mixed house mean? Twice everything? Twice the studying? Twice the hand-slapping? Twice the bubbling cauldrons of processed pork blood and seasoned chicken's feet? No repeat visits from friends who didn't understand the Chinese scrolls on the walls or bitter dried plums on the coffee table instead of cheese balls and peanuts, who had to bend over at the door and take off their sparkly high-tops? Would she make us learn Chinese? Agree with my father when he said dinner was for eating, not talking? Would I feel twice as out of place in my own home?

The following weekend, the photograph woman became three-dimensional. We met her in the cavernous auditorium of the Chinese Culture Center, where we spent every weekend. Theater had brought my father and Ines together. My father performed in Chinese drama, and rehearsed at the center. Ines, as a favor to her sister-in-law who acted opposite my father, agreed to be an extra. I put my book down to watch this five-foot woman float toward my father. His eyes widened, and then he grinned. I almost didn't recognize him. At ten, I couldn't know what it was, but later I realized I was witnessing my father's heart soften.

"Girls, *lai*. Boy." My father called us over just as he always did after rehearsal. Normally, we would stand there, his little ducklings tucked behind his back, and wait for our next directive. What would I do if he demanded, "Hug her"? Did I have to do it? Could I stand in defiance and defense of my mother? Would my sister join me in a front against this woman, this foreigner, my father's girlfriend? My sister and I exchanged glances. Elliott seemed fine, oblivious. How could I escape the photograph woman becoming real? If I didn't smile, would she leave and never come back? They turned together to face us, their hands entwined. I could see only the tips of her fingers, her hands were so small. We were brought before her like an offering, part of his dowry. As if introducing a queen, he said, "This is E-nus." Eventually my father would call her "*Lao Boi*," or "Wife" in Chinese.

"It's nice to meet you," she said, in her small voice.

We bowed our heads and each shook her hand. I couldn't be obstinate. She was too nice, too kind, too demure. "My daughters are here, they can take you to our house for a while." She didn't ask outright if we wanted to go, but just presented the opportunity as a gift. "No reason for you to stay here and do nothing."

Baba said, "Girls, go, go with them. I pick you up later or we spend the night there." Spend the night. A ripple of excitement coursed through me. Toni and Georgette were sixteen and almost thirteen and lived with Ines and Ines's mother—coveted older girls, the access point into the life of a teenager. Toni drove us to their house on the other side of town. It must have had seven bedrooms and just as many bathrooms, long corridors of closed doors. About an hour after we got there, my father came with "lunch boxes," what he and his friends called takeout. I spent the night with Toni in her four-poster bed and Addie spent the night with Georgette. A Chinese man's voice poured out of Toni's boom box. Poster upon poster of Chinese rock stars covered the walls of her room. Georgette taught Addie numbers and colors in Chinese. Maybe it would be all right, all this Chinese stuff. Maybe I could become half-American and half-Chinese, rather than just American with a Chinese name and an exotic look.

Somehow the girls' very existence softened the blow of my father's courting, and I got some questions answered. Ines, who was from Taiwan, had married her high school sweetheart, who turned into a rich businessman. They had four daughters—Yaya, Wawa, Toni, and Georgette. Yaya and Wawa (their nicknames were Duck and Doll in Chinese) were fraternal twins a year younger than Addie and me. As part of Ines's custody agreement with her ex-husband, she got Toni and Georgette and he got the twins. Ines and her husband had been divorced a few years, not nearly as long as Baba and Mom had been.

Over the short year before Baba said "I do" to Ines, I investigated my father's new girlfriend as if she were a crime scene. I was determined to find a piece of evidence that would deem her inappropriate for our lives. I couldn't. Not only was Ines a far better mother to us than our own—she showed up, on time, and spent time with us—she was the yin to my father's yang. He was hot-tempered, she was soft-spoken and patient. He made our decisions, she asked our opinions.

He was a project manager, she was a mom. Gone was the punishing routine of getting ready with my father. Sitting in a hard wooden chair as he pulled my hair in pigtails so tight my eyes went slanted, eating a breakfast of oatmeal he'd cooked the night before and left out, inheriting Elliott's hand-me-downs that my father laid out for us. Ines introduced our hair to the French braid, took my mother's rose at Mother's Day pageants (Mom rarely showed, or came too late), made American kid food like grilled cheese sandwiches and French toast, packed our lunches with a note, feminized our wardrobe, told my father what we were afraid to.

The night before my father got married, Ines played Super Mario Brothers with us in our living room while my father was at a meeting. "I-N-E-S T-S-A-I," she entered on the screen after earning a hundred points.

"That's not your name," I said. Seeing my name next to hers felt like a punch in the stomach. Even Mom had never gone by Tsai. It belonged to us—me, Addie, Elliott, and Baba.

"But it will be. After tomorrow," she said with the same ecstatic enthusiasm any bride would.

"But it isn't your name. That's *our* name!" I screamed and ran from the room.

"Emma!" my sister shouted. "What's the matter with her?" I heard her ask Ines.

"Just leave her. She'll work it out."

I was too proud to go back in without being begged and so I cried and I waited. No one ever came. That is, until my father whispered me awake two hours later.

"*Guai guai*, you a good girl."

I lifted my head and looked at him. He was smiling. He was happy. I flew toward him in a hug, holding on to him as if he had announced he was leaving me in the morning. "You ready for me to get married tomorrow?"

"No." I wasn't. I loved Ines already, but I hated her too. I hated that she did a better job than my mother did, I hated that she was Chinese, I hated that she was so . . . nice.

"You're just saying that because your mother told you to," he retorted, the smile turning to an angry line. That was true, actually. My mother *had* pushed all of us to take a stand against the marriage. A part of me wished I could take what I'd said back, and a part of me threw my words down as a gauntlet.

"If you aren't ready for the answer, don't ask the question." I had never spoken back to my father, but in that moment I was too desperate to be scared.

"Emma, go to sleep," he said. The sound of my name stung. He almost always called me *Guai Guai* (precious) or Girl, only Emma when I had done something wrong.

It took a year, maybe two, before I saw how Ines transformed our lives. My father bought her a new house and a new car and he yelled at us less often and she wouldn't let him insult our mother and the food was better and my father was happier. Little details fixed themselves in my mind, that slice of life in the day-to-day I hadn't realized the divorce had cut out of my father's existence. How she took his hand in hers the minute they sat down in a movie theater and rubbed the length of his hand with her thumb. How they started taking ballroom dance classes together and practiced in the living room. How we not only got a new mother, but my father got a new wife.

"I am strong," she told me, "but I am also a wife."

A Chinese wife, I thought. Get ready to give up your rights. Serve him hand and foot as he sits around a coffee table with the men, playing gin and snacking on watermelon seeds. Then smile sweetly when he forbids you to drive on the highway or any street with a speed limit of fifty, or grocery shop after seven, or ride your bike on residential streets, or wear high heels or makeup or sleeveless dresses, or take a night out with the girls. Swallow whatever criticism he dishes out.

Hand over your paycheck and bow to the $200 a month he gives you for yourself. A part of me wanted to roll my eyes at her subservience.

But in demonstration her subservience looked like love and respect. She ladled vegetables and meat onto my father's plate, even if the serving dish sat right in front of him. She did every single chore with rare help from my father: all the cleaning, dishes, cooking, laundry, grocery shopping. She did it all even though she was hardly a housewife. Whether my father allowed it or she demanded it, Ines spent her weekends with her kids and he spent his weekends with us. She got up around seven every Saturday, spent a couple of hours cooking my father's favorite dishes, then went to see Toni and Georgette, who were too close to graduating high school to move in with us. All this and she worked full-time as a realtor, later changing jobs to manager of a shipping company.

My father returned her love. Ines liked to travel, so my father faced his fear of flying and took her to the Bahamas for their honeymoon. She liked to dance, so they started ballroom dancing lessons. Even though my father was and still is obsessively frugal, he bought her designer shoes (on sale, of course) once or twice a year.

It wasn't long before I called Baba and Ines "my parents." Mom drifted in and out of our lives as she followed men and jobs wherever they might take her—first to Phoenix, then to South Korea, where she lives now. Even though I would never call Ines "Mom," that's what she's been for the last twenty years. She was there at every recital and graduation, to take me shopping for a prom dress, to rub my hair over every rejection, to talk me down from every fight with my father. When I got lupus, she came to the hospital with my father—my mother was in Shanghai then—and when I had my first child, she came to hold him hours after he was born, my mother still in South Korea.

Now that I am married with children of my own, we all come together on holidays, and at weekly Sunday lunches. Every single time I see it again: the wife I want to be now that I am married, the mother Ines is to me. She serves a ten-course meal without help, her cute little hand on my father's back. She bows her head and tells me to "sit down, sit down and eat, Emma, I made this fish for you, and these vegetables, you sit here." She brings me a bowl of chicken soup, the same chicken broth she hand-fed me when I was in the hospital that morning she pulled my dad out of the chair he'd been sleeping in and made him go home to rest.

What if? What if my father had listened when I told him I wasn't ready? What if he hadn't married her? How different would my life be? I'd hate everything Chinese, as I did before I met her. I wouldn't have "parents." My father wouldn't have found his smile. I would have only seen marriage as what it shouldn't be: two hurt people screaming at each other in a driveway. Instead, even twenty years later, I see a touch, a look, a nudge, a smile, a laugh. I see maternity. I see marriage. I accept myself as what I am: half-Chinese.

EPIPHANY

• • •

sallie wagner brown

My eighty-eight-year-old father lies on his kitchen floor propped on one arm, grimacing in pain. He stares at my stepmother, tries to get up, but can't. She leans over him, holding a glass of wine. "Can't you just move your big, dumb feet instead of tripping over them? I can't take much more of this," she barks, spattering spittle.

I shock myself almost as much as her as I drop the bag of Kentucky Fried Chicken I've just brought for dinner and stride toward her, afraid she might kick him. She backs up behind the kitchen island, wide-eyed. I've been patient with her for four decades. Enough is enough.

"He is sick and old and he doesn't deserve this!" I shriek. "Can't you ever think of someone besides yourself?"

I know yelling at her will only make things worse, but I can't help myself. My husband picks up the bag of Kentucky Fried Chicken and sets it and the drinks he was carrying on the kitchen counter. He helps my father get up off the floor and guides him to a wingback chair in the den just off the kitchen.

"You won't let him read the paper because it makes noise when he moves it." I glare at Pat, literally seeing red. "You won't let him go to the bathroom until a commercial because he 'clomps his big feet,' then you get mad if he has an 'accident.'"

Pat's back is against the wall ovens. Mouth open, she says nothing, though she tries to form words. She's never seen me like this.

"You make him bend over and pick up crumbs from the floor in the middle of his meal. He can barely stand up! What are you thinking? How can you be so cruel? What would you do if someone treated you this way?"

Dad is fifteen years older than Pat. She's lost her golf partner and his help now that he's aging, but she doesn't get to take it out on him. They had no children together; they have no other family left alive. My husband Butch and I are all they have, and we will help them, both of them, but I cannot, will not, stand by when she's so abusive, so mean. He's a kind, gentle, loving, intelligent man. My heart breaks to see him suffer the pain, the humiliation she causes him.

I leave Pat pressed against the wall and go to my dad. He tries to smile. I'm shaking as I touch his shoulder and ask softly, through tears, if he is okay. I press my cheek to his forehead, then stumble out to our car without looking at Pat.

I inhale deliberately, slowly, as I wait for Butch. I'm as angry with myself for the venom I've spewed as I am at Pat for her selfishness, her meanness.

Butch grins as he bends his tall frame into the driver's seat.

"Your dad is okay, Pat is still stunned." He can't resist a chuckle.

"Oh, Butch! It's not funny. I can't believe I went after Pat like that."

Butch smiles. "She deserves it, you know."

"But I don't want to turn into her." I stare at their front door for a moment. "She had to know when she married an older man that he wouldn't be able to keep up with her at some point."

Butch starts our Escape SUV and turns to back out the drive. "They had at least forty pretty good years."

"True. She treated him a lot better before his years caught up with him." I sigh and stare at my hands, remembering how she used to fling comments about big feet at me, not him, or how she'd get after the kids for making noise scraping the last bits out of their cereal bowls. God forbid.

Butch pulls into a parking spot right in front of Starbucks and opens his car door. Some people might need a good stiff drink at this point, but he knows a Grande, triple-shot mocha is what I need.

I put my hands on my cheeks and look sideways at him, so he closes the door again. "This is a tough time for her. I should have tried to be more understanding. Oh, what if I've just made her more upset . . . and she'll be even worse to him?"

"Whoa! You just gave her a pretty good reason to think twice before going after him or anyone else, no matter how sorry for herself she's feeling."

I drop my hands and look at him doubtfully. "Maybe, but I hate how I feel when I act like that. I hate feeling so angry."

After a quiet moment, Butch smiles, and we get out of the car. He takes my hand and we walk into Starbucks for some chocolate therapy.

A week later, I rally the courage to visit Pat. She opens the door, then sullenly turns, walks to her spotless living room, and sits in a chair across from a stylish but uncomfortable, high-backed beige couch.

I sit on the edge of the couch. "Pat, we need to get past this. It's hard on the whole family when one of us is . . ." I don't know what to say to get a conversation going without setting off an ugly emotional scene all over again.

She fixes her eyes on mine, frowning. At the word "family," she stiffens and looks away. With a cold, rough voice, she says, "I try, you know, but I'm just not a caregiver." She emphasizes the last word as if it's distasteful and beneath her.

Too quickly I say, "Being a caregiver isn't a personality trait, it's a choice."

"Maybe for you it is, but I'm just not a patient person, never have been." She grimaces as she continues, "And noise is very upsetting to me."

I stop myself before retorting that maybe it's not always about her. I knew this conversation would be difficult. I want her to think about her part in the family, not play defense, so I pick up on the "noise" issue and twist it into a different approach. "I admit, being part of a family can be trying, but there are benefits as well."

Her face softens a little, so I continue, "It's nice to have people around you know you can depend on." I feel absolutely slimy making such a gross reference to the free slave labor available to her if she'll just be a little nicer, a little more inviting to her relatives, but less tension in the family is worth a little slime.

"I do appreciate Butch. He's a good man, and so tall and classy."

"True." I'm hesitant to push too far, but I may not get a chance again. "You'd find Devon a good man, too, if you gave him a chance. He is Tricia's husband, after all, and your grandson-in-law!" I'm really going out on a limb here, but the only person she treats worse than my dad right now is my daughter's husband.

She wrinkles her nose and looks away.

"Couldn't you have just let it go when he shaved his head? He'll think you don't like him."

"I don't like him."

"But do you have to make it so clear all the time?"

She lifts her chin, frowns, takes a deep breath, and starts to answer but thinks better of it. Finally, with a sigh, she barely whispers, "I *guess* not."

That's a big step for her, so I choose to hope.

Only two days later, my daughter calls crying, unable to talk clearly.

"Tricia, calm down. You're not driving now, are you?"

"No, Mom. I pulled over."

I can hear her breathing as she struggles for control. "I just left Pat and Grandpa's house. Oh, she's so awful! Poor Grandpa!"

Oh, no. I thought I'd made some progress with Pat. "What happened?"

"Mom, it was crazy. When I drove up, she was outside watering her roses. Before I could even get out of the car or say 'hi' to her, she started yelling at me!"

"Yelling at you? For what?"

Hiccups interrupt her story. "She said that she knew I was not there to see her. She was really mad. I thought she was going to throw the water sprayer at me." Tricia pauses again to calm herself.

"I said I was there to see her too, but she told me to just go in and see my grandpa and not even talk to her. Mom, I could barely keep a cheerful face for him." She starts to sob again. "What have I done to her to make her act like this?"

"Oh, Tricia." I force myself to speak calmly, soothingly. "You did let Grandpa know you love him. You are doing the right thing. That's all you can do."

Tricia doesn't respond, but her breathing calms and the hiccups cease. I am heartsick—for my dad, and for Tricia.

Within six months, dementia overtakes my father. He has no way to stay engaged with the world besides staring out the window because most other activities make too much noise for Pat. He dies a year later at ninety-one.

Five years after my father's death, we stop at a rest area on our way to our family cabin for Pat's eightieth birthday. On that sunny, cool September afternoon, Pat steps out of our car, has a stroke, falls, and breaks her hip. The hip-replacement surgery doesn't go well, and the stroke leaves her with some dementia. In one swift event she is no longer able to take care of herself, physically or mentally.

Butch and I had agreed thirty-five years before to be trustees of my dad and Pat's estate. Her memory issues and physical disabilities are severe enough that we will be managing her care and her finances for the rest of her life.

While she recovers as much as she can, I am with her every day for weeks. We take care of her little Schnauzer, and arrange for her care at a skilled nursing center near our home so we can continue to help her when they've done all they can for her at the hospital.

One afternoon, when I arrive at her room, she looks particularly tired in her flimsy, blue print hospital gown. She leans her elbow on the side rail and holds out her hand to me. "I know this has been hard for you. You've been doing so much for me, being here every day, driving so far."

I'm stunned. She's never been this docile, and she's never been sincerely appreciative or recognized someone else's difficulties, that I can remember. Could the stroke have affected the "sympathy centers" in her brain?

We sit there for a moment, holding hands, then she drops my hand, looks at the ceiling, and pronounces, "But really, I am the one suffering. I have to lie here all day, in pain."

I surprise myself by not feeling hurt or disgusted at her selfishness. Really, any other response just wouldn't be Pat.

She lies there, bottom lip jutting out, a frown on her face as her stare bores holes in the ceiling. For heaven's sake! She looks like a pouty little child.

She is often childlike: her temper tantrums, the way she takes care of her own needs without concern for the needs of others. Still, I expect her to be a mother, to act unselfishly as a mother would, because she took on that role when she married my dad.

Or did she?

Tension is gently sucked out of me. I feel hollow. She has fallen asleep clutching her hands together below her chin. My hollowness fills with softness and warmth as I realize the mistake I've made. A mistake I can fix.

"I can't fix her, but I can fix me," I whisper. Tears stream, but they don't sting inside like tears of anger or grief. These are tears of relief, tears that cleanse.

I gave her the role of mother. Furthermore, I based the requirements of that role on my aunt who had gently, unselfishly raised me, who had put my needs ahead of hers, and who died fifteen years ago when I still needed her.

Pat was almost forty with an established career as a university administrator when she married a man with a nineteen-year-old daughter. She'd never felt the unselfishness and deep love real mothering requires. She'd based her whole life on her own needs and wants.

I'd been trying all these years, especially since my aunt died, to force Pat into a mother role, to set expectations for her, to expect her to fill a commitment she didn't make. Without the emotional baggage of those expectations, I could have accepted who she was, warts and all, thereby finding peace myself.

I might have seized the opportunity to show my kids the elegant art of accepting difficult people with grace and loving them unconditionally, instead of teaching them to feel sorry for themselves when Pat mistreated them.

Relief overcomes regret as I sit against the cold pane of glass behind the windowseat next to Pat as she snores and mutters in her restless sleep. The physical chill intensifies the sun's soft light as it soothes my soul.

Part 5 | *Reflections*

TAPESTRY OF GRACE

• • •

stephanie cassatly

Three teenagers exited the jetway into the gate area of the New Orleans International Airport where my parents, brother, and I waited anxiously. I was nine years old, standing close to my mother, waiting to welcome my two newly discovered half-sisters and half-brother.

The night before, my parents had sat my brother, Steve, and me down in our living room and carefully explained that my father had three children from a previous marriage who were coming to visit us for the first time. I felt something between excitement, as if a magician had just pulled a rabbit out of a hat, and confusion. *Why had my parents never mentioned any of this before and what other secrets could they be keeping from us?* This was my first awareness of the complexity of my family and my parents' sins of omission.

After my father introduced everyone, we five children, ranging in age from nine to fifteen, stood awkwardly in front of each other, trying to absorb our striking resemblances: thick dark hair, angled jawbones, and deep-set, almond-shaped eyes.

Back at our house, my three new half-siblings, Carlos, age fifteen, Annie, fourteen, and Susie, thirteen, sat on the sofa together while Steve, eleven, and I sat with our mother on a nearby love seat. My father, a handsome Cuban businessman, sat in a tall armchair amidst all of us, clumsily trying to drum up conversation while fidgeting with my Slinky on the coffee table. Shy and silent, we children were all data collecting, developing profiles, and trying to understand this new terrain.

"Tell me, Annie, do you like to play the piano?" my mother asked, knowing that their mother was a pianist and teacher.

"It's okay. I don't like to practice, though. It's boring." Annie twisted her long braid draping over her shoulder.

"That sounds familiar. Stephanie plays the guitar and hates to practice as well."

My mother leaned back so we kids could see each other. Our eyes met and then darted toward the carpet. Despite my mother's best intentions, our relationship could not be forced. We had to find our own way because we were old enough to know what was real and what was not.

"Steve can beat a fine rhythm on the drums," my father said.

"I can beat a fine rhythm on Susie's back," Carlos chimed in. We all laughed, grateful for some comic relief.

Taking Carlos's lead, my father picked up a pair of maracas from the coffee table. "Check out *this* rhythm." He began dancing in the middle of the room, tripping over himself, acting like a drunk doing the cha cha. Everyone howled. There he was, center stage and under the limelight he always enjoyed, making everyone laugh and temporarily diffusing the underlying discomfort I'm sure we all felt.

Later that evening, as my mother kissed Steve and me goodnight in my bedroom, she said, "It may feel strange at first, but they're part of our family. You'll see. It'll get easier with time."

More than strangeness, I felt tenderness toward my half-siblings, because I knew they were growing up without a father. But I wondered about my father—about his complete absence in three of his children's lives and his difficulty making things right. He'd abruptly dispelled my belief that all parents give their children an equal measure of love. I wondered for the first time if he could abandon me in the same way. His lighthearted humor now seemed like a form of denial or a small Band-Aid for a deep wound.

Carlos, Annie, and Susie occupied Steve's bedroom across the hall. After lights were turned off and doors pulled shut, we all lay awake next to our full-bloods, silent at first, letting the darkness finally relax our minds and release the tension of the day.

"They seem nice," I whispered to Steve.

"Yeah, it's weird, though. They look like us."

"Yeah, Annie looks like me and Susie looks like you. Carlos is a blend, don't you think?" I asked.

"Maybe. He seems kind of funny."

"Funny ha ha or funny weird?"

"Funny ha ha. Did you notice he laughs a lot like Dad?" Steve said.

"Sort of. Why do you think Dad never sees them?"

"No clue."

The weight of the question hung heavily between us.

I imagined that Susie, Annie, and Carlos must have been speaking similar words among themselves across the hall. My parents, finally alone in the den, were talking in muted tones, assessing the day's progress, until the sound of my mother's crying and father's angry voice broke through.

"It's the least we can do. You haven't paid alimony in years and she feeds them on food stamps," my mother pleaded.

"Why should I pay her anything? She's poisoned them against me."

"The children are innocent in all of this. You and I are the ones who must atone," she said, her voice cracking.

What were my parents guilty of? My stomach tightened, as it always did when they fought. I lay awake long after I could hear Steve's breath become regular with sleep. At nine, I did not understand the challenges or history of my parents' marriage. I only understood that they fought often, that there were secrets from the past, and that my mother seemed more invested in my half-siblings than my father.

This first visit with my half-siblings lasted a week. By the end of it, the five of us had found enough common ground to look forward to seeing each other again. Over the following summers and holidays, they came for longer visits, where we fell into some semblance of a rhythm. Steve and Carlos shared a passion for horseback riding and worked together for hours every day at the stable in front of our house. Carlos's sense of humor was infectious and Steve was drawn to him as the older brother he never had. Annie, Susie, and I played games, worked in the garden, and baked together. They were tender with me in my youthful awkwardness. The disparity between their lives and mine must have been striking to them, but if they felt any jealousy toward me, I never perceived it.

Little mention was ever made of their mother, though I was secretly curious about her. *Who was she? Why had she and my father divorced?* The only mention ever made of her was when my father angrily cursed her. Strangely, my mother always seemed to defend her. One day I asked my mother about her. She paused to gather her thoughts.

"Well, she is Cuban, like your father. She is a very accomplished pianist. They met when they were young and your father says she loves her music first and foremost."

"Is that why they divorced?"

"Your father wanted a homemaker who placed him first in life," she offered, gazing downward.

So Susie, Annie, and Carlos were growing up with a mother who focused on music and a father who was angry and absent. *How were these kids managing?*

Several years later, my father decided he wanted a younger secretary, not a homemaker, for a wife. Late in my high school years, after twenty years of marriage, my parents went through a bloody divorce, which left a large schism between my father and me. We did not speak for almost two years. I boycotted his wedding out of respect for my aggrieved mother, and joined the ranks of Susie, Annie, and Carlos as another child he was capable of writing off.

When it was time for me to choose a college, my mother serendipitously urged me to attend school in Atlanta, Georgia, just two hours from Augusta, where Annie, Susie, and Carlos lived.

In the second semester of my freshman year, Steve, who was attending college in New Orleans, surprised me with a visit. *How wonderful! A visit from home*, I thought, as he appeared in my dormitory. But in a flash, his stricken face registered. On unsteady ground, I asked, "What is it?"

He took my elbow and guided me into my dorm room, closing the door behind us. "Mom's been shot. She's gone." It was a convenience store holdup by a drug-crazed addict stealing money for his next fix. She was in the wrong place at the wrong time.

After my mother's funeral, I returned to Atlanta alone to try to find a new normal, but that no longer existed. Disoriented and bereft, with Steve still back in New Orleans, I felt as if I had been dropped off a train in a strange land, blindfolded, with no ticket to return home. Annie, however, the older of my half-sisters, had received a phone call from our mutual aunt, my father's sister, telling her about my mother's death. She began showing up in my life. She frequently drove two hours to Atlanta for weekends, or I would hop a Greyhound bus with my guitar in tow to spend a holiday with her and my other half-siblings in her small apartment. They reached out in a hundred small ways, each one a vital life preserver. The age gap between us slowly closed as I accepted a new vision of my family.

My father, now fifty-five, with two ex-wives and two sets of children with whom he rarely communicated, relocated with his new wife to Hong Kong for his work. Perhaps because I was the youngest or most in need of parenting, I tried to compartmentalize my hurt and made peace with my father before he left. To his credit, he rose to the occasion by including me in his new life. Although I was unwilling to call her my stepmother, his new wife embraced me as well. Whether or not her grace was born of the same guilt for which my mother had reached out to Annie, Susie, and Carlos, I chose to feel it was genuine and that perhaps she could be woven into my life.

Just as travel can expand the mind, my father and his new wife's invitation to visit them in Hong Kong also expanded my heart and broke down barriers. I was twenty-four and granted a leave of absence from my job in Atlanta. During the days, when my father worked, my stepmother and I traveled to strange seaside markets, Buddhist temples, and into the New Territories of Red China. We developed an elusive but lasting friendship that provided a bridge, not only in age but also in communication, between my father and me.

Toward the end of my visit, my father and stepmother announced they were having a baby. This was the first of two pregnancies that would introduce two younger half-sisters, Heather and Holly, into my life. By now I was beginning to think I needed a flowchart for people who asked about my messy and confusing family, so I frequently skimmed over the details of three marriages, multiple affairs, two divorces, three sets of children, and a murder.

Eventually my father and his new family returned from Hong Kong and settled in Connecticut, close to New York City, where I had moved with my new husband. My career in advertising had blossomed and I worked sixty hours per week, but on the weekends and holidays we welcomed a break from city life and drove out to visit my father, stepmother, Heather, and Holly. I saw with wonder how the girls shared similar physical traits with the rest of my siblings and me. Young and oblivious to our family history, they accepted me freely, as I did them. Perhaps because of our age difference—they could have been my daughters—there was no jealousy, only love. I reveled in having two younger siblings, fed them, baked and played with them, giggled, and even changed their diapers when they were little. My husband and I were asked to be Holly's godparents, an honor we took to heart.

When Heather was in kindergarten, my stepmother arranged for me to take her to school one day and spend the morning. I entered the classroom holding Heather's hand and introduced myself to her teacher. "Hi, I'm Heather's sister, here to visit this morning."

"You mean her aunt?" she said, not so much a question as a declaration.

"No, actually I'm her older half-sister . . . it's complicated," I stammered. "I hope it's okay for me to stay a bit." I had decided early on not to label, and somehow limit, my love for my siblings by using the word "half." Inevitably, though, I had to explain or else tolerate quiet looks of confusion.

"Oh certainly, of course." Her face flushed as she guided me over to Heather's cubby, where Heather was intently unpacking her crayons from her backpack.

Shortly, I was sitting next to Heather, our bodies touching, in circle time. We listened to *The Very Hungry Caterpillar* and sang unabashedly as we did the hand motions to "The Wheels on the Bus," both of us smiling ear to ear.

Tragedy struck again, however. When my father was just fifty-nine, he was diagnosed with pancreatic cancer and died within a few short months. Heather and Holly were five and three. On his deathbed, he held my hand and pleaded, "Please do not forget about them. They don't have anyone else."

Soon to be an orphan and still feeling like a child myself, I promised I would do my best.

Despite some softening through illness and age, my father delivered his final blow to Annie, Susie, and Carlos at his own funeral. A business friend read the eulogy my father helped him write before he died. At the very end, after espousing all my father's business accomplishments, he named my father's survivors—everyone except Annie, Susie, and Carlos. All seven of us sitting in the front row were stunned by this omission. Although I had been named, I was sickened with disappointment in him and brokenhearted for my older half-siblings. Carlos and Annie appeared stoic, or maybe just hardened after so many years of feeling invisible in their father's eyes. But Susie promptly tumbled out of her pew, ran from the chapel to her car, and broke down in uncontrollable, heaving sobs. Carlos, Annie, Steve, and I followed her out to the parking lot. We stood huddled together on a cold winter day, speechless, each one touching Susie, trying to help her catch her breath, supporting her—and each other. *Had my father simply forgotten to include them? Was he that cruel?* How strange that through his neglect, or in spite of it, he had brought us all together.

Soon after my father passed, my husband's work took us to Florida, but I stayed in touch with my stepmother and younger half-sisters, visiting them whenever I could. When the girls were finally old enough, they traveled to see me for occasional summer and holiday visits. Yet, as if some curse continued, Heather and Holly suffered an even earlier loss of both parents than I had. When they were fourteen and seventeen, their mother finally succumbed to late-stage breast cancer. I was gutted by their sorrow, as if it were mine all over again, and I wondered if I had the stamina to help them in any way.

At their mother's funeral, I sat with Heather and Holly in the front row of the church. After so much loss, I contemplated the notion of poetic justice, because the only parent still alive was my father's first wife. She decided to have the girls move in with close neighbor friends and finish high school in Connecticut. I couldn't help feeling I had somehow failed my half-sisters by not bringing them to live with me, but I renewed the promise I had made to my father by visiting them more frequently and calling them on a weekly basis.

At thirty years old, with two young daughters of my own, it was as if I were standing outside a long dark tunnel, looking at Heather and Holly walking toward me from the other end. Just as I had traversed a decade of my own grief and darkness, they were beginning their journey of healing. As Annie and my other older half-siblings had done for me, I would do what I could for them.

When they were in college, I invited Heather and Holly to spend summer vacations with me in Florida. Heather worked in my husband's office, while Holly took online classes from my home. One day, Holly asked me, "Do you have any old family recipes? I really want to learn how to make black beans and rice, *ropa vieja*, and *flan* like my mom did."

In fact, I did, from our father's Cuban heritage. Within the hour we were buying saffron, bay leaves, and other necessary ingredients.

Later at the stove, as if the aroma was conjuring spirits, Holly put her arm around me.

"Even though I don't really remember Dad," she said, "there is something about cooking this food with you that makes me feel connected to family."

I pulled her into my arms, thinking my heart might burst. On that evening, and many more, the stove became a conduit for connecting us to our mutual roots.

Over three decades have passed since I lost my mother, two decades since my father, and one decade since my stepmother. After all the losses, and perhaps because of them, these tragedies have helped my half-siblings and me exonerate each other from jealousy or guilt for the sins of our parents. What have endured beyond all measure and reason are a certain love and respect among us, where relation labels, age, and the amount of blood we share are secondary to the experiences and relationships we choose, or do not choose, to create.

It would be dishonest to say that we all came through our fractured family experiences unscathed, but we all make the effort, to the best of our abilities, to separate the choices our mutual father and different mothers made from those we make for ourselves.

Although we are scattered throughout the world, we have shared occasional birthdays, holidays, vacations, graduations, weddings, and funerals. We now range in age from twenty-four to fifty-eight and are a colorful and intricate tapestry, woven over several generations from a messy spool of thread. My connection to this untraditional family is steadfast. We gather around each other's kitchen tables, cabins in the country or at the lake, at hotels—just about anywhere—for laughter and tears, always in the spirit of grace.

A TALE OF TWO STEPDAUGHTERS

• • •

amy hudock

Chloe walks away from the car, turns, gives me a half smile, then straightens her shoulders and hitches up her backpack, slung low over one arm. I stand, waiting in front of her new dorm, not sure what to do.

"Do you want me to come with you?"

"No, I can do this."

I watch her as she goes, until she is out of sight. Like a plane lifting into the air, I feel a moment of weightlessness and find it hard to breathe—she is so beautiful and strong. Her wheels are pulling up as she rises into her new skies. The possibilities in front of her stun me.

I wish her mother were here to see it, the girl becoming a woman. It's something a mother should see. My chest tightens, and I feel a sob building. I am merely the stepmom, and I feel that I am gobbling up glory that I don't deserve.

Her mother and father couldn't be here, so I have just helped her move into her dorm. I am the backup person, the default, the consolation prize. Chloe would much rather have one of her parents here with her. I know this. But I know if it weren't for me, she would be making the transition to college living with no parental-type person at all. So, I guess I am better than nothing.

Earlier, we drove from Charleston to the University of South Carolina campus in Columbia in three cars—Chloe, her friend, and I. We carried boxes and shoved them in all the open spaces of the dorm room. I took her and her friend to lunch. And we went to Target to buy some new bedding to fit her tiny dorm room. To buy something to cover these awful walls, to get a lamp, to make it a bit more like home. Then, we unpacked, rearranged, organized. I acted the role of mother to a stepdaughter who sees me as an older friend, perhaps the only time in our relationship that I have acted the role of "mother."

She was a senior in high school and on the way out of the house when I married her father. She worked, went to school, had a boyfriend, lived half the time with her mother. She breezed through the house at odd hours, a teenager rushing to become an adult. The only real time we spent together happened because of horses. I am a rider, and I own two horses. Chloe took lessons for years before I ever met her, and had developed into a good equestrian. When I could, I tried to get her to come to the barn with me. There, we had something in common. There, we had something to talk about. There, we had the horses to act as a bridge between us.

Once, we went to Burger King after riding. She was in a vegetarian phase, and I remembered from my vegetarian years that they had a decent veggie burger. We sat, sipping our sweet iced tea and eating our veggie burgers, bathed in the scent of cooking meat and frying potatoes, and we had our first real conversation. About her childhood. About her parents' divorce. About her conflict with her mother.

About her own future. I can't repeat that conversation because it would break the code of privacy I know she would want honored. It's not my story to tell. But I saw her differently after that. I saw her more as a whole person, someone who had depth and character and strength, rather than the cardboard teenager she had become in my mind. I also learned that I mattered to her, that I made a difference in her life. I didn't expect that. And I felt honored.

But, ultimately, it didn't change the fact that she has a mother, and although I know I make some kind of difference, I am peripheral to her life. I have accepted that role—until now. Today, I get a center seat. And I find that I am crying.

Because this isn't the first time I have felt this. Or done this. You see, Chloe was not my first teenage stepdaughter. I had one before. And her name was Phyllis. I was married to her father years before, in a place far away. She had lost her mother to cancer, and when I met her, she herself was fifteen years old and not well. She was struggling to come to terms with her mother's death, and she was losing herself to eating disorders. Despite all that was difficult in her father, he knew he couldn't care for her alone. He needed help. And I lived next door.

I found her standing in the road one day. Her face was gray, she was sweating, and I could smell bile. I imagined she had recently thrown up. I took her hands and had her sit down on a rock alongside the road, and we talked for hours. About her dead mother. About her dead grandmother (who had helped raise her). About school. About everything. She was so far gone, she couldn't even cry. I simply listened, and it seemed to help. From then on, she came to my house. We drank tea together, and I tried to help even more.

Eventually, I became her stepmother, a role I had not imagined for myself. But there I was. Together through two years of a difficult marriage, me giving birth to a little girl, her healing from eating disorders. I cooked for her, took her to doctor appointments, helped teach her to drive, protected her. I watched her grieve her mother. She loved me. She needed me. In fact, I once traveled to North Carolina to visit my family, and she called every day, begging me to come home. I left early for her. Yet, regardless of the primary role I took in her life, I felt that in the comparison between her memories of her mother and realities of me, I came up short. But I didn't mind. I forgave her everything because she was a motherless child who had lost her way. And I wanted to save her.

Unfortunately, the marriage was ill chosen from the start. I stayed long enough to get Phyllis out of the house, into college, and on her own. I couldn't stay longer. But I couldn't leave until she was out and on her own. I wanted her to be safe.

When she started packing her bags to become a freshman at the University of California, Berkeley, I was packing to go teach at the University of South Carolina. One day, before I got on a plane to cross the country back from California to South Carolina, I drove her to the UCB campus for her college orientation. I pulled up alongside the campus so she could hop out of the car.

"Do you want me to park and come with you?"

"No. I can do this."

She got out of the car, turned, gave me a half smile, then straightened her shoulders and hitched up her backpack, slung low over one arm. She turned her face toward Sproul Plaza and all the possibilities there. She walked away, so strong and beautiful, and never looked back. And I felt a moment of weightlessness, and I couldn't breathe. I cried and talked to her mother, hoping that somehow she could hear me, so she would know that her girl was going to be okay. That she was healing. That she was out on her own now. That she had made it. I wanted her to know that despite all that had happened, her girl would be okay.

That Thanksgiving, Phyllis came to visit my family and me in North Carolina. I drove in the middle of the night to pick her up from the Greenville airport and bring her back to my hometown of Kinston. As she came off the plane into the humidity of the South, she smiled at me as if I were a birthday present, wrapped and sitting next to a cake. We hugged, and she said, "You are my family. You make me feel like home." I still have a framed picture of that holiday. In it, Phyllis is walking through a soybean field close to my father's house. Her little half-sister, Sarah, is following behind her, trying to walk in her muddy footprints. They are both smiling and looking forward, as if to keep walking forever.

A year later, Phyllis and I would no longer be speaking. In a conflict between her father and me, her father required that she choose between us. I never required that of her, but he did. She chose blood and took her father's side. And I felt the difference that blood makes. She called to tell me, "I never want to talk to you again," and as I heard those words, I sank down to the cheap kitchen linoleum of my rented house thousands of miles away from her, feeling the distance between us crystallize, become brittle and finite. The phone went dead, and in the silence I curled up on the floor and cried. Despite all that happened, despite all that I gave, all that I became to her, I was still only the stepmother, and I was not necessary.

I honored her request to never contact her again—so much in her life was out of her control. I wanted her to be a willing participant in any relationship we might have. But back then, and still now, years later, she has not chosen me. I go online to find glimpses of her as I track her from college, then to one graduate school, and then to another, lurking in the unseen ether of her life. I hope she is happy, and that she has found peace with her past and inspiration for her future. I wish only the best for her, my stepdaughter, the child who was not of my blood but stays in my heart.

My two teenaged stepdaughters have taught me some important lessons. I wish I could say that I learned that the love between stepparents and children is magical and wonderful and that it's the same as the love of a biological family. But I have to be honest, and say that I learned that, at least for me, it isn't.

I learned that it's not about me. It's never about me. It's always about the mother I am not. In both situations, one where the biological mother had died, the other in which she had been divorced, I was simply a placeholder for the absent mother. The mother role is so large, so encompassing of hope and desire and hurt and love and pain, that even a biological mother has problems filling it. A stepmother evokes the role, but can't fill it. In trying, I felt the longings of a mother, to love and be loved, to care and be cared for, and I believe my stepdaughters, in their own ways, reached out to me at different times in an effort to make me into their mother. But, ultimately, we failed, not because we didn't try, not because we didn't love, but because the distance between the ideal of mother and the reality of stepmother was too great.

However, once in a while, the blazing glory of a shared moment washes out the shadow of the absent mother, the stepmother/daughter roles, and the stepmother and stepdaughter can see each other more clearly, with more focus. And it is those moments, as few and far between as they are, that make being a stepmother worth the stress of blending families, facing the mother-stepmother conflict, and accepting my own insignificance. I remember those moments, like when I took my stepdaughters to college, as some of the most important of my life. I may have birthed a child with my body, but I helped birth these two girls into the larger world. I wasn't there when they took their first steps, or got their periods, or went on their first dates, but I watched them take their first leaps into independence. I helped make it happen. And for that, I will always be proud. I will always love. I will always be their stepmother and, in some small ways, a mother to them.

NIGHTSHADE LOVE

• • •

nancy antonietti

An extended family gathers to send off their child. Lingering goodbyes are fraught with emotion and promises to reunite soon. A military deployment scene, perhaps? What if I told you it was the end of a four-year-old's day?

I recently attended a concert at my son's preschool. Few feelings compare with watching your four-year-old belt out a song with all his heart. As only a parent can, I discerned his sweet voice above the chorus, and my soul sang along.

As the evening ended, something captured my attention. The various age groups at this preschool were assigned to classes named after different fruits. A friend of Nick's, whom he called Krysty Blueberry, stood outside her classroom with quite an entourage. Krysty's mother had once confided to me at pickup that she was divorced, derision for her former husband bulging in her words. Both of

Krysty's estranged parents had attended the concert that evening, as well as a set of grandparents on the mother's side. It was the father's night to take Krysty, and the "losing" family members were carrying on like bad actors in a third-rate production. Their overdone sentimentality would have been comical if I didn't know the lasting effect it could have. As Krysty's father stood five feet away, holding his daughter's jacket and lunchbox, the others took turns kissing and hugging Krysty goodbye.

"We'll see you soon, darling," the grandmother said, smothering Krysty's face in her bosom.

"Mommy will come pick you up tomorrow, honey," the mother cooed, taking Krysty's hand while the grandmother continued to hold her captive.

When the grandmother finally released Krysty, I saw the father take a step forward. But the mother still had hold of her hand, and as the little girl started toward her dad, the mother exerted a steady pressure to pull her back.

"Mommy's going to miss you, baby," she said, and kissed Krysty's hand.

The father then took two steps toward them and held the jacket out to his daughter. But his ex-wife still was not done. She reached out to brush a strand of hair off Krysty's forehead and smooth it back behind her ear.

"You be a good girl, now, and I'll see you before you know it," the mother said.

The father raised his head and inhaled a breath of self-control at the insinuation that the visit with him was a hardship to be endured. Who would pay this much attention to another family's goodbye, you might ask? Probably only someone who had lived through the same situation. Watching Krysty and her family, I was transported to a similar incident thirty-four years ago. My dad had come to take me for a court-awarded visitation with him, my stepmother, and my new baby brother. Upon entering the house in which I'd lived since my mother died three months after giving birth to me, Dad spoke to my grandfather for a bit, then came into the living room. I was sitting on the floor doing my favorite board puzzle. My father gave me a hug, then said he had to use the bathroom and we'd leave when he was done.

I continued to play quietly while he passed into the next room. I turned each wooden puzzle piece by the little red knob in its center, putting them in their places to form a picture of a mother bear and her cub. The mother was carrying a picnic basket, and the piece that would have been her right leg was missing.

My grandma came into the room and found me working on the puzzle. "Honey, you don't have to go this weekend, if you don't want to," she said, and I remember it clearly because of the queer look on her face. It wasn't her usual expression. Her lips stretched thin, and her eyes opened wide. "We're planning to go out for pizza, and to the drive-in. You could stay and come with us." Something else was out of the ordinary. Ma's voice had a singsong quality to it, coming out a little louder than usual, inflecting and stretching the words so that they seemed to have an extra-special importance today and required more of her breath. This confused me, and I didn't answer, but concentrated on the wooden shapes in my hands.

Of course I was going. Ma had already helped me change into my good clothes. While four years later she still wore black for my mother, the young daughter she had lost, Ma fashioned brightly colored clothes for me. She had made the pleated skirt that I wore, and its matching red jacket, on the old sewing machine that sat beside the television set. The sewing machine popped out of a small table when you opened the hinged top, which I thought was the neatest thing.

At this point, through the thin wall, I heard the toilet flush. My grandma stiffened beside me, and her abrupt straightening caused me to look up at her. Her face had turned a funny color and her nostrils opened up as she breathed in.

The door opened and my dad strode out, wiping his damp hands on his pants. I wanted him to smile at me, but he didn't. Silent, he held out his hand. I stood up and slid toward him, my bare knees pocked with the imprints of the carpet fibers. When I didn't give him my hand, he put his outstretched one on my shoulder. The skin on my neck felt hot and prickly, and I didn't feel as if I needed the jacket that lay on top of my weekend bag. We took it anyway.

That's why I can relate to Krysty. Although she is not being told in words that her dad is a bad guy, she is definitely getting the message. Krysty walks to her father, her steps slow and halting, the divide magnified to the width of a canyon rather than simply a few of her small strides. She looks back over her shoulder for reassurance that she doesn't get. Krysty has many years of this routine of goodbyes left, and the effects will accumulate. I hope that she will be able to see through this manipulation and not allow it to color her perception of her father. But I doubt it.

Manipulation, a strong word. Is it warranted to accuse these loving relatives of such behavior? The real question is, is this a willful manipulation? Do they engage in this subtle slander, this emotional abuse, consciously? And that is a big question. One would think that an adult would be smarter than to do that, more heedful of the best interests of the child than of his or her own. But, as I've told my teen and preteen sons, sometimes grown-ups don't act very grown-up.

What could the adults possibly hope to gain by placing the child in the middle of their conflict? More of the child's love? Impossible. The child's love is already boundless, infinite. Perhaps the adults seek a greater percentage of the child's love than is allotted to the other "team"? As if love were a game, with points to be hoarded?

Why do I speak so harshly? Surely there are worse fates than to be wanted too much. Well, here's the rub. My childhood played out amidst the same animosity that swirls around Krysty, between the most important people in my life, my father and my stepmother, and the people who raised me until I was five, my grandparents. Although I was not yet fluent in the words the world uses, I was nonetheless very emotionally attuned to these adults I loved and trusted. I suffered the constant anxiety of my belief that by not renouncing one set of parents I was displeasing the other. A child is not equipped to make heads or tails of such a situation, and into that void of misunderstanding creeps guilt that can ruin relationships.

There is a photograph of me taken outside my dad's church on a May morning in 1978. I am wearing the lacy white dress of a Catholic girl's First Holy Communion. My grandparents are standing on either side of me. The smile on my face engages my lips only. I hold my arms stiffly at my sides, my shoulders square with the tension of knowing that my grandparents must feel unwelcome and that there is nothing I can do to help them. They have driven over an hour to sit on a hard, cold pew for the ceremony, but they are certainly not invited to the dinner party that will follow. I remember, at age eight, sweating over this impoliteness.

In another instance, my grandparents were anticipating a court-ordered weekend visitation, but after driving to Methuen at the appointed time on Saturday and then again on Sunday to try to pick me up, both times they had gone back to Gloucester alone. They hadn't found anyone at my dad's house, because he had taken me away, not willing to change his plans for his family's weekend in order to accommodate the visitation for my grandparents. I don't recall where my father brought me that weekend, but I do remember that Ma and Pa came to my elementary school early the following Monday morning, probably wanting to make sure that I was whole and safe and well. They had had absolutely no contact with my dad or explanation for my absence. My first-grade teacher, a young woman who shimmered in the glow of my adoration, let them sit with me for a while.

"Your grandparents love you very much," my teacher said when they had gone. I already knew that.

Conversely, on more than one Sunday afternoon when I was over-due to have been returned to my dad, I remember the phone at my grandparents' house shrilling unanswered in the hall. Listening to it, my insides were twisting, because each loud ring accused me of my complicit betrayal. After all, I was not screaming and kicking to be brought home; I went along with the pretense that it was okay for me to stay with them for another few hours.

What is amazing to me, looking back as an adult, is how tied-in I was at the tender age of eight to the emotional undercurrents of these experiences. Whether the issue of right or wrong was ever addressed with me directly or not, I was aware of it. Definitely.

That set of experiences led to a very dysfunctional relationship between my dad and me that had been oh-so-delicately painted in shades of negativity. I have a recurring dream in which I'm at a family function and I have to scurry between the table where my parents sit and the one at which my grandparents are seated, scrupulously met-ing out my attention. In my waking hours, my dad was so hurt by my continued allegiance to my grandparents that he forbade me to stand by the window and wait for them on the mornings that they would come to reclaim me. From repeated comments directed my way, he made it clear that he didn't want me to acquire, through prolonged exposure, the qualities he despised in my grandparents. I took his concern to mean that he already saw me as tainted by my association with them, interpreted his watchfulness as judgment, and felt I never got a passing grade. I remember trying to portray myself in a better light whenever I could, believing that deflecting the blame for my childish misbehaviors would make him more likely to love me, when

in fact I was reinforcing his perception that I was as prone to pre-
varication as my grandmother. These feelings were the basis for our
troubled relationship as I grew into early adulthood.

If I had chosen to try to figure out who was wrong and who was
right, I could have cut myself off from one side of my family at age
eighteen, when the allotment of my time was no longer under the
jurisdiction of the courts. That would have extended the circle of
pain to many more people: aunts, uncles, cousins. Instead, I found
peace by realizing that most people act in a way they can justify. They
may react to what they feel has been done to them, and then their
behaviors escalate, but they each think they are doing their best with
the circumstances that exist. Looking at the situation that way, I recognized that there was culpability in the actions, without condemn-
ing the people. I was able to continue to love both sets of "parents" in
spite of the hurt they inflicted on me and on each other.

But my relationship with my father had been fractured beyond
what we had the emotional capacity to completely repair. Besides an
infrequent "I love you," the most expressive statement I ever made to
him was after I had driven him to one of his doctors' appointments
when his health began to fail. After a day at Mass General Hospital, we went out for dinner and shared some great conversation. I
basked, that afternoon, in his company. When I dropped him off at
home, I called him back to me as he walked down his driveway. "Hey,
Dad? I really enjoyed spending the day with you." It may have seemed
anticlimactic to the ordinary person.

With the understanding that I have grown into, my nightmares
have stopped. My dad was fun-loving, kind, generous, and very
tolerant, I realize in retrospect, to have put up with the way he was
portrayed to his own daughter. Unfortunately, I lost my dad to his
illness before we could totally overcome the damage.

As Krysty's mother and grandparents followed her out to the
parking lot, my heart ached for this little girl who was just beginning

to recognize the nuances in the attention being paid to her. Even another adult might not see it, for the scene appears innocent to someone who doesn't feel what she feels. In fact, this little girl might be envied as someone who has so much love in her life. Don't be fooled. This kind of love is like nightshade, beautiful to behold, but unquestionably dangerous.

Through the plate-glass windows of the preschool, I watched Krysty get buckled into her dad's SUV. I said a prayer for her, that her family would become mindful of the effects their conduct could have on her, and that she and her father would enjoy their precious time together. Scooping up my own little boy, I prayed that Krysty would find her way.

IN AND OUT OF STEP

• • •

candace walsh

On the subject of stepfamily, I used to be more pessimistic than not. In every other area of my life, I'm a bouncing, furry ball of puppy-like enthusiasm and optimism. But when it came to the step experience, I had a tendency to be as crusty, tough, and resigned as the owner of a biker bar right before the 684th fight breaks out. Luckily, life has handed me some grounds to reconsider.

After years of frustration, disrespect, and two-facedness, I've given up on having any kind of relationship with my stepmother. I don't talk to stepfather number one (because he almost choked me to death) or stepfather number two (because we don't have anything in common). Stepfather number three is a sweetheart, but given that I'm forty-one and live thousands of miles from immediate family, it's not like he has a meaningful presence in my life. My ex-husband's new girlfriends have also come on the scene all friendly and talking the evolved blended family talk, but both times, the dynamic has soured.

"Why were my stepparents so nightmarish?" I asked my therapist once.

"When people with issues divorce, they attract more people with issues," she said. Instead of containing their dysfunction as a married couple, my mom and dad doubled it when they hit the singles circuit post-divorce.

One of my pet theories is that when people get married the first time, they are attempting to step into an aspirational reality of the best life they can imagine. They're being guided by what they want to be. They find others who reflect back that same idealism. But when they go out looking for number two while they're bitter and disenchanted, dug into the negative characteristics that contributed to the end of marriage number one, they end up clicking with other bitter, disenchanted people.

Are you thinking about becoming a stepparent? Here's a news flash for you. You will find it tiring and you will feel underappreciated. You will tell kids to pick up their socks, turn off the lights, wipe their mouths, wash their hands, say please, close the fridge, put their bowl in the sink, and promise never to clean their rooms by shoving everything under the bed again. And again. And again. You're going to feel resentful about sharing your partner. You're going to dislike that the kids have their mother's or father's eyes or nose or mouth or jawline. You're going to be told, "You're not my mom/dad." You're going to spend money or other resources on them, and they will not appreciate it enough. When you lose your temper, your partner will get more upset with you than they would the kids' other biological parent.

Stepparents often complain that they're not treated like real parents. Well, guess what? That repetitive, day-in, day-out grind *is* the life of a real parent. Biological parents have learned to refine their vision, to see, notice, appreciate the subtle thanks, the benefits, the gratifications of parenthood: a small sticky hand stroking your arm unexpectedly, the trust communicated when a child falls asleep in your arms, a crayoned, uncommissioned portrait of you that looks more like a grinning praying mantis. The way that a kid sings along in the car with you to a catchy song on the radio, or starts saying one of your signature expressions, or loves your green chile tortilla casserole. They'll be more honest with you than you're accustomed to, because they trust you and haven't figured out how to be false-to-be-kind yet.

Stepparents have to change their expectations as well. If they expect kids to be as effusive as their BFFs or a business colleague, they'll be disappointed. One of the joys of being a kid is accepting crucial nurture without having to write thank-you notes in return.

You have to be all that a parent is, but you don't get the halo. Nobody gets "Stepmama" tattooed in a heart on a kid's bicep.

You also don't inherit the lifelong heartache that parents develop the second their children are born; the constant hum of worried love that never really goes away, flaring up with the advent of a mysterious bump or symptom, dying down to glowing embers when the children are in their presence, the picture of health.

When my daughter evaded a near-kidnapping at the playground, my ex's former girlfriend was upset—but not because we almost lost our child. She was upset because it happened on her birthday. My mother was hysterical on the East Coast and needed to be sedated by her doctor, I was crying and traumatized for months, my daughter's dad was deeply freaked out, but his serious girlfriend, who had spent thousands of hours with the kids, was primarily pissed off that this event disrupted her special day.

You might love their dad or mom, but you need to get over yourself. Soldiers don't get all pouty and huffy about having to wear the uniform, go into battle, hump pounds of equipment, and eat shitty food during their tour of duty. They signed up for it. They took the time to research what they were getting into, and if they skipped that step, nobody feels sorry for them.

It's your job to sort it out on your own time, not to take it out on the kids. It comes with the territory and it will never change. I'm not trying to say it's easy to be a stepparent. It's probably harder than being a biological parent at times. So unless you are really committed to doing it right, to making it your spiritual practice, don't get involved with a parent. It's like being a surgeon. If you open up that child's heart, you can really do some lasting damage unless you're conscious, aware, strong, and driven by good, healing intentions. Love is not going to conquer all. Being a stepparent will pull every ugly, unresolved scab off your soul, dip it in hot sauce, and stick it up your nostril. So have your self-help books, your journal, your friend-to-vent-to, your therapist, and your self-care in place.

I also have these hard-won observations in the form of a don'ts list.

Don't come between your partner and the kids. You might win in the short term, but it's an ugly, ugly thing to do and the karma will make you wish you were never born (in your next life, when your soul finds itself in the body of a dung beetle).

Don't pretend to like the kids if you really don't. They will pick up on it on some deep level, and spend a big portion of their lives confused about what love is supposed to feel like.

Don't throw the other parent under the bus. When the kids come to you complaining about their mom or dad (your partner's ex), sympathize with them. Kids have the potential to pit parents and stepparents against each other, to misrepresent situations. Don't let them run with it.

Don't be unpleasant or rude to your partner's ex. Treat him or her the way you would treat your boss's friend. The kids aren't your bosses, but causing or fueling drama is a lose-lose situation. It stresses out the kids and makes you look bad. Stress is harmful to people's health, and interferes with these children's sense of inner peace and even ability to concentrate. If you can't engage in a healthy way with the other biological parent, don't engage at all. Leave the logistics and horse-trading to the two people who conceived these children in the first place.

Don't blame the kids for what their biological parents didn't teach them. Manners. Respect. Responsibility. Whatever. Bring it up with your partner, research what the kids are capable of developmentally, step up and fill in the blanks as a teacher and a parental figure.

Don't have your own kids with the parent and then start marginalizing the first batch. Love is not finite. There's plenty to go around and you don't have to hoard it.

Except for my mom's current husband, I was not a winner in the good stepdad and stepmom lotteries, which was especially difficult because my biological parents didn't really have their acts together when I was young. It would have been nice to have a "do-over" parental figure come in and be solid. I also didn't get lucky in the department of having a congenial relationship with my ex's partners. But one thing having step presences in my life has delivered: the ability to disengage from a relationship when it isn't promising. I am an expert at letting go, instead of throwing good money after bad, emotions-wise, hoping that people and dynamics will change.

Have I ever been a stepparent? No. But I have married one.

I didn't leave my first marriage bitter and disenchanted. I was sad and regretful, but also eager to live out the rest of my life with the blinders off, the gate flung open. That's a good part of the reason that my kids did win the stepmom lottery with my wife Laura.

She thinks that the kids have such a great relationship with her because she took things really slowly. I dated her for three months before introducing her to the kids. She was an unobtrusive presence, preferring to have a low-key role for quite a while. Her attentiveness picks up where mine leaves off; she makes sure the kids are signed up for swimming lessons, that their outgrown clothes are removed from their dresser drawers. She also reprimands them for ignoring me, tuning me out, or being disrespectful, when I'm too distracted to notice. Her love for me raises the bar on how the kids should behave.

And yes, she gets frustrated, but she's quick to remember what it felt like to be a kid, and to put herself in their shoes. Because Laura never shames them or makes them feel inadequate about how much they should be appreciating her, they abundantly appreciate her.

Laura and I felt so strongly about the children's importance in the formation of our family through marriage that we wrote them into our wedding ceremony.

I vowed: "Laura and I promise to give you a steady home filled with love. We know that you have built our family love nest as much as we have, and you have shown me what it means to love someone so deeply that you can't believe you ever lived your life without that person. We are happy that you will see our lives continue to intertwine through the coming years, that you will see us on good days and bad days, remain committed and patient, kind and connected. Laura and I promise to be there for you, to teach you and feed you and listen to you and hold you, and to help you discover your own true selves, where you find the most peace and happiness. We will always be there for you."

And Laura vowed: "Honorée and Nathaniel, we promise to respect you, love you, and care for you. We promise to try our best to teach you how to love, to trust, to respect, to learn, and to hope so that in good times and not-so-good times you will always have those impulses. We will tell you and show you both that you will always be appreciated and loved for who you are, and for who you are not. And we promise to nurture our little family so that we grow together, supporting each other no matter what, because together we are strong."

To us, anything less wouldn't add up to being a family.

But Laura and I do have certain privileges. As two women, we have a certain latitude in creating our family together. Why is that? We're not a man and a woman, coming together in a parental dyad, within the Template. The Template nudges women into one role, men into another—and to do things differently is to sit down and reinvent the paradigm. A single dad with kids is going to have a certain unspoken expectation of what role his new wife will play within his family. And a potential stepmom will often seek to fill those traditional mother's shoes without questioning or negotiating with the man she loves. She's not just taking on a new family; she's taking on the outlines of a female archetype.

So when stepparents find that these roles are irksome, they often blame it on being a stepparent, not being a parent, a person pressed into a restrictive familial role that requires them to give up autonomy, freedom, and gratification.

Because Laura and I don't have a context for how to create our roles, we do so consciously and tentatively. It's a series of experiments without too many assumptions, and we learn from each one, refining as we go. Sometimes she does the dishes, sometimes I do. I send the kids to her when they have astronomy questions and she sends them to me when the matter is hygiene related. If we were entrenched in gender roles, it would have been a lot easier for us to grow resentful about our inherited, not chosen, sets of responsibilities.

Do I think men and women, coupled together, can't accomplish the same level of ruminative role defining? No, I don't. Scores of couples are as conscious. They do have to choose to bring more consciousness to bear, given how automatic (how unlike choices!) the choices seem.

My relationship with Laura has caused me to reconsider my pessimism around stepfamily dynamics. It is possible to be a steady, reliable, and loving stepparent who isn't spitting-mad all the time. It is possible to be a child resting in the river of love flowing from three or four adults committed to that child's well-being.

I always wanted to give my kids what I didn't have: a happy family made up of Mom and Dad in an intact relationship. When that wasn't possible, I felt as if I had let them down. But in the end, my children ended up with something even better: Mom and Mom, plus Dad and Mom. "You have three moms?" my son's friend once asked incredulously. "No fair!"

STEP ON THE GRASS

• • •

cassie premo steele

As I write, a waning winter moon hangs before dawn out-side my window. A space heater hums to warm my studio, and a votive candle glows. The coffee is creamy and sweet at my elbow. The house is quiet, in this dark time, predawn, when I wake to do yoga and meditate and write. The subjects of my writing—my stepfather and my stepdaughter—are long gone. One is dead and the other has moved away. And I miss them. Daily.

At the beginning of the step-relationship, the future possibility of absence, of longing, of the empty space their leaving will create in your heart—all this is the furthest thing from your mind. When a step-person first comes into your life, he or she will appear to you as an intruder, an interloper, an invader of your peace and the plan you had for your life.

Invasion Scene One: I am in middle school and my mom, divorced since I was eight, has had a few dates with a guy from work. My sister and I call him Wedgie Man since his pants were too tight when he came over for lunch one Saturday and we had to look at his wedgie while he walked hand in hand with our mother in front of us.

She is about to go out on a date with him again, and I am standing at the top of the stairs of our suburban townhouse, yelling down to her at the front door. "I'm telling you, if you keep dating him, you are going to fall in love with him, and then you will F him, and then you will marry him, and then our lives will be ruined!"

That's pretty much what happened. To my thirteen-year-old mind, anyway.

Invasion Scene Two: I am grown and dating a man who has a three-year-old daughter. He lets her sit in the front seat when we go out to dinner (this was before the seat laws were passed for kids, but still) and I sit in the backseat and watch them as if I am a silent audience member at a movie. At one point, she leans over to him and stage whispers, "Daddy, you know what?"

"What?" he says.

"Cassie has greasy hair," she says, and they giggle. I am the nerd ostracized by the popular kids, and these popular kids have more power and cool than I will ever have.

And yet I stay. Six years later, he and I get married.

The story of how one negotiates the emotionally treacherous waters from those first scenes until where I am now—feeling unconditional love and deep peace and gratitude for the existence of both of these people in my life—is an important story to tell. Because there are too many wicked stepmothers in movies and real life. Too many evil stepfathers, too. And bratty stepkids. And broken families. Not just blended, but broken, inside and out.

Here are the steps, pardon the pun, that may help you navigate your way from the scenes of invasion to love: Grow, Recognize, Accept, Scare, and Sail. Together they form the acronym GRASS. As in, your ass is.

As my mother said to me before I got married and became a step-mother, "It's like you've been gypped. You know how hard parenting is now, so you can't have your own baby blindly thinking it'll be fun."

Grow Scene One: I read somewhere, back in the early years of dating the man with the young daughter, that I should never try to be her mother. Instead, I should think of myself as an aunt, someone supportive and kind but fairly distant. Let her come to me. Let him do the emotional work of parenting. Looking back, this was the first, best move I could have made. What it meant was that he could grow as a parent because I did not move in with him, which meant he had to do the laundry, the bathing, the bedtime, the grocery shopping, the caretaking that many men never do. He grew as a parent, she grew as a kid, and I grew two hundred miles away in graduate school for a few years.

Often we get into relationships with people because we hope they will heal us. Resist this. Grow first. Then marry.

Grow Scene Two: My stepfather loved to cook. One year in high school, before my mom had married him, he offered to cook dinner for a group of my friends before a big dance. He made his famous chili. There was music. People had fun. But he didn't socialize. He was shy. He stayed in the kitchen. One of my friends came up to me and said, "What's up with him? Why is he in the kitchen?"

"Leave him alone," I said. "He made the dinner."

I had enough sense, a few years after my screaming scene on the stairs, to know that he made my mom happy and he was a good guy, and never in a million years would my mom have said, "Sure, I'll cook for thirty of your friends." So I was growing to see what he could give me—could provide for me—as a man in my life.

And when you let someone Grow into who they can be, you can begin to recognize them for who they truly are.

Recognize Scene One: It wasn't all chili and parties with my stepfather. As a budding writer, I would often give him my poems to read and critique. He called them "mood pieces," which meant they were not poems at all. I resented this, and yet I enjoyed having a writer in the family. I saw that he was not publishing, maybe, as he'd always dreamed of doing, but this too was a lesson in recognition for me. At a level that lodged like a tiny arrow in my ribs, the message he gave me in criticizing my writing was, "Keep going. Get better. Don't be like me. Be better. Be a writer."

I did.

Recognize Scene Two: Soon I had finished all my coursework at the grad school two hundred miles from where the Man with the Kid lived, and we decided I would move in. We got engaged and set the date for two years from then, which would give me time to write my dissertation and graduate first. I wanted to be a PhD before a Mrs.

One morning, I was putting on makeup in the bathroom, and the Kid (who was now seven) looked at me and said, "Where are you going?"

"I'm going to Atlanta to meet with my dissertation committee," I said.

She paused, those big blue eyes looking at me, and asked, "Are you coming back?"

I crushed her into my arms and said, "Oh, yes, Kid, I'm only going for a few days. I'll be back. I'm not leaving permanently."

She loved me first. I gave her space and acted like an aunt for enough years for her to come to recognize me for who I was—and to love and accept that person.

Which leads, very quickly, to Acceptance.

Acceptance Scene One: When I published my first poem, one summer when I was living at home with my mom and stepfather in my early twenties, my stepfather went out and bought me a pair of Bass sandals. Bass was very "in" at the time, and as a broke grad student, I wouldn't have bought them for myself. I loved those shoes in a deep, deep way. They felt like an award to me. They were. They were the award he had given me as my stepfather, who was saying, "I am proud of you."

One morning I woke up and there was mud all over the shoes. My younger sister had worn them out clubbing the night before. The fight that ensued was not suitable for younger viewers. I beat the crap out of her. We weren't yet very enlightened as a family.

Acceptance Scene Two: Fast-forward four years. My husband and I are married, and we have just had a baby. My stepdaughter is eleven. She comes with her mom to the hospital to see us. She brings three things. One is a stuffed black cat for the baby because we have a cat named Kali at home and that is *her* cat and she wants the baby to have a cat too. The second thing is a book of art about motherhood, signed by both her and her mother. What this means is that we are all, truly, family now. The third thing is her violin. She plays for the baby, for the family, for all of us, right then and there. Later, my daughter's first words will be "Wawa," for her sister, Laura, and "wawawa," for the music that her sister plays on the violin.

"Now comes the scary part," as my high school boyfriend once said as an excuse to put his arm around me at a movie theater. The film was *Tootsie*.

Because this is what it means to be family: there is Growth and Recognition and Acceptance, but there is also a scary part.

Random Scary Scenes:

My stepfather and I get too drunk together at Thanksgiving.

My husband and I separate, and when I try to talk to my step-daughter on the phone, she won't talk to me.

My stepfather gets deathly ill, and when I bring my three-year-old daughter to visit him, she sits carefully on his bed so she doesn't knock over the oxygen tank, and he calls her his "sunshine."

My husband and I reunite and my stepdaughter says, "He was fine without you. He was over you."

My stepfather dies.

My stepdaughter isn't included in his obituary.

My stepdaughter leaves for college.

And this is when you reach the end of the treacherous waters. Your boat lands on the opposite shore just as your heart sets sail.

The thing about step-relationships is that at some level you *choose* them. You cannot blame biology or genetics or the repetition of generations. You choose to make a family with this person, and somewhere along the way, it happens. You become family. Which means you love them. But they hurt you. And you heal from it. And you are all crazy. But you laugh together. And then they get sick and leave and die. And it all happens so fast.

Sail Scene One: My mom was right, back when she said that being a stepmother would give me an inside scoop on mothering. I often say my stepdaughter trained me to be a good mother. Because she was not "mine." Because I had to be more careful. Because she had two other parents who did a wonderful job and I wanted to be a working member of that team.

But my stepdaughter taught me something else that many of my friends who have children my daughter's age do not yet know: they leave.

Kids leave. They leave for college or the army or a marriage or a job. And that's it.

They are gone.

Sure, they come back. Sometimes. And they call. Or text. But the house is empty without them. And if you have not been tending to your own soul—finding ways to Grow, Recognize, Accept, Scare, and Sail for yourself, you will be very lonely.

So, no matter what happens in your step-relationships, learn to step on the grass.

Sail Scene Two: When I asked my mother for a story about what she thought my stepfather meant in my life, she told me this: The day he helped take me to college for the first time was the proudest day of his life. He rented the U-Haul case to strap to the top of our little red Honda. He drove my mom and me to the middle of Virginia, and he helped me take my boxes to the third floor of the dormitory in the late August heat. And when they walked away, he told her he was so glad he was able to be there for me—because he had never been able to do this for his own son—and it was the proudest day of his life.

I had not known this. I burst into tears when she told me.

I remember, at the time, being annoyed at them in the way teenagers are, and wanting them to leave so I could unpack and listen to my music and get used to being alone.

I am crying now as the birds begin to chirp outside the window and the sky is lightening for the coming dawn, thinking of how much this story means to me. How I wish I could go back and be present for him in that moment. How I wish I could go back and say thank you. To both of them. My step-people. My family.

A STEP AT A TIME

• • •

marge piercy

My brother was married four times.
The middle two produced three
children, whom he abandoned
as men did and do, dropping

each like a pair of old shoes
to be raised by those of us
who cared enough. Step
fathers, aunts, grandmothers

a gaggle of stepchildren
who sometimes loved them
and sometimes not—that
was and is the gift of men

who deposit babies and shrug
them off like biting flies.
Stepmothers are cursed
in fairy tales, cruel, abusive

but how many offspring
would wizen with neglect
without those added families
after that sharp subtraction?

Held, cuddled, coddled, even
adored, with luck they move
into a warm place that may
begin to heal that gaping wound.

My mother's dearest friend
was not a blood sister, but
taken in because she needed
to be fed, clothed, loved.

Among eleven born in family
Florence stood out like a daisy
in a pansy patch—taller,
blonde and equally prized.

Contributors

NANCY ANTONIETTI is a retired engineer from New Hampshire who has given up design of experiments in favor of crafting dialogue and spinning narrative. Her writing has been honored by PEN Nob Hill and Seacoast Writers Association and published in *Strut Magazine*, *In the Fray*, *Words and Images*, *A Cup of Comfort for the Grieving Heart*, *A Cup of Comfort for Christian Women*, *Americal Journal*, *The NH Mirror*, and *Italianicious* magazine. She is currently working on a novel while learning to quilt and occasionally harvesting a handful of tomatoes from her container garden.

SHANNON BARDWELL and her husband, Sam, live in the Mississippi prairie along with their aging deaf cat, Jack, three goofy but lovable ducks, and varying numbers of goldfish. Shannon is a columnist for *The Commercial Dispatch* newspaper and *Catfish Alley* magazine. Her published short stories include "Ninety-Nine Nights in a Tent," "Little Red, a Squirrel Dog," "Delta Child," and "Momma and the Hoochie Coochie Club."

SALLIE WAGNER BROWN is a writer, a traveler, a dog-lover, and the mother of adopted, step-, and biological children. She lives on Hood Canal in northwest Washington state where the breathtaking view both distracts and inspires her in her writing. Her stories about her kids who think they are grown-up and her dogs who think they are her kids have been published in *A Cup of Comfort*, *Chicken Soup*, and *Not My Mother's Book* series.

STEPHANIE CASSATLY earned her MFA in Writing at Vermont College of Fine Arts and her undergraduate degree from Emory University. Her work has appeared in *Fourth Genre*, *Harvest Times*, *A Cup of Comfort*, *The Palm Beach Post*, and *The Jupiter Courier Journal*. Her essays have received notable mention in *The Best American Spiritual Writing* and *New Millennium Writings*. Most recently, she was awarded first place in *Writer's Digest*'s annual writing competition. She is currently working on her memoir and teaching writing part-time at Palm Beach Atlantic University.

KERRY COHEN is the author of six books, including the memoirs *Loose Girl: A Memoir of Promiscuity* and *Seeing Ezra: A Mother's Story of Autism, Unconditional Love, and the Meaning of Normal*. Three more books are forthcoming. Her essays have been featured in *The New York Times* "Modern Love" series, *The Washington Post*, *Brevity*, *Literary Mama*, *Brain, Child* magazine, and many other journals and anthologies. She lives in Portland, Oregon, with James Bernard Frost, her two children, and her two stepchildren.

BETSY GRAZIANI FASBINDER has been awarded the Floyd Salas Award for Fiction, a Jack London award, and two East of Eden awards for both fiction and memoir pieces. Four of her works have been produced as Readers' Theater in the historic Nevada Theater in Nevada City, California. She is the coproducer of Words Off Paper, a quarterly writer event in Marin County, California. Her debut novel *Fire and Water* was released by She Writes Press, March 2013, with the audio version released in April 2014. Her blog, *Art Finds a Way*, can be found through her website at www.betsygrazianifasbinder.com.

JAMES BERNARD FROST is the author of the novels *A Very Minor Prophet* (Hawthorne Books) and *World Leader Pretend* (St. Martin's Press) and the travel guide *The Artichoke Trail* (Hunter Publishing), which won a Lowell Thomas Award for Best Travel Guide. His articles, essays, and reviews have appeared in *The Nervous Breakdown*, *The Los Angeles Review of Books*, *Role/Reboot*, *Trachodon Magazine*, *The San Francisco Bay Guardian*, and the *Farallon Review*. He has been a contributor to the *San Francisco Examiner* and Wired Online, where he wrote food, travel, and culture reviews. He teaches creative writing at UC Berkeley Extension, Gotham Writing Workshop, and the Red Earth MFA Program.

ELIZABETH KING GERLACH is mother and stepmother to four great young men. She is the author of *Just This Side of Normal, Autism Treatment Guide*, and *Apples for Cheyenne* (Future Horizons, Inc.) She wrote and published the children's book *One Lucky Flower* (Four Leaf Press). Her essays have appeared in *A Cup of Comfort*, *Exceptional Parent Magazine*, *Mainstream Magazine*, and *Autism Asperger's Digest*. Her website is www.fourleafpress.com.

ARIEL GORE is the editor and publisher of the Alternative Press Award—winning magazine *Hip Mama* and the author of eight books. Her latest, *The End of Eve*, chronicles her years spent caring for her dying mother and has been called *"Terms of Endearment* meets *Whatever Happened to Baby Jane?"* She also teaches The Literary Kitchen online workshops.

MELISSA HART is the author of *Gringa: A Contradictory Girlhood* (Seal Press, 2009) and *Wild Within: How Rescuing Owls Inspired a Family* (Lyons, 2014). Her work has appeared in *The Los Angeles Times, The Washington Post, Mothering, Orion, High Country News, Horizon Air,* and *Brain, Child* magazine. She is a contributing editor at *The Writer* magazine and teaches at the School of Journalism and Communication, University of Oregon. More can be found at her website, www.melissahart.com.

AMY HUDOCK, PHD, is a writer, professor, and editor in South Carolina. She is the coeditor of the books *Literary Mama: Reading for the Maternally Inclined* (Seal Press, 2006) and *American Women Prose Writers, 1820–1870* (Gale, 2001). Her work has been anthologized in the *Chicken Soup for the Soul* and *A Cup of Comfort* series, as well as in *Torn: True Stories of Modern Motherhood, Ask Me About My Divorce, Mama, PhD,* and *Single State of the Union.* She is a cofounder of Literary Mama, an online literary magazine chosen by *Writer's Digest* as one of the 101 Best Web Sites for Writers (2005 and 2009) and by *Forbes* as one of its 100 Best of the Web (2005). Her work has also appeared in *Skirt!, Equus, The Post and Courier, ePregnancy,* and *Pregnancy and Baby.* She teaches writing (creative and other) at Trident University.

LIZABETH P. KINGSLEY is a New Jersey-raised, over—extended mother of two and stepmother of three who lives with her girlfriend in New Jersey and tries to get up a little earlier and go to sleep a little later every day to cram more in. A poet, she's a longtime student at The Writers Studio in New York City, where she cultivates her passion for writing and helps to run the program. She enjoys writing online columns at www.jerseymomsblog.com, poetry (*New Ohio Review*), her column "Blended" in *The Alternative Press*, personal essays (*Union County Family*

Magazine), and short stories (*William and Mary Review*) about the incidents and emotions both small and large that fill her ever-lengthening days.

BARBARA STRAUS LODGE's essays have appeared in *Literary Mama* (2014), *The New York Times* "Motherlode" column (2013), *Elohi Gadoji Literary Journal* (2014), *The Examined Life Journal* (2013), the "LA Affairs" section of the *Los Angeles Times* (2012), *The Sun Magazine, Amarillo Bay Online Literary Magazine,* and *Whole Life Times Magazine.* Her essays have been anthologized in *Exit Laughing— How We Use Humor to Take the Sting out of Death,* (North Atlantic Books/Random House, 2012), and, under her pen name Leigh Stuart, in *Dear John, I Love Jane* (Seal Press, 2010), which was a Lambda Literary Award finalist. Recognizing her personal truth while simultaneously uncovering her husband's secret life is the subject of her nearly completed memoir, *Revolution.* Her website is www.Barbarastrauslodge.com.

JENNIFER MARGULIS is an award-winning writer, a former senior fellow at the Schuster Institute for Investigative Journalism at Brandeis University, and a former Fulbright Award recipient. Her articles have appeared in *The New York Times, The Washington Post,* and *Smithsonian Magazine.* Her fifth book, *The Business of Baby: What Doctors Don't Tell You, What Corporations Try to Sell You, and How to Put Your Pregnancy, Childbirth, and Baby Before Their Bottom Line* (Scribner, 2013), was a finalist for a Books for a Better Life Award. She lives in Ashland, Oregon, with her husband and four children. Learn more about her at www.JenniferMargulis.net.

MELANIE SPRINGER MOCK is a professor of English at George Fox University, Newberg, Oregon. Her essays and reviews have appeared in *Christian Feminism Today, Literary Mama, The Chronicle of Higher Education,* and *Mennonite Weekly Review,* among other places. Her most recent book, *Just Moms: Conveying Justice in an Unjust World,* was published in 2011. Her book *The Spirit of Adoption* will be published by Cascade Press in 2014, with another book, tentatively titled *Meant to Be,* forthcoming from Chalice Press.

JESSICA PAGE MORRELL understands both sides of the editorial desk—as an editor and author. She is the author of *Thanks, but This Isn't for Us, A (Sort of) Compassionate Guide to Why Your Writing Is Being Rejected; Bullies, Bastards & Bitches: How to Write the Bad Guys in Fiction; The Writer's I Ching: Wisdom for the Creative Life; Voices from the Street; Between the Lines: Master the Subtle Elements Of Fiction Writing;* and *Writing Out the Storm.* Her work also appears in anthologies and *The Writer* and *Writer's Digest* magazines. Morrell founded and coordinates three writing conferences. She has been a columnist since 1998 and is a popular speaker at writers' conferences throughout North America. She lives in Portland, Oregon, where she is surrounded by writers and watches the sky in all its moods and permutations.

C. S. O'CINNEIDE lives deep in the trees of a small Ontario town with her Irish husband and a collection of their Canadian progeny. She contributes as a regular satirical news columnist to *Paper Droids,* an online magazine for women in geek culture. Check her out there or at her blog, *Misery's Company with Ocinneide* (misenysco.blogspot.com).

REBECCA PAYNE has written poems and essays for publications such as *Friends Journal, Canary, Washington Square Review,* and *Our State: Down Home in North Carolina.* She has also published political/social articles for local newspapers, and has contributed to an anthology by Wising Up Press. She is currently working on a memoir about her harrowing stepfamily life.

MARGE PIERCY is the author of seventeen novels, including the *New York Times* bestseller *Gone To Soldiers*, the national bestsellers *Braided Lives* and *The Longings of Women*, and the classic *Woman on the Edge of Time*; eighteen volumes of poetry, including *The Hunger Moon* and *The Moon is Always Female*; and a critically acclaimed memoir, *Sleeping with Cats.* PM Press has been republishing several of her early novels with new introductions and has just brought out Piercy's first and only collection of short stories, *The Cost of Lunch, Etc.*

MARY FAITH POWERS is a full-time freelance writer. She lives in the beautiful Ozark Mountains with two men, two dogs, and eight cats. Writing is the only way to have her voice heard above the din. This is her debut in the publishing world.

GIGI ROSENBERG's "My Secret Father" was adapted from *How I Lost My Inheritance: A Mother/Daughter Memoir*. She's performed at Seattle's On the Boards, been a guest commentator on Oregon Public Radio, and been published by *Poets & Writers*, *Writer's Digest*, and *Parenting*. She was a 2014 Jack Straw Writer and is the author of *The Artist's Guide to Grant Writing* (Watson-Guptill, 2010). Gigi lives in Portland, Oregon, where she works as a coach to entrepreneurs and artists. For the latest, visit: gigirosenberg.com.

SUE SANDERS's essays have appeared or are forthcoming in *The New York Times*, *Salon*, *Real Simple*, *The Rumpus*, *The Morning News*, *Parents*, *Family Circle*, the *Seattle Times*, and *Brain, Child* magazine, among others. Her book *Mom I'm Not a Kid Anymore*, a collection of parenting essays, was published in May 2013 by The Experiment. Sue lives in Portland, Oregon, with her "official family."

ALAINA SMITH loves a good story. Her true tales appear in multiple anthologies, including four *Chicken Soup for the Soul* books, six *Chocolate for Women* books, five *A Cup of Comfort* books, and more. She enjoys writing, working for a nonprofit organization, and movie-going with her husband, Frank.

MARCELLE SOVIERO is the editor-in-chief of *Brain, Child: The Magazine for Thinking Mothers*. Her award-winning essays have appeared in various online and print publications, including *The New York Times*, Salon.com, *Eating Well*, *New York Metro*, *Fairfield Parent*, *Big Apple Parent*, *Babble*, *Literary Mama*, and *Upper East Side Magazine*. In addition, her essays have been featured on American Public Media's syndicated radio show, *The Story*. She is the author of *An Iridescent Life: Essays on Motherhood and Stepmotherhood*.

CASSIE PREMO STEELE, PhD, is the author of twelve books—poetry, fiction, and nonfiction—about the connections among mothering, healing, creativity, and our relationship to the natural world. Her next book, *13*, is poetry in the voices of a mother and daughter after divorce. And on Earth Day 2015, her long-awaited book, *Earth Joy Writing*, based on her years of work as a writing coach, will be published by

Ashland Creek Press. To contact her about individual or group writing coaching, visit her website at www.cassiepremosteele.com.

DEB STONE's writing has appeared in *The Oregonian*, *Portland Tribune*, *Portland Upside*, *Asylum*, *Poetic Voices*, and *Oregon Gourmet Foods*. Her essay "Mr. Potato Head's Secret Life" was selected for Portland's inaugural *Listen to Your Mother* show, and her essay "Skipping Stones" is included in *The Truth of Memoir: How to Write About Yourself and Others with Honesty, Emotion, and Integrity*. She has been a birth, foster, step-, and adoptive parent to over thirty children, and a court-appointed special advocate for another two dozen abused and neglected kids in foster care. Deb recently completed her memoir *Mother Up*, and is currently writing the sequel, *Mother Enough*.

ELLEN SUSSMAN is the nationally bestselling author of four novels, *A Wedding in Provence*, *The Paradise Guest House*, *French Lessons*, and *On a Night Like This*. She is the editor of two critically acclaimed anthologies, *Bad Girls: 26 Writers Misbehave* and *Dirty Words: A Literary Encyclopedia of Sex*. She teaches through Stanford Continuing Studies and in private classes. Her website is www.ellensussman.com.

EMMA KATE TSAI is a writer and editor in Houston, Texas. Her work can be found online in such journals as *Intellectual Refuge*, *Elephant Journal*, and *Connotation Press*. She has also been published in *Loving for Crumbs*, edited and self-published by Jonna Ivin, and *Drinking Diaries: Women Serve Their Stories Straight Up*, edited by Caren Osten Gerszberg and Leah Odze Epstein and published by Seal Press. Emma is currently working on a memoir about identity in identical twins.

CANDACE WALSH is the author of *Licking the Spoon: A Memoir of Food, Family, and Identity* (Seal Press, 2012), a New Mexico–Arizona Book Award winner; coeditor, with Laura André, of *Dear John, I Love Jane: Women Write About Leaving Men for Women* (Seal Press, 2010), a Lambda Literary Award finalist; and the editor of *Ask Me About My Divorce: Women Open Up About Moving On* (Seal Press, 2009). She is the managing editor of *New Mexico Magazine* and was the features editor at *Mothering* magazine. Her articles and essays have been published in various national publications, the Huffington Post, and in the anthologies *The Good Mother Myth* and *Spent*. She recently served as faculty at the Wild Mountain Memoir Retreat with Cheryl Strayed, and at Bird by Bird and Beyond with Anne Lamott. She also works as a writing coach and book consultant. She's on Facebook (facebook.com/ WriterCandaceWalsh) and on Twitter (@candacewalsh). Learn more at candacewalsh.com and author-it.net.

CYNTHIA WHITCOMB spent thirty years as a screenwriter and has had thirty full-length scripts produced for prime-time national television. She has been nominated for the Emmy, Writers Guild, Cable Ace, and Edgar Allan Poe awards. Whitcomb has written two books on screen-writing. She has created roles for Jason Robards, Anjelica Huston, Martin Sheen, Ellen Burstyn, Kevin Spacey, and Melanie Griffith. Since 2007 she has been a full-time playwright for which she has twice been a finalist for the Angus Bowmer Award. She has taught writing for more than thirty years. She has two children, two stepchildren, and two grandchildren.

KEZIA WILLINGHAM, a former high school dropout, earned her bach-elor's degree from Oregon State University and her master's degree in Social Work from University of Washington. Her writing has appeared in *Hip Mama*, *Literary Mama*, *The New York Times* "Motherlode" column, *The Seattle Times*, and xoJane.com. She lives in Seattle with her family, which includes six cats and four dogs, all rescues.

Credits

Acknowledgments

Thanks to Krista Lyons for believing in this book and guiding its development. To Marcia Gerhardt who sparked the idea for an anthology on step-parenting and then graciously handed me the controls to fly solo. To Candace Walsh who championed the book with Seal Press. To Cynthia Whitcomb who read my first response from Seal Press and insisted, "That's not a rejection. That's an invitation." To Cassie Premo Steele who provided my first fishing list of talented writers, and the golden words, "Writers are generous."

Wild applause for the amazing contributors who had the courage and tenacity to explore often-painful memories and share their poignant, sometimes funny, sometimes heart-wrenching, always inspiring stories.

A virtual bouquet of damask roses to my mother, Helen Hinckley Jones, who consulted with me on my first novel when I was in second grade and encouraged me on through adulthood in all my writing endeavors. I owe any success to her guidance. Kudos, too, to writing mentors Colleen Sell and Molly Gloss who believe in me when I lose faith in myself.

Thank you to colleagues Margo Bowman, Jay Arzadon, Kimila Setzer, and Jeanne Silaski who read the introduction and made editorial suggestions at least a thousand times. More thanks to Jeanne for our late-night brainstorming sessions on the organization and details of the book.

My husband Ray deserves special credit for his never-ending support of my writing. I know he'd rather we were hiking, but says only, "Oh, you're still in your office."

About the Editor

Samantha Waltz has been writing since childhood. She sold her first story at age eleven to a local newspaper. Her next stories were published in *American Girl,* and she later worked as a guest editor and assistant editor for *Mademoiselle.* Her books include *Parenting: Four Patterns in Childrearing* (New York: Hart Publishing), *Parenting Gifted Children* (Salem: Oregon State Department), and *Gifted Child: Master Piece in the Making* (Oregon Association of Talented and Gifted). Her personal essays have been published in *Redbook, The Christian Science Monitor,* and more than sixty anthologies, including the Seal Press anthologies *Ask Me About My Divorce* and *Why We Ride.* She lives in Portland, Oregon, with her husband and frequently spends time with her three children, five stepchildren, and their families. Her early work is under the names Samellyn Jones and Samellyn Wood.

SELECTED TITLES FROM SEAL PRESS

For more than thirty years, Seal Press has published groundbreaking books. By women. For women.

The New I Do: Reshaping Marriage for Skeptics, Realists, and Rebels, by Susan Pease Gadoua and Vicki Larson. $17.00, 978-1-58005-545-1. A new perspective on the modern shape of marriage, this guide offers couples a roadmap for creating alternative marital partnerships.

Break Free from the Divortex: Power Through Your Divorce and Launch Your New Life, by Christina Pesoli. $17.00, 978-1-58005-535-2. An easy-to-follow, all-in-one guide to navigating the perils of divorce and returning to solid emotional ground.

Stop Signs: Recognizing, Avoiding, and Escaping Abusive Relationships, by Lynn Fairweather. $18.00, 978-1-58005-387-7. A go-to manual for women containing the life-saving information needed by anyone who is living with abuse, knows someone who is, or wishes to avoid becoming involved in a potentially life-threatening relationship.

Prude: Lessons I Learned When My Fiancé Filmed Porn, by Emily Southwood. $16.00, 978-1-58005-498-0. This humorous memoir reveals the author's bizarre journey to conquer her discomfort around porn—and how she ends up finding herself and ultimately fixing her relationship for good along the way.

The Good Mother Myth: Redefining Motherhood to Fit Reality, edited by Avital Norman Nathman. $16.00, 978-1-58005-502-4. This collection of essays takes a realistic look at motherhood and provides a platform for real voices and raw stories, each offering an honest perspective on what it means to be a mother.

Licking the Spoon: A Memoir of Food, Family, and Identity, by Candace Walsh. $16.00, 978-1-58005-391-4. In *Licking the Spoon*, Walsh tells how she turned to cookbook authors real and fictitious to learn, unlearn, and redefine her own womanhood, and recounts the meals, memories, and cookbooks that touched her along the way.

FIND SEAL PRESS ONLINE
WWW.SEALPRESS.COM
WWW.FACEBOOK.COM/SEALPRESS
TWITTER: @SEALPRESS